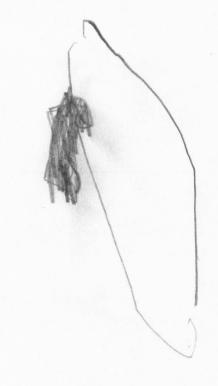

THE TWO WORLDS OF
SOMERSET MAUGHAM

THE TWO WORLDS OF
SOMERSET MAUGHAM

by WILMON MENARD

SHERBOURNE PRESS, INC.
LOS ANGELES, CALIFORNIA

For

DIANE

Who graciously and readily forgave the long separations
of too many years while I raptly followed the resplendent
sea-trails of Somerset Maugham among the exotic islands
and ports of the South Seas and the Far East.
For her charming forbearance
this volume
is
lovingly dedicated

ACKNOWLEDGMENTS

Sherbourne Press gratefully acknowledges the permission granted by Mr. and Mrs. Philip I. Berman, of Allentown, Pa., to reproduce on the back cover of this book the famous Gauguin-on-glass. They purchased this painting from Somerset Maugham, and have contributed a great deal to stimulating American interest in the works of Paul Gauguin.

Sherbourne Press wishes to thank the Tate Gallery, London, for permission to reproduce the Graham Sutherland portrait of Somerset Maugham on the front cover of this book.

The author, Wilmon Menard, is especially grateful for the above-and-beyond personal interest which the publisher, Louis Linetsky, and the editor, Froma Sand, have accorded the editorial treatment of his manuscript.

"This mysterious, divine Pacific zones the world's whole bulk about; makes all coasts one bay to it; seems the tide-beating heart of earth."

Herman Melville

"The Pacific is inconstant and uncertain like the soul of man . . . the trade wind gets into your blood, and you are filled with an impatience for the unknown . . . you forget your vanished youth, with its memories, cruel and sweet, in a restless intolerable desire for life . . ."

Somerset Maugham

CONTENTS

VI THE SEARCH

THE WRITINGS OF
W. SOMERSET MAUGHAM

Illustrations appear after pages 182 and 214

I

THE MEETING

1. Introduction at Rapallo

I had been warned, before meeting William Somerset Maugham for the first time, that the encounter, socially and conversationally evaluated, might not be too lucrative. It could even be disastrous to one's poise and pride. I had heard countless tales of his polite animosity and chilling candour. I knew that the British playwright and novelist was rabidly reticent by nature, almost forbidding at times in his discomfiting aloofness, and prone to frigid stares and cynical remarks that could forever vanquish and estrange anyone not included in his select circle of close friends.

Nevertheless, the formal introduction did take place. It was in the early 1950s, and the setting was Sir Henry Maxmilian Beerbohm's Villino Chiaro in Rapallo, between Portofino and Genoa, on Italy's Ligurian seacoast. The occasion was a small gathering to celebrate Max's return to Via Aurelia, 47, from a hillside Catholic rest-home on Rapallo's

3

Montallegro, where the British essayist, critic and carica-
turist had temporarily migrated to escape the oppressive heat
of the Italian summer.

I had driven up with invited friends from Viareggio,
knowing that Maugham would be present. It had been
through Maugham's superb stories of peoples and places below the equator that my first literary interests—and my later
travels—had been seriously directed to the South Seas and
the Far East, so I was eagerly anticipating the meeting.

But Max had prepared me for a possible rout.

"When Willie arrived I made the mistake of mentioning
to him that one of your critics, Edmund Wilson, might
be here today, too," he said ruefully. "Fortunately, Wilson
couldn't make it. Anyway, because Willie loathes Wilson for
some rather uncomplimentary things he wrote about his
talents—and for the possibility that they might have been
in the same company—he's thoroughly provoked at me, and
is in the library, sulking. However, he is alone, and perhaps
by now he's simmered down a bit. Let's hope so."

I recalled that Edmund Wilson, once notorious for his
Memoirs of Hecate County, had given Maugham's *Then
And Now* a scathing review when it was published in 1946.
He had taken the opportunity to make a disparaging summa-
tion of all of his writings, and had included a most unflat-
tering character-analysis as well.

Wilson had relegated him, with perverse waspishness, to
the category of a second-rate author, accusing him of shoddy
craftsmanship, character delineation and plotting; he insinuated that Maugham had venomously used his position as a
"popular writer" to attack far superior writers,[1] and had also
attempted to promulgate false standards of morality and un-
dermine the precepts of Christianity. Specifically Wilson had

---

[1] Thomas Hardy and Hugh Walpole under the character-names of
Edward Driffield and Alroy Kear in his *Cakes and Ale*.

said: "It has happened to me from time to time to run into some person of taste who tells me that I ought to take Somerset Maugham seriously. Yet I have never been able to convince myself that he was anything but second-rate . . . My experience with Maugham has always been that he disappoints my literary appetite and so discourages me from going on . . . He is a half-hashy novelist, who writes badly, but is patronized by half-serious readers who do not care much about writing." It would have been much better, he sneered, if Maugham had continued with his early medical career and had left serious writing to those better equipped.

Such was the cause of the unpropitious climate at the time I was to meet Somerset Maugham.

Nevertheless, Max, past eighty and frail—but still elegant in a double-breasted grey flannel suit and blue skull-cap—led me through the living-room into the small library of Villino Chiaro and bravely introduced me to a brooding Maugham, seated under a wash-drawing of Thomas Carlyle striding cantankerously along a Chelsea embankment.

With serene high-domed forehead and disarming very blue eyes, Max had fortuitously added to the rather cautious introduction: "He's not even half your age, Willie, and he's been to just about every place in the South Pacific and the Orient that you've visited for your stories, not once, but two and three times—so you two should really have something to chat about."

Maugham, holding like a scepter a half-finished triple Martini, served in a champagne goblet, averted his frozen stare into the circular Regency mirror on the adjoining living-room wall. I saw that the orbital glass afforded him a view of both rooms, and that he was indulging in his favorite pastime: observing humanity in perspective. He nodded coolly, ignoring my outstretched hand, and resumed his study of reflected lip-movements and gestures.

More to himself he mused: "That old and marvelous mirror, because it's convex and concentrates everyone in the room, adjusts them to one focal point, making an entire image. Max's father bought it at the Paris International Exhibition of 1867, and for years now Max has had it, first in the nursery, now here. I think he intended writing an autobiographical novel about that mirror. That would have been interesting, very interesting. But he never did. Pity, really."

I had a brief few moments to study the British author. A near octogenarian himself, he resembled a mummified Chinese mandarin, disinterred after long entombment and placed into position for ancestral worship. The thought frivolously passed through my mind: if a movie studio ever decides to film a remake of James Hilton's *Lost Horizon*, he would now be ideal for the original Sam Jaffe role as the ageless Grand Lama of Shangri-la. The beaked nose, the wrinkled parchment skin, the hooded falcon's eyes, and cynical mouth, for more than a decade, had delighted artists and photographers—and I recalled Graham Sutherland's inspired Maugham portrait.

Then, suddenly, with aroused import, his gaze shifted from the burnished Regency mirror to me.

"Oh, so you've b-b-been to the islands of the South Pacific," he said, with a slight stammer. "The islands and natives fascinated me. At the time of being there, one is never conscious of their almost occult effect. There is a strange affinity with the sea and man, of nature and the universe, that is not readily perceivable in any other latitude, except perhaps India. In Polynesia one is drawn subtly into its spell, and, even after just a short visit, one is never quite the same again."

His appreciation of green islands in summer seas, to which I also had a deep attachment, allayed somewhat my uneasiness. And it was extremely interesting to hear Maugham in

6

his advanced age, more of a cynic than ever on spiritual forces, speak so feelingly of the isles of Polynesia. Relaxing a little, I sat down.

"My trips out of Europe to the South Pacific islands, the Indies and the Orient," he continued, "changed my writing program considerably."

Maugham, up until the First World War, had concerned himself solely with writing plays and novels. For twenty years he had ignored the short story form. But when he made his voyages into the South Pacific he found actual characters and their emotional involvements that stimulated his imagination. It was like a miraculous resuscitation, and he returned to short story writing with astonishing fervor and productivity. His notebooks were soon filled with sufficient data to keep him occupied for years. Six of these stories of Polynesia—Hawaii, Tahiti, and Samoa—adjudged his most perfect and powerful, were published in book-form under the title *The Trembling of a Leaf.* (1921) He was well over forty when he wrote one of the short stories of that volume, *Miss Thompson,* his best known short story, which later was dramatized by John Colton and Clemence Randolph under the more arresting title of *Rain,* earning in stage, movie, radio and television royalties more than a million dollars.

The Moon and Sixpence (1919), based on the life of the French neo-impressionist painter Paul Gauguin, with its concluding setting of Tahiti, is claimed by most critics to be his finest novel, and for which the intellectuals, who had previously spurned his writings, nearly accepted him.

As Maugham had frequently remarked: "I have never been able to write anything unless I had a solid and ample store of information for my wits to work upon."

He found a superabundance of literary material in the islands of the South Pacific.

7

The short story, *The Fall of Edward Barnard,* in *The Trembling of a Leaf,* is an example of a departure from his customary simple, lucid and pungent style of writing, influenced perhaps by Shakespeare's advice that "an honest tale speeds best being plainly told." In his stories of Polynesian islands and peoples he became more lyrical, sharing his enchantment of palms, blue lagoons and surf-fringed coral reefs with his readers, who, later, to the delight of steamship-travel agencies, actually followed Maugham's colorful sea-routes through the South Pacific.

Maugham's reputation as a writer is more solidly established on his Chekhov-de Maupassant influenced short stories. His collection of short stories of the Far East and the Orient, under the titles of *The Casuarina Tree* (1926) and *Ah King* (1933), and his travel-essay volumes, *On a Chinese Screen* (1922), and *The Gentleman in the Parlour* (1930), the latter a superb chronicle of a journey from Burma, through the Shan States of this country, into Siam, to the destination of Haiphong in the then French Indo-China—and his favorite of all his writings—reveals clearly the effect that exotic countries and people had upon him. As he wrote: "Then it seemed to me that in these countries in the East the most impressive, the most awe-inspiring monument of all antiquity is neither temple, nor citadel, nor great wall, but man . . . I travel because I like to move from place to place, I enjoy the sense of freedom it gives me, it pleases me to be rid of ties, responsibilities, duties; I like the unknown: I meet odd people who amuse me for a moment and sometimes suggest a theme for a composition; I am often tired of myself, and I have a notion that by travel I can add to my personality and so change myself a little. I do not bring back from a journey quite the same self that I took."

The Far East, and the South Pacific islands, in particular, did elicit from Maugham an outpouring of poetic prose,

8

florid descriptions, charming metaphors and similes, which in his temperate-setting tales he had heretofore studiously avoided or shunned.

And another surprising departure in his South Pacific stories is that, although he dealt roughly with white women in the tropics, he wrote with respect and understanding, almost admiration, of the sexually provocative native women.

I ventured to make a comment upon his kindly treatment of Polynesian females.

He smiled slightly, nodded. "Yes, I have respect for the island women because of their honest attitude on sex. I found that they did not have in their sexual congress the obnoxious deceit and shrewdness of European women. The Polynesian women have no pretenses or trickery about coition. They accept their femininity and their normal sexual appetites as a rightful heritage and a normal biological indulgence, not as a cruel and psychological weapon. They give themselves in venery as they might casually bestow a smile or a wreath of flowers. Quite commendable, really.

"Frankly, I prefer a free-loving, passionate woman to a frigid and selfish one, a promiscuous one to a stupidly virtuous female. With a Polynesian *vahine,* sexual infidelities do no damage to her pride or her heart."

I listened. He was embarked on a subject which I knew he would pursue to some length, knowing that I would have some comprehension of such a controversial topic.

"The refreshing difference between an island woman of strong sexual drives," he continued, "and a European woman with an incessant sexual itch is that the Polynesian *vahine* is a sensualist in the purest form, a true voluptuary without inhibitions, as perhaps all women were originally intended, whereas her European white sister is invariably a boresome psychopath, a frustrated female plagued by Freudian neu-

9

roses, who imposes on any man that truly loves her, but whom she does not care for, as much cruelty as she is capable of."

This was Maugham, the true misogynist, expounding!

"Yes, I am convinced that sexuality is only understood and performed by the natives of the South Pacific islands, particularly Tahiti and Samoa. They know that the keenest pleasure to which the body is susceptible is that of sexual stimulation—and they have no mental traumas about gratifying this healthy appetite."

As he spoke his sardonic gaze shifted about the library, now resting briefly on an illustration of the Elizabethan comic actor, Dick Tarlton, as the Harlequin; scanning a shelf of books; roving back to the Regency mirror to follow with disillusioned eyes a person's pantomime, movement, or transit of the living-room, cataloguing in his amazingly retentive mind a unique gesture or facial expression. I had the impression that he might be an expert lip-reader.

"I spent some time in Tahiti and Samoa," he said, "but not long enough. It was during the First World War and I was, due to a recurrent lung ailment, between assignments with the British Intelligence Office. They requested, after a trip of convalescence to America and the South Pacific, that I go to Russia to influence the Menshevik Party, by supplying them money for arms and newspaper support for their plans, to continue the war against Germany. Therefore I couldn't remain as long as I wanted to in the islands. But I was there long enough to convince myself that Europeans were sexually deranged and the Polynesians sexually sane."

He irritably shoved his goblet at me. "That Max! He serves warm martinis! Unforgivable, really! Sinclair Lewis once complained that I served warm martinis! So now I'm complaining! Would you be kind enough to see if you can do something about this abominable martini, or have Miss Jungmann take care of it?"

When I had brought him back a fresh, properly chilled martini, with an almond-stuffed olive, he resumed the equatorial discussion.

"I went to Tahiti to talk with anyone who had known Paul Gauguin, in preparation for what was to be my *The Moon and Sixpence*. Previous to going to Tahiti I had read considerably about French Oceania, and I remember what the early Pacific discoverer, Captain James Cook, had written about the morals of the Tahitians: he was convinced that there was less platonic love in Tahiti than in any other country of the world."

And Monsieur Louis Antoine de Bougainville, the French navigator and explorer, had reaffirmed this publicity about Tahitians. He had called the island the New Cytherea, and explained why: "The name which I intended for it was suited to a country, perhaps the only one in the world, where men live with vices, without prejudices, without necessities, without disputes. Born under a most beautiful sky, nourished on the fruits of an earth which is fertile without tillage, ruled by patriarchs rather than kings, they know no other god but love . . . The whole island is a temple of love . . . the act of procreation is an act of religion . . . following the tender impulses of a consistently pure instinct, because they have not degenerated into reason."

"Captain Cook gave a rather lurid description of a sexual rite in Tahiti," continued Maugham, "that elicited an enthusiastic endorsement from Voltaire, who, curiously, seems to be remembered only for his *Candide*."

Cook had invited the Queen of Tahiti and her Court to religious services, and she had reciprocated with an island ceremony. In his chronicles he described her "religious" service:

"A young man, nearly six feet tall, performed the rites of Venus with a little girl about eleven or twelve years of age,

11

before several of our people and a great number of natives, without the least sense of its being indecent or improper, but, as appeared in perfect conformity to the custom of the place. Among the spectators were several women of superior rank, who may properly be said to have assisted at the ceremony; for they gave instructions to the girl how to perform her part, which, young as she was, she did not seem much to stand in need of."

Voltaire, the French writer and philosopher, had written: "Being unable to travel, I have been reading the Captain Cook *Voyages around the World*. I know nothing more instructive. I see with great pleasure that what Monsieur de Bougainville has told us is true. When the French and the English are in agreement we can be sure that they have not deceived us. I am still in the island of Tahiti, I am admiring the diversity of the scenery, I see with edification the Queen of the country taking part in the communion of the Anglican Church and inviting the English to 'Divine Services' as conducted in her kingdom. This divine service consists in making a young man and a girl, quite naked, have intercourse in the presence of her Majesty and 500 ladies and gentlemen of the Court. It can be affirmed that the inhabitants of Tahiti have preserved the oldest religion on earth in all its purity."

Captain Cook had also written about another charming custom of the Tahitians:

"There is a scale in dissolute sensuality, which these people have ascended, (note that he indicates *upward,* instead of the missionary-prescribed downward slide into perdition) wholly unknown to every nation whose manners have been recorded from the beginning of the world to the present hour, and which no imagination could possibly conceive. Sisters, daughters, and even wives, are offered to strangers, either as a courtesy, an act of hospitality, or as a reward . . .

It cannot be supposed that, among these people, chastity is held in much estimation."

Maugham captured the olive on his tongue, chewed it reflectively, his expression oddly wistful.

"I genuinely enjoyed Tahiti. I decided that the islanders were the most normal people that I had come across in any of my travels. I remember that Henry Adams, a rather dull American, a sarcastic, class-conscious prig, who imagined himself to be a revered cardinal-at-large—and whom I knew as an old man when he was writing some heavy historical tomes—had assisted the Nineteenth Century Queen of Tahiti, Arii Taimai, in writing her memoirs, and he quoted her as saying: 'Tahiti has plenty of vices, and is a sort of Paris in its refinements of wickedness; but these have not prevented the Tahitians from leading as happy lives as have ever been known among men.'"

A truck roared up Via Aurelia, on its way to or from Genoa, and the library became a sound-box for its din.

Maugham winced, muttering: "I can't understand why Max has lived here so long. The pandemonium of modern machines! Noise can kill slowly, you know. How I appreciated the peace and quiet of the South Pacific islands!"

We waited until the flatulent back-firing of the truck faded away into the distance.

"I met an extraordinary assortment of people in Tahiti. There were pearl traders, skippers of copra-schooners and pearling luggers, beachcombers, rascals and wanted criminals —and they all had a story. All I had to do was to make myself comfortable with a gin drink on the verandah of the hotel, and just listen. But there was one salty character, whom I had to avoid. His name was Captain Joe Winchester, off a trading-schooner servicing the Tuamotu islands north of Tahiti, and he spun more lies than a Welsh barman. I understand that he later became James Norman Hall's father-in-law, but I'm sure that Hall never used him as a source of information for the *Bounty* trilogy.

"An enormously fat, part-Tahitian woman of about fifty ran the Hotel Tiare[2] where I stayed in Papeete. Her name was Louvaina Chapman,[3] and she was a gracious friend to everyone who came to Tahiti, beachcomber, seaman, or millionaire. She had befriended Paul Gauguin many times when he was in need, and she knew a lot about him. I learned many interesting things about Gauguin from her. She had a heart as big as her body, and anyone in need of a free meal could get it at the Tiare Hotel; there was a lot of credit in her bar ledger that she knew she'd never collect.

"What a bright and happy sight she was sitting in the small kitchen attached to the verandah dining-room, dressed in her pink Mother Hubbard and small straw hat, superintending the Chinese cook, smiling, singing, now shouting out a hearty greeting to a passerby. Everyone knew and loved her.

"Her nephew Johnny Parè Gooding,[4] in his twenties at the time I was there, was the only happy half-caste that I ever met. He didn't brood about his Polynesian blood, there was no false shame in him. He was a plumpish young man, with black curly hair, and a cherubic face; he wore flowers in his hair. He would become very excited when conversing upon a topic that interested him, his voice keening to a shrill falsetto, to C above High C. He was a valuable fund of information about the customs, legends and morals of the Tahitians.

---

[2] The Hotel de la Fleur of Maugham's *The Moon and Sixpence.*

[3] Who was the corpulent "Tiare Johnson" of the same novel. Rupert Brooke had written of her kindness and generosity, and Elinor Mordaunt, who wrote the scathing *Gin and Bitters* attack on Maugham as a reply to his *Cakes and Ale,* had described her with affection.

[4] Johnny Gooding was not her nephew, but her son, the result of Louvaina's marriage to Samuel Gooding.

"For some time after I left Tahiti we corresponded. He knew I planned to use his aunt in my Gauguin novel, and he wanted to be certain that I treated her with the respect due her. Later, he ran a hotel on the waterfront of Papeete, the Aina Pare, and he wanted me to know that he had a print of Queen Victoria and The Battle of Copenhagen over the stairway to the second floor.

"One night when I came back to the Tiare Hotel, I found a young Tahitian girl in a *pareu*-sarong reclining on my mosquito-draped bed. She was the younger sister of one of the hotel's chambermaids, and Louvaina had sent her to my room, having decided that it was time I had a *petite amie*.

"I gave the giggling girl, who couldn't have been more than thirteen or fourteen, a few francs and sent her on her way. The next morning, when I stuck my head in the kitchen to say *bon jour* to Louvaina, the dear, sweet soul burst into tears. Her feelings were deeply wounded that I had not kept the nubile maiden for an all-night dalliance. To her it was the same as if I had rudely tossed a beautiful gift back into her face. Johnny later told me that any man who comes to Tahiti and doesn't shortly sleep with a Tahitian *vahine* is watched with suspicion and distaste; the natives are sure that something is not quite right with him. I understand that the morality of the Tahitians has changed very little since my visit there.

"I've never forgotten the Tiare Hotel and Louvaina. She was one of the most kindly and amusing women I have ever met. Johnny wrote me that she died in the influenza epidemic that struck Tahiti in 1918-19. I shed some tears over that sad news. I was very upset. I had hoped to see her again."

2.   A View of the Polynesians

I had never read of Maugham expressing any sentiment over a woman in any of his writings, save perhaps his mother, who died when he was quite young, eight years to be exact. She was a beautiful and intelligent woman, her affection and love too short-lived for the sensitive younger son, and Maugham never recovered in his lifetime from the shock of her wasting death by tuberculosis in 1882. He had wept over the death of an obese native woman in faraway Tahiti, yet he had been known merely to raise a cynical eyebrow and give an indifferent shrug of his shoulders when advised of the death of a woman within his circle of European friends.

I thought, too, about his rejection of the sexually precocious Tahitian girl, not through impotency or continence, but purely because of an inbred caution that he had developed early in life, the result of the unhealthy moral environment of his unhappy youth in the vicarage of his Uncle

Henry at Whitstable in Kent. This slothful, penurious, dictatorial man was later to become the *Reverend William Carey* of his *Of Human Bondage*. This novel was autobiographical and told of Maugham's life as a medical student and intern in St. Thomas's Hospital on the Thames, directly across from the Houses of Parliament, where he administered to the disease-ridden dwellers of the Borough of Lambeth. In his capacity as an obstetric clerk he had delivered almost 70 infants into the slum-world of Lambeth. This was the setting of his first novel *Liza of Lambeth* (1897), written at the age of 22, and based on a true case-transcript.

Working as an *accoucheur,* he had witnessed only the ugly and loathsome aspects of venery. He had become then, and had remained all his life, a detached observer, viewing from the safe range of growing repugnance the sordid results of sex manifested in squalor. He was intrigued and at the same time repelled, finally becoming contemptuous of the monstrous physical penalties and emotional anguish precipitated by concupiscence. All his life he had been a little too squeamish, too finicky, to indulge riotously in all the vices he accorded the heroes and heroines of his short stories and novels.

He had expressed his personal philosophy concerning amorality in his *The Summing Up*:

"Philosophers and moralists have looked at the body with misgiving. They have pointed out that its satisfactions are brief . . . The keenest pleasure to which the body is susceptible is that of sexual congress. I have known men who gave up their whole lives to this; they are grown old now, but I have noticed, not without surprise, that they look upon the years as well spent. It has been my misfortune that a native fastidiousness has prevented me from indulging as much in this particular delight as I might have. I have exercised moderation because I was hard to please. When from time to time I have seen the persons with whom the great lovers satisfied their desires I have been more often astonished by the robustness of their appetites than envious of their successes. It is obvious that you need not often go hungry if you are willing to dine off mutton hash and turnip tops."

Maugham had turfed the Tahitian trollop out of his room in the Tiare Hotel because of his inbred aversion to fornicating with a brown-skinned girl; it wasn't quite the thing that a thoroughgoing British gentleman would do. He approved of Polynesian sexuality, but he was having none of it himself.

And he still wanted to examine all facets of the islanders' eroticism.

"It's unjust to accuse the Tahitians or the Samoans of being debauched because they enjoy promiscuous fornication; they cannot be judged by Christian concepts or standards. To them it is normal to copulate, as habitual as eating, drinking or sleeping. They do not in their uncomplicated minds associate any details of wickedness or nastiness with it, which is perhaps why they shock white visitors by talking or joking about sex so openly."

It was apparent, too, that the Tahitians, for example, being closer to nature, have constantly, from childhood, witnessed the creation of plant, animal, sea and human life on more intimate terms. Although appearing lewd and outspoken concerning coition between the sexes, the Tahitians do not dwell morbidly on the erotic details as do the people of more highly civilized countries.

"It is very clear to me," said Maugham, "that the Tahitians do not think romantic sensations are centered in the heart or brain, as Europeans are led to believe. They are convinced that the physical attraction between man and woman is in the stomach, loins and genital organs. I was curious to find out if, in the Tahitian vocabulary, there was a word for *love*, as we know it. It did not exist, either in simple meaning or suggestion. Louvaina and Johnny explained to me that their definition of *love*, the instinctive physical magnetism between male and female, had only one word, *héré*, and when I asked what the true meaning of that word was, they said it meant the physical act of a man and woman sexually coupling."

Sexuality has been, and is today, a very dominant influence in the culture of the Polynesians, and it was interesting for both Maugham and myself to observe, while in Tahiti and Samoa, that the psychotic aberrations found in the Western world, because of prudery, prohibitions and unwholesome concealment, did not take possession of them. The Hawaiians, Samoans and Tahitians even today, as has been verified, are not suffering from any guilt traumas over their open indulgences in promiscuous sexual intercourse; they do not consider coition sinful, indecent or shameful, even though the missionaries strove fanatically to reshape their centuries-old traditions of venery. Therefore, the Polynesians, particularly, gratify their sexual appetites without any feeling of impropriety. Chastity for a woman in Polynesia is not considered a virtue, rather her sexual dexterity and promiscuity are considered an asset, a mark of successfully fulfilling her role as a truly feminine woman.

"The factor that set in motion the great social revolution in the Western world, the rather incredible change in relations between the sexes," said Maugham, "was the invention and general dissemination of modern contraceptives. Now any modern young lady understands that what used to be called *chastity* or *virginity* was a social code based on fear. The theme of adultery in a story today can only be one of comedy or satire."

Many white visitors to Tahiti and Samoa and Hawaii, especially the bigoted and fanatical missionaries, accused the islanders of being lustful, depraved and shameless in their sexual activities.

"I was most gratified to find out that the Polynesians were not the animals that the missionaries imagined," said Maugham. "I had an opportunity, in Hawaii, Tahiti and Samoa, to study their sexual culture. I was astonished with the native delicacy and refinement and affection they expressed in sexual congress. While living in the Hotel Tiare in Papeete, the life there was so free and easy that I didn't have to peek over transoms or through keyholes to see what was going on. The doors at night were left wide for the cool trades to blow through, with only a half-length lace curtain fluttering in the open doorways, and men and women came and went at all hours. I had been told by Louvaina that even the chambermaids of the hotel awaited their lovers on their sleeping-mats freshly bathed, with all body odours and unsightly hair under their armpits and also pubic hair removed. When they sallied forth, singing and smiling, for sexual assignations outside, they wore attractive gowns, their bodies anointed with an emollient made of coconut oil and fresh tropical flowers, and wore chaplets and neck-wreaths of spicy, or heavily scented flowers. I felt that the Polynesian women were essentially the pure feminists, with a commendable awareness and acceptance of the difference of the sexes. Such cannot be always said of European women."

Paul Gauguin had cynically observed:

"In Europe intercourse between men and women is a result of love. In Oceania love is a result of intercourse. Which is right? The man or woman who gives his or her body is said to commit a small sin. That is debatable, and in any case sin is wholly redeemed by Creation, the most beautiful art in the world, a divine art in a sense that it continues the work of the Creator. The real sin is committed by the man, or woman who sells his or her body. . . . Their (women's) nature is to love, but love of a special kind, one that conceives and in conception gives itself completely. Woman only fulfils herself. She will be free—and healthier —on the day when her honor is no longer placed below her navel."

Another refreshing attitude that I found in the South Pacific, markedly in Tahiti, was that sexual antagonisms did not exist, and that affection and anger, jealousy and revenge, sadness and bereavements were as short-lived as their passing tropical showers. Although I watched for signs, I couldn't find a neurotic or frustrated *tane* (man) or *vahine* (woman) in the islands.

Maugham elaborated further:

"Perhaps one of the reasons for their free disposition in sexual congress is the conditions under which the islanders live. Their familiarity with venery commences in childhood.

"In the Hotel Tiare there were many children playing on the verandahs and in the corridors and garden. They had only to glance into a room to see men and women indulging in sexual intercourse. I speak now of the Tahitian servants, not the European guests of the hotel.

"And out in the country, when I visited in the districts of Mataiea and Tautira, I noted that although many of the better class Tahitians had European-type wood frame houses, there was, customarily, just one large dormitory-style room for sleeping. At night-time, sleeping-mats were spread over the entire space, and children and adults of both sexes bedded down there, side by side. The families were large, and most times there were visiting relatives, even young newlyweds on honeymoon. It is apparent that the young men and women had little privacy to copulate. But the idea of privacy did not bother, or deter, them. And they did not think it vulgar to indulge their sexual desires, even though there was a night-light, a kerosene lamp, always burning low, to dispel the evil spirits of which all Tahitians are superstitious, regardless if restless children might awaken and guilelessly watch them for a minute or so. Therefore, the children, the teen-agers, have always been accustomed to scenes of unrestrained fornication. And so they became, at puberty, eager for experiments in coition."

I once asked a nurse of the Government Hospital in Papeete at what age the island girls usually lost their virginity. She replied that she had never examined a young girl over the age of 13 years who had not already been deflowered.

And a balmy climate, an abundance of edible foods, a perfect balance of nature, provided the ideal *ambiance* for eroticism. Captain Cook, as Maugham pointed out, nearly two centuries ago had expressed his awareness of this blessing: "The earth produced spontaneously, or with so little cultivation, that they seemed to be exempted from the first general curse that 'man should eat his bread by the sweat of his brow.' "

Maugham had noted, too, that the Tahitians changed sexual partners casually. And he approved. The moralists and missionaries condemned them for what they considered to be a dissolute and unsentimental indulgence, but their abhorrence of the Tahitians' erotomania could be tempered by the fact that it did release the islanders, at a very early age, from the all-consuming disease of jealousy, sparing them the more serious emotional disturbances common in European monogamous relationships. The easy exchange of native girls in sexual play eliminated the curse of exclusivity and possessiveness. Such sexual freedom did not permit these neuroses to develop.

Maugham had expressed himself frequently about European eroticism:

"Here in Europe, in America, Scandinavia, or anywhere in the 'civilized' countries of the world, the customary result of man's cohabitation with a woman, however sanctioned by society, is to make him a little more petty, a little meaner than he would otherwise have been. The majority of women are physiological messes, and not many of them, for sex, are worth more than a fiver, unless you're in love, of course. But then, love is, essentially, only for the very stupid or the very poor."

And if they were disappointing as sex partners, they were atrocious as mothers: "Few misfortunes can befall a boy, which bring worse consequences, than to have a really affectionate mother. Your writer Philip Wylie wrote an excellent book on the 'Moms' of America in his *Generation of Vipers*. These carnivorous females drive a husband out of the house and the sons into homosexuality."

Maugham always wrote a play, a short story, or a novel, to explain fully something he felt that he must translate for the public. His play, *The Breadwinner,* lampooned the abominably precocious juveniles and their art-phoney, rattle-brained mothers.

Maugham in his writings constantly deplored the European attitude on sex: "One of the misfortunes of human beings is that they continue to have sexual desires long after they are sexually desirable. I suppose it is not improper that they should gratify them, but I think they would do better not to talk about it . . . There is nothing about which men lie so much as about their sexual powers. In this at least every man is, what in his heart he would like to be, a Casanova."

And he had made a caustic comparison between heterosexual relationships in the Western world as opposed to those in Polynesia:

"Here in Europe the only relief the great mass of people have in the deadly monotony of their daily work is during that relatively short period when their sexual instincts are active and they can indulge in charitable lechery. In Tahiti and Samoa and the other Polynesian islands, sex is an accepted legacy of pleasure, not rationed by the calendar, the 'rhythm-cycle,' a bribe, or proffered as a bonus for being a good provider, butlering to a woman, or being a law-abiding member of the community.

"That love is chiefly the instinct for the propagation of the species shows itself in the fact that most men will fall in love with any woman in their way, and not being able to get the first woman on whom they have set their heart, soon turn to a second. It is but seldom that a man loves once and for all; it may only show that his sexual instincts are not very strong.

"The islanders are very promiscuous, so their sexual instincts must be very strong, at least we'll just have to accept that explanation.

"The fact is that what we call love depends on certain secretions of the sexual glands. When that love dies, it sometimes turns into affection. But however comforting affection may be, it is not love. That is what makes marriage so difficult. The fact is, two persons don't want to have intercourse with one another indefinitely. With few exceptions, the only way to keep it going is for one or both to have some fun on the side. At least, the Polynesians subscribe to that doctrine."

Max Beerbohm passed the library doorway, then reappeared almost immediately, his eyebrows flying up on his lofty, baby-pink forehead; his moustache seemed to quiver with consternation. He appeared completely bewildered that Maugham and I were still talking animatedly. He nodded, gave me a celestial smile over Maugham's shoulder, and withdrew.

THE MEETING

I was myself quite astonished, but complimented, that Maugham, on our initial meeting, was conversing with me at such length and with such a personal candour. He was customarily testy when meeting a stranger, particularly with writers, his suspicions aroused that they would be conniving for an interview, which he loathed to grant. He was fanatically averse to ever reading anything about himself, or afraid that a fledgling author was promoting a glowing endorsement from him for the dust-cover of a first, mediocre novel. "I refuse to let any writer climb onto my back to get ahead!" he had often snorted.

I'm sure that Maugham's rather incongruous amiability toward me, and the sustained flow of conversation, was established by our mutual appreciation of islands and natives of the South Pacific and the exotic ports of the Far East. It was obvious that he considered the Pacific area, which covered a third of the surface of the globe, the most colorful and fascinating in the world.

Herman Melville had acquainted him with the shimmering expanses of the South Pacific, the green islands, and "savage woodlands guarded by horrible idols," in his *Typee, Omoo* and *Moby Dick.* He had great admiration for this writer of the sea and forgotten islands. "His style reached its perfection in *Moby Dick* . . . it has copious magnificence, a sonority, a grandeur, an eloquence that no modern writer, so far as I know, has achieved. It is a great, a very great book."

Melville had written of the Pacific: "It rolls the mid-most waters of the world, the Indian Ocean and the Atlantic being but its arms . . . The same waves lave the faded but still gorgeous skirts of Asiatic lands . . . while all between float milky-way of coral isles, low-lying, endless, unknown archipelagoes . . . This mysterious, divine Pacific zones the world's whole bulk about; makes all coasts one bay to it; seems the tide-beating heart of earth."

And Maugham found the Pacific, endorsed by Melville, Robert Louis Stevenson, Joseph Conrad, Pierre Loti, Louis Becke and Lafcadio Hearn, the most soul-stirring sea that he had ever sailed upon.

Maugham wrote: "The Pacific is inconstant and uncertain like the soul of man . . . the trade wind gets into your blood, and you are filled with an impatience for the unknown. The billows, magnificently rolling, stretch widely on all sides of you, and you forget your vanished youth, with its memories, cruel and sweet, in a restless intolerable desire for life . . . You sail through an unimaginable silence upon a magic sea . . ."

The best of Maugham's short stories and novels, according to a poll of critics, are of the South Pacific islands and the Orient. They are the ones which have earned him acclaim and several millions of dollars, and have been enthusiastically accepted by readers in all lands. They are masterful in character delineation and plot and, most important of all, have stood the test of time. His *Miss Thompson*, the story of a blonde prostitute cast adrift in the steamy port of Pago Pago of American Samoa, is a matchlessly cut gem of a story, and is contained in the volume of short stories, *The Trembling of a Leaf*, the title a quote from *Sainte-Beuve*: "L'extrême félicité à peine séparée par une feuille tremblante de l'extrême désespoir, n'est-ce-pas la vie?" Such are the stories in this volume of Polynesian-island settings, their power derived from their taut construction, restrained tension, cumulative effect, sharp character portrayals and bold climaxes.

"For the short stories in *The Trembling of a Leaf*," Maugham said, after sipping the last of his triple martini, "I had the good fortune to know first-hand the islands, the natives and the Europeans in the different groups of Polynesia. Because of their somewhat remote and languorous disadvantages where the white man was concerned, the enervating tropical torpor and boredom, the soul-eroding effects of succumbing to the sexual proclivities of native women, the South Pacific islands were held to be the most compatible latitude for Europeans, male or female, to deteriorate physically and spiritually, become involved in violent emotional conflicts, and to suffer dire consequences because of their trangressions.

"The popular expectation concerning any white man who ended up in the tropics in any capacity, was for him to be described as a rum-sodden human derelict, sprawled under a coconut palm, his arm hugging the bare waist of an island strumpet, while another tramp-steamer sailed away without him. Anyway, demoralization was supposed to take effect more quickly in the tropics than in a temperate climate, which might be true. Therefore, it was the accepted backdrop for human derelictions, and where, in the end, a white man's sins would catch up with him, subjecting him to all the horrors of purgatory.

"And, quite unexpectedly, I did find real men and women in the islands of the South Pacific struggling against physical and moral decadence, unable to adjust themselves to the alien environment, in spite of its lush tropical beauty. I was soon filling my notebooks about them. All of them appeared to be playing a losing game against tangible or imaginary forces of fate. I'm sure they would have gone to pot just as quickly in Iceland. Most of them had come to these equatorial islands to find peace of mind, and to attempt a reconstruction of their lives, which in another clime had been only ones of failure and frustration. These sometimes desperate characters were moved by the faintest emotional zephyr, which could stir them either toward happiness or despair, and so their destiny was actually contingent, and determined, lightly, fragilely, upon the barest 'trembling of a leaf.'

"In Europe, and other 'civilized' countries of the temperate zones, habit and tradition are more firmly established for the white man, civilization being the matter of centuries of conditioning. In London, for example, or even New York City, mankind is subjected to just about the same sort of standardizations, controls and influences in his economic, political and social life. He's rather heavily insulated, and it takes a patient literary surgical-planing to skin-peel him down to the true subcutaneous personality level. The rare individual in the cities is hard to come by who will set into motion a story-line, or who, in himself, is worthy of an entire character study. Every person has his traits, his idiosyncrasies, his secret desires, his sensitivities, the element of nonconformity and mysterious reactions to life, which make him unique; and most times a writer has to do a considerable amount of searching to locate someone in a city who will generate an idea or suggest how he can be worked into a story. And this isn't easy to detect in a man or woman who wears his or her civilization too heavily.

"I travelled for about six months in America and the Pacific area, and what I found on that first trip into the South Seas made me impatient to return later, to make an intensive coverage. And at the end of the First World War I did go back, extending my travels into Malaya, Java, Siam, China, Borneo, and many back-of-beyond places. I was looking for living men and women who were acting out some sort of a real-life drama or comedy. I wasn't disappointed. I found them aboard ships, in hotels, in railway carriages, in government offices, on rubber plantations, in bars, in palm huts living with native women, and on lonely, forgotten coral beaches. I travelled in luxury liners, aboard copra-reeking schooners, by native *pirogue*, by car, by sedan-chair, on horseback, on foot, and even by bullock cart to reach them. I was constantly alert for that priceless ingredient called character, or personality, the unusual facet of individuality.

"I knew that the odds were in my favor in the islands of the South Pacific and the Far East. Here white men were living under less civilized restraints, at least the habits and routine of a European city were considerably relaxed. The customs and traditions were those of the native, which required only a rather tolerant respect for aboriginal etiquette. True, many white men did maintain a certain dignity and self-respect by dressing formally for dinner every evening, but this was only a pretense. Deep down most of them had begun to disintegrate, this brought on by the intolerable climate, the endless days of boredom, too many *stengahs,* and too many idle hours of soul-searching.

"There were other contributive factors, too, a complaining, restless wife, the temptation of native women of easy morals, and, in many instances, a hard-driving superior whom they despised.

"The majority of them were quite uncomplicated, and I was able to sort out most of them after a short observation or conversation. And they told me stories about their lives or other people's, which I'm sure they never would have had I been a permanent resident of the jungle compound or even the huge bustling seaport. I had the advantage of being in transit, and he or she knew that the chances of their ever seeing me again, or talking to me, were very slight. I was the sympathetic listener to a secret story, someone to break the monotony of their existence, and most of them seemed eager to lay bare the soul.

"In just a few hours, sitting on a screened verandah of a Malayan rubber-plantation bungalow, over a siphon and a bottle of whiskey, I've learned more about my fellowman than I could ever hope to if he had lived next door to me for twenty years.

"So I travelled through the Pacific and the Orient because I was interested in human nature, and needed characters for my stories.

"In those early Empire years, white men, out in the South Pacific or Far East, were in the alien environment for pre-scribed reasons: escapism; a curiosity about exotic places and peoples; enforced exile, because of incompetency, to a lesser government post; a desperate bid to get-rich-quick in a steaming, fever-ridden jungle; self-banishment because of some failure or tragedy in their past; or to indulge in the final stages of dissolution away from the embarrassing cen-sure of friends and family. Today, air travel has changed that concept. But, then, the South Seas and the Far East were considered *very remote* and rather unsuitable places, reached only after a long, uncomfortable ocean voyage, where a white man went only if he were desperate for a job, or was trying to rehabilitate himself.

"Therefore, most of them *were* real characters. I tried to make use of them, and their problems, as capably as I knew how. That I didn't always portray them, or their emotional circumstances, as attractively as they imagined them to be, earned me, of course, considerable criticism and hatred. On my return visits to many of those places a lot of doors were rudely slammed in my face, I was publicly insulted, and some even threatened to do me bodily harm. But I learned to ac-cept all that. One can't deal with people long without making enemies. I saw them the way they were, and I didn't intend to 'gild the lily.' If they didn't like the way I honestly thought them to be, then to hell with them—confidences and privacy be damned!

"A writer is like a paleontologist trying to reconstruct the extinct beast from a fossil bone: he can only compose from what his experience, research and his imagination are able to make tangible. A man can be unique, but that doesn't mean that he doesn't fall into one of the small number of basic categories, and an experienced writer of considerable travel acumen and observation can usually sort him out very quickly. He is able to tell immediately, by a sort of clairvoyance, when a place or a person promises something of value.

"When we meet people we see them only in the flat, they offer us but one side of themselves, and they remain shadowy: we have to give them our flesh and our bones before they exist in the round. That is why the characters of fiction are more real than the characters of life."

3. On
People, Places and Writings

My extensive travels had taken me through the South Seas, southeast Asia and the Orient, and it was all too true that displaced men and women in these settings were, or seemed to be, more unusual. Likewise, they appeared to be, as Maugham indicated, more vulnerable to a swifter physical and spiritual impairment than in temperate climes. If they were colorless clerks in an import-export house in London's Mincing Lane or Fenchurch, somehow in their transfer to a branch office in Singapore, Borneo or Shanghai, their ordinariness seemed to take on character, as if, suddenly emancipated, they were able to develop unusual aspects of that ordinariness. They became *conspicuously* ordinary people. In London, Maugham would have ignored them. But set against an exotic background, they seemed to stand out, their ordinariness enhanced, or perhaps ennobled, by the encom-

33

passing ambiance of tropical or oriental beauty. And they seemed to get along quite well.

The truly extraordinary men and women who came out to the tropical Pacific and Far East were in the minority and they appeared to suffer the most through lethargy, the enervating heat and humidity, and the lack of mental stimulation. They were abruptly cut off from the cultural benefits of London, smart spectator sports, and brilliant drawing-room or country house gatherings. At home their moral fibre was more durable, due to their conformity to a serious career, or their family and social image. But in the equatorial Pacific, or China, restlessness seemed to consume them; they couldn't, or didn't care, to adjust to the alien environment; they lost their grip on self-respect more rapidly, and moral dry-rot set in. Released from perhaps a life of quiet desperation, these particular men and women committed unaccountable, tragic and sometimes monstrous acts in the South Seas and the Far East. And Maugham was the first writer of any ability, after Conrad, to come along and record them accurately. His *The Letter, Footprints in the Jungle* and *The Book-Bag* are examples of real-life dramas in that exotic part of the world.

The majority of Maugham's stories of the South Seas and the Far East, based on more fact than fiction, were heavily flavored with marital infidelities of the whites, cohabitations with native women, and the soul-torments of the misfits. Sometimes Maugham condoned their bizarre deportment with atonishing liberality, at other times he scourged them with the most heinous penalties.

For many, many years now white men have been going to the South Seas and the Orient to get away from it all, or to find, for a sexual banquet, the erotic women initially described by the early Pacific and Far East navigators, and later confirmed by the whalermen, adventurers, beachcombers, painters, writers and professional voyagers. These whites went to Polynesia, Melanesia, Micronesia, Malaysia, the Indies and the Orient, as government workers, apprentices, planters, or remittance men, men from all walks of life, ranging from chronic drunken drifters to brilliant administrators. A large percentage of them were wayward sons of outraged, wealthy families in England, some were congenital crackpots, escapists, drunkards and satyrs. And they were deeply disturbed humans, who were hopeful that the islands below the equator would provide the necessary change for a complete reformation, or the antidote for their sexual proclivities.

The bachelors invariably encountered trouble in their faraway posts, either through their involvement with the promiscuous wives of officials or planters, or with native women. Sometimes the outcomes were homicidal, as actually happened in the case of *The Letter, Before the Party*, and so many others.

Maugham ran across many white men in Tahiti, Samoa, Malaya, Java, Sumatra, Siam, Borneo and China who had no illusions about women. They were not about to dance attendance on their wives or try to play the role of the perfect lover. Because native women were so easily accessible they preferred to indulge their extracurricular sexual experiments with them on the side.

There is a certain male species, particularly British, who finds a certain relief in surgical sex, wherein there is no absorption of individuality, no particular invasion of privacy, no rigid rules of fidelity or responsibility, nor the hazards of becoming too emotionally involved. This idea held for many of the real-life Maugham characters. White women became furious when they discovered their husbands or lovers were cohabiting with native women. The real-life heroine of *The Letter,* Leslie Crosbie, shot and killed her lover.

It was obvious that if these men were misfits at home, they were to become worse misfits in the tropics. The South Seas and the Far East most certainly didn't settle their psychological problems. When surfeited with the scenic attractions of palms silhouetted against technicolor sunsets and blue lagoons and reefs foamy with spent surf—and especially the voluptuous and amorous native women—they found that the equatorial islands had actually less to offer than the place from where they had come—and so alcohol and amoral escapes became their only means of temporarily relieving crushing despair. This is not exaggerated. They are still out there today, not in such large numbers because of the changing of sovereignty in so many once British-held areas, and it is not difficult to recognize them. Both Conrad and Maugham gave readers accurate case-histories of white men in the South Seas and the Orient under dramatic or calamitous or ludicrous circumstances; they knew well the characters they fictionized.

"In considering the men and women who went out to the South Seas and the Far East," Maugham explained carefully, "and who provided the protagonists for many of my short stories and novels, you must understand that they were the human precipitations of Great Britain's industrial revolution, when the country changed from agriculturists to articled clerks and tradesmen. Although the landed gentry never admitted it, the industrial middle-class soon determined policies in our colonies, and just who were to be sent out as administrators, civil servants, planters and apprentices.

"The type of person who did leave Great Britain for faraway posts had no particular tradition to uphold, as did the landed gentry. He was most times an incompetent, a rank opportunist, or a troublemaker. On the way out he changed and stored his woolens in the emporium of Simon Artz in Port Said, where he was completely outfitted in tropical attire, solar topee, general necessities, malarial pills and contraceptives. There he would leave his temperate-climate clothes in moth-balls until, on leave home to Great Britain, or at the termination of his contract, he would claim them again. Port Said was then the change-over point.

"Many of them never returned to take their gear out of storage at Artz's. They had been buried in Malaya, Borneo and China. I understand that even as late as 1950, when the director of Simon Artz cleaned out the storage rooms, there were old-fashioned suits and boots, some a half-century out of date, still awaiting the call of the owner or the claiming by the wearer's executor-of-estate.

"Many of the white men had to come out to the tropics as bachelors, because they couldn't find a woman willing to face the uncertain future in a 'primitive country' under physically trying conditions. Those who did bring their wives out had real trouble on their hands. White women were scarce, and the bachelors were fair game to the neglected wives of overworked civil servants or planters. They all ran true to form, bitches and sluts. Most of them were of no particular social standing in Great Britain, but, with servants available, they became insufferable tyrants. Such were the 'ladies' who lost us our possessions in Africa and elsewhere. Most times they were morally loose, and the effects of tropical heat, inertia, and boredom, converted them into pathological nymphomaniacs. As I've had some training in medical science, especially in obstetrics, wherein the female genitalia is an object of constant study, it was instantly obvious to me what physiological messes these females in the tropics were. But their predatory and promiscuous activities were doubly dangerous in such places as Malaya, Borneo and China, because their world was a small one, although the series of plantations might be spread out in a wide area. Gossip was vicious and all-destructive.

"In many parts of the world, even today, I am *persona non grata,* and hosts and hostesses still rant about my violations of confidences. I have been accused of cruelly portraying real-life men and women in my stories. I do not think I have done this. All I have done is to bring into prominence certain traits that many writers shut their eyes to. The contrast that I have found in people has interested me, but I do not think I have unduly emphasized it. The censure that has from time to time been passed on me is due perhaps to the fact that I have not expressly condemned what was bad in the characters of my invention and praised what was good. It must be a fault in me that I am not gravely shocked at the sins of others unless they personally affect me, and even when they do I have learnt at last generally to excuse them. I take the goodness of the good for granted and I am amused when I discover their defects or their vices; I am touched when I see the goodness of the wicked and I am willing enough to shrug a tolerant shoulder at their wickedness. I am not my brother's keeper. I cannot bring myself to judge my fellows; I am content to observe them. My observation has led me to believe that, all in all, there is not as much difference between the good and the bad as the moralists would have us believe.

"Secretiveness always involves pride. And so the story invariably comes out of secretiveness; therefore, the pride is wounded when the guarded memories are exposed by a writer.

"Among other things not too flattering, I have been accused of not particularly liking people. One doesn't have to like people to be a writer. It's whether he understands them. Dickens was quite anti-social, and so were Melville, Tolstoi, Dostoievsky and Balzac. I wouldn't say that they were the finest craftsmen in their writings, but they had a keen insight into human motivations and thoughts. That is why they were splendid writers. If a writer is interested in a person, even though you dislike him, it won't prevent him from finding that person valuable in a short story, novel or play. A writer's active imagination and personality make a story worthwhile. A writer's observation is the important talent.

"A writer is more likely to depict a character who is a recognizable human being with his own individuality, if he has a living model. Often a reader will recognize a trait he knows in himself, or a description of a place he lives in and, in his conceit, jump to the conclusion that the character described is a portrait of himself.

"The model a writer chooses is seen through his own temperament, and if he is a writer of any originality what he sees need have little relation to the facts. He takes only what he wants of the living man. He uses him as a peg on which to hang his own fancies. For example, I never even spoke one word to the real-life trollop who became the heroine of my *Miss Thompson*, although she travelled on the same boat with me from Honolulu to Samoa and stayed at the same boarding-house in Pago Pago. I can't even remember her real name. Many people have conceitedly claimed to be the real models for some of the more popular characters of my short stories and novels. This practice of ascribing originals for the creatures of the writer's fancy is a very mischievous one.

"In my travels, particularly in the South Pacific and the Far East, I have been more concerned with the obscure than the famous, with back-of-beyond places rather than the accepted trippers' sightseeing spots. I can't work up much enthusiasm over the great wonders of the world; too many platitudes have been bestowed upon them already. I found more beauty in tiny native huts on stilts over a muddy canal in Bangkok than the Alhambra in Granada. The commonplace man interests me more than the important, affluent one, because he appears to be a more genuine fellow. He displays his oddities because it has never struck him that they are odd. The so-called great man is too often all apiece. It is the little man that is a bundle of contradictory elements. For my own part I would much rather spend a month on a desert island with a beachcomber than a bank president. So travel became a very integral part of the business of writing, at least for me."

Maugham's travels in America, Hawaii, Samoa, Tonga, Fiji and Tahiti were made during the First World War years and composed his first long extended trip. In 1920, after he had recuperated from tuberculosis in a sanatorium in the north of Scotland, he travelled through China; and the following year found him in the Federated Malay States, Indo-China, and then returning to China. In 1922 he was in Australia, the introductory setting of his *The Narrow Corner*, continuing to some of the islands of the Malayan archipelago, with a three months' stay in Java. In 1923 he visited Central and South America; in 1924 he was back in the Malay States, Borneo and Siam; in 1929 he was in Borneo again. In 1937 he went to India for a winter holiday.

"Rudyard Kipling had encouraged me to go to India with the idea of a series of modern stories. I felt that Rudyard had written all there was worth writing about this huge strange country, but when I went there I saw that he had written about only one aspect, which now was long outdated. But I was too old then to tackle such a complex country, and I no longer seemed to have the knack of devising a story out of stray bits of dialogue or a brief encounter. The only thing I got out of India was some material for *The Razor's Edge,* which I, and my critics, are in agreement is not my best novel by far.

"Kipling, who had spent a holiday in the West Indies, also tried to encourage me to go there to look about, but, again, it was too late in the day for me to take on a new area. The South Seas, the Far East, and the Orient were my favorite and familiar areas.

"Voyaging through the South Seas and the Indies, I kept a notebook on places, peoples, brief jottings of observations, reminder-impressions and dialogues. I rarely went to my ship's cabin or lagoon-side hotel room without writing down a description of a special scene of the day, or of some conversation with a special character that I might be able to use in a future story.

"A writer always needs an incident or a character for a starting-point, but I always exercised imagination, invention and a sense of the dramatic to make it something of my own. I have known authors who declared that none of their characters was ever even remotely suggested by anyone they had known, but in most cases their characters were wooden and lifeless. It is certain that many excellent writers have based the persons of their stories on persons they have known in real life. A good novelist must work from life. But though they have in mind a particular person, this is not to say that they have copied him, nor that the character they have devised is to be taken for a portrait. It is unjust then for the critics to blame an author because he draws a character in

41

whom they detect a likeness to someone they know, and wholly unreasonable of them to expect him never to take one trait or another from living creatures.

"Using notes I have taken, not as a story outline which would limit and constrain me, but usually of character observations, or pertinent descriptions of certain settings of the story I have devised in my imagination, I find that the story comes to me in a straight line. I am convinced that the subconscious does the really difficult work. I sit down with a fountain pen and unlined paper and the story pours out. However lousy a section is I let it go. I write on to the end. Then the subconscious mind has done what it can; what is to be created is there. And the rest—the rest is simply effort. You may go over and over, polishing, rewriting the lousy parts, sometimes rewriting a page for the whole day, going over a chapter time and time again, until, though you know it isn't right, it is the best you can do. But that is the labor of the conscious mind, the effort of a craftsman. It is the first draft, the creative draft, that is basic."

It is obvious, after reading *A Writer's Notebook* (1949), in which are published the condensed and edited material of the 15 thick notebooks he kept from 1892 to 1944, how valuable his notes were for future stories. "By making a note of something that strikes you, you separate it from the incessant stream of impressions that crowd across the mental eye, and perhaps fix it in your memory . . . When you know you are going to make a note of something, you look at it more attentively than you otherwise would, and in the process of doing so the words are borne in upon you that will give it its private place in reality."

As an example of the value of some of his notes, a reader finds these jottings on his voyage from Honolulu to Pago Pago:

"[The prostitute] . . . Plump, pretty in a coarse fashion, perhaps not more than twenty-seven: she wore a white dress and a large white hat . . . She had left Iwelei,[1] (Honolulu's red-light district) after the raid . . ."

And his observation of the missionary aboard the same southbound vessel: "He was a tall thin man, with long limbs loosely jointed, hollow cheeks and high cheek-bones . . . He had a cadaverous look, and a look of suppressed fire."

And of the setting of his eventual *Miss Thompson*, the steamy South Pacific port of Pago Pago, American Samoa: "It is a great land-locked harbour, and all around it rise, high and steep, the green hills . . . It is terribly hot and very rainy. From out of a blue sky you will see heavy grey clouds come floating over the mouth of the harbour, and the rain falls in torrents."

And of the famous boarding-house itself: "It is a two-storey frame house with verandahs on both floors. Below is a store in which are sold canned goods, pork and beans, beef, hamburger steak, canned asparagus, peaches and apricots; and cotton goods, lava-lavas, hats, rain-coats and such like . . . The rooms are almost bare of furniture, a poor iron bed with a ragged mosquito-netting, a rickety chair and a washstand. The rain rattles down on the corrugated iron roof."

On these brief notes Maugham composed the short story *Miss Thompson*.

"But I needed more than a pencil and a note-pad to get stories," said Maugham, his eyes fixed on the Regency mirror again. "I am not myself a good mixer, inclined to reticence and impatience with the general run of people one meets aboard ships, or in hotels. As a boy I was not in good health, I had no interest in games in school which are important

---

[1] *Iwelei* is the correct spelling, but Maugham always wrote and spoke of it as *Iwelei*.

in the social life of students. I was shy and I stammered badly, a nervous affliction occasioned by the early death of my mother, and being shifted about to relatives, bedevilled by classmates, and bullied by stupid masters.

"For perhaps one or more of these reasons I was inclined to withdraw from society, and so at an early age I found it difficult to enter into any familiarity with others. I have retained this anti-social trait throughout my life. I don't like people en masse, but I have loved individuals. I have never liked anyone at first sight. I do not think I have ever addressed someone I did not know in a railway carriage, or spoken to a fellow-passenger on board ship unless he first spoke to me. I have an allergy to excess alcohol, so I'm not one to spend my time in a bar roistering with characters, who I'm sure could provide many splendid types of stories, because man becomes more coherent and understandable when his inhibitions have been diluted with alcohol. As you can understand, I had some grave disadvantages for a writer seeking material.

"I was very lucky to have, on my journeys into the South Pacific and the Far East, a companion who had an inestimable social gift. He had an amiability of disposition that enabled him in a very short time to make friends with people in ships, clubs, bar-rooms and hotels, so that through him I was able to get into easy contact with an immense number of persons whom otherwise I should have known only from a distance. So I made acquaintance with them with just the degree of intimacy that suited me.

"My travelling companion-secretary was Frederick Gerald Haxton, an American, whom I had met in France at the beginning of the First World War in the Red Cross ambulance unit to which I was attached. I had admired his energy and adventurous nature. So when I planned my South Seas travels, I contacted him in Chicago and he agreed to go along.

"We were not twenty-four hours at sea before, with his good nature and humour, he knew everybody aboard ship. A charming fellow, really. But for him I never would have collected the characters that were to spark my imagination for the book *The Trembling of a Leaf*. He, also, accompanied me in 1920 to China, and from that trip came *On a Chinese Screen*. He was with me in Australia and Malaya, which resulted in *The Narrow Corner*.

"To give you an idea of how Gerald helped me, I can cite this instance, among many, which is a good example. Gerald and I had gone to Sumatra and were staying at a place which which I called Tanah Merah in the story he was to uncover for me here. I set a time to dine at the white man's club, but Gerald, as usual, became involved with some friends in the bar. I was very hungry, and became finally very provoked waiting for Gerald, knowing his addiction to drinking and gambling.

"I was nearly through dinner when he staggered in. I was thoroughly out of sorts, and about to raise a stink about his inconsideration, when he said: 'I'm sorry, I know I'm drunk, but as an apology I've got a corking good story for you.' And he sat down, and I coldly listened to him. When he was through my anger had dissolved. What he told me became one of my best short stories, *Footprints in the Jungle*, a true murder story of a wife and her lover who had killed her husband.

"Critics accused me of writing that story in my customary cynical vein, condoning the crime. I only followed the facts. I learned that the planters, traders, agents, doctors and officials of the community had accepted them after the slaying, and, from all accounts, the husband, being a sadistic bully,

deserved what he got. Later I met the couple. I found them
very gentle and friendly, and I couldn't bring myself to be
revolted by what they had done. They didn't appear to
be suffering from any remorse, and it didn't seem to mar
their happiness in their marriage later on. Very nice people,
really. Yes, human nature is very odd.

"That was just one of many stories that Gerald dug up for
me. And he was so helpful in so many other ways. When the
Nazis invaded France and the Vichy Government was established, I had to clear out of my villa on Cap Ferrat. I was, as
a suspect spy because of my *Ashenden* espionage stories of
the First World War, on Hitler's list to be arrested and
brought to Berlin. I was warned to get out of France, as
rapidly as I could, to a safe country. My villa was filled with
valuable paintings and art objects, I had to take care of my
staff, there were cars and a yacht to think about. And there
were all my books and manuscripts. It was a pretty kettle of
fish, I can tell you! But Gerald took charge. He told me:
'You've got to leave right way! Don't worry about anything!
I'll attend to everything!'

"And he did. With the aid of kind neighbors he hid my
paintings, manuscripts, cars, yacht, everything of value that
the Nazis would loot. When I came back, after the war, I
found I hadn't lost a single item. He was a good and trusted
friend, and, although he had a fondness for the bottle and
roulette, very capable and dependable when the occasion
demanded. Brave, too.

"Once, in Sarawak, in 1922, a freak tidal-wave, called a
bore, upset the boat in which we were travelling down river.
I would have drowned if Gerald hadn't rescued me.[2]

"During World War Two, he finally returned to America

---

[2] Related in detail in *A Writer's Notebook*.

and stayed with me for a short time in South Carolina, where I was sitting out the war. Then, for the war effort, he obtained a job in Washington. But he suddenly became very ill in 1944, and four days after an emergency operation he died, at the age of 52. His death was a bitter grief to me. We had known each other for many years, we had taken the bad with the good, and I had come to consider him like my right arm. It is difficult to estimate how many miles we travelled around the world together, or how many stories he found for me."

Maugham's Far East and oriental travels, in essay form, have been published in part in such volumes as *On a Chinese Screen*, and *The Gentleman in the Parlour*, the latter a series of vignettes and character sketches of his trip from Rangoon, Burma to Haiphong in the then French Indo-China. *Gentleman* is his favorite collection of travel impressions, and his *Chinese Screen* is an excellent tableau of pre-Communist China. These two books reveal a keener insight into Maugham himself, who is more of a sentimentalist than he cares to admit.

But Maugham eventually became surfeited with travel.

"Finally, after a half-dozen or more of these voyages to faraway islands and countries of the South Pacific and Asia, people became too much alike. I kept meeting too many of the same types. I found my interest in them waning. I had come to the point where I found it difficult to sort them out, to give them individuality. The fault was with me, not them. They were still the same, but I no longer had the faculty to lift them out of their ordinariness, to give them my special touch of characterization to make them humans with arresting traits. They definitely had, living in an alien atmosphere, distinct peculiarities that made them characters, but I had lost contact with them. I suppose I had become too indulgent of their standard frailties. I ceased to consider them as real

47

people. I came to the conclusion that travel offered, for the future, small benefit. I had sufficient notes in my pads to keep me writing for a century or more. Succinctly, I had become thoroughly bored with distant humanity. What I now felt about mankind, I had occasion once to have a man pronounce whom I had met aboard a ship in the China Seas: 'I'll give you my opinion of the human race in a nutshell, brother,' he said. 'Their heart's in the right place, but their head is a thoroughly inefficient organ.'

"Nevertheless, the Pacific and the Far East, and the whites I encountered out there, provided me with the best material for my most popular, and my favorite, essays, short stories and novels."

It is evident that Maugham had a very genuine affinity with the South Seas and Asiatic countries. His jottings in his notebooks affirm this: they were longer, more colorful, more enthusiastic than earlier impressions; it was as if he were seeing beauty in nature and man for the first time. They did not carry the cynical overtones of his other notes penned in Europe.

As for example, an evening on a Tahitian lagoon:

"At sunset the sea turns to a bright purple; the sky is cloudless and the sun, burning red, sinks into the sea, rapidly, but not so rapidly as writers lead one to believe, and Venus shines. When evening comes, clear and silent, an ardent, frenzied life seems to break out. Countless shelled animals begin to crawl about at the edge of the water, and in the water every living thing seems to be in action . . . In the quiet of the lovely evening there is something mysterious about it . . ."

His impressions of a native bazaar in Kuching, Malaya:

"On the banks of the river are the native huts, and here, living their immemorial lives, are the Malays. As you wander in the crowd, as you linger watching, you get a curious, thrilling sense of urgent life. You divine a happy, happy, normal activity. Birth and death, love and hunger; these are the affairs of man."

And of Ceylon:

"The Jungle. There is a moment just before sundown when the trees in the jungle seem to detach themselves from the great mass of forest and become individuals . . . in the magic of the hour they appear to gain life of a new kind so that you can almost imagine that they enclose spirits and with the sunset will be capable of changing places . . ."

His enchantment with Burma:

"Mandalay by moonlight: The white gateways are flooded with silver and the erections above them are shot with silhouetted glimpses of the sky. The effect is ravishing . . . it has a beauty which you can take hold of and enjoy and make your own . . . Those other beauties need the frame of mind to be enjoyed and appreciated, but this is a beauty suited to all seasons and all moods."

An observation aboard ship:

"The Skipper: he is a little plump man, without angles, with a round face like the full moon, red and clean-shaven, a little fat button of a nose, very white teeth, fair hair close-cropped, with short fat legs and fat arms . . . He is not without charm. He never speaks without an oath, but a good-natured one. He is a jolly soul. He is American, of thirty perhaps, and he has spent all his life on the Pacific. He lost his ship and with it his certificate, and has now come down to the command of this dirty little tramp. It has not interfered with his good humour . . . He is fond of his whiskey, and fond of the Samoans, and he tells vivid, funny stories of his success with them."

Although Maugham wrote many fine short stories of the

South Pacific islands, the Far East and the Orient, the reading public identify him immediately and more readily with *Miss Thompson*, or *Rain*. Although the short stories *Mackintosh*, *Red*, and *The Pool*, also of a Samoan setting, are almost as well written, few readers associate them with him. The response is always the same: *"Sadie Thompson?* Oh, yes— Somerset Maugham."

I had, for some years, wondered why Maugham himself had not undertaken the conversion of the short-story, *Miss Thompson*, to the stage-hit *Rain*. He had, after all, first become famous as a playwright, not as a short-story writer or novelist, and at one time, early in his career, in 1908, he had four plays running simultaneously in London: *Lady Frederick*, *Mrs. Dot*, *Jack Straw*, and *The Explorer*.

Now I had the opportunity to put the question to him.

He smiled wryly.

"Frankly, I never saw *Miss Thompson* as anymore than just a good short story, and I still feel the same way, which might explain why I didn't adapt it for the stage, as I did *The Letter*, for example."

An American writer, J. C. Furnas, visiting Pago Pago many years after Maugham's visit, had made this comment: "A magazine publisher stood beside me at the rail twelve years ago as the liner *Mariposa* sailed from Pago Pago in American Samoa. His eyes fell on Centipede Row, a line of cottages inhabited by married officers of the miniature U.S. Navy base. 'Six little bungalows,' he said dreamily. 'Six little bungalows at Pago Pago. Ah, if only Willie Maugham were here!' "

Willie Maugham most certainly had been there, under circumstances more propitious and rewarding, story-wise, than six little naval cracker-boxes.

II

HAWAII

4. The
Red=light District of Iwilei

Furnas had passed through Pago Pago in May of 1947, and
the only hotel for transients was appropriately named the
Saddie Thompson Hotel, with a misspelled first-name sign
commemorating the long-ago deported strumpet of Honolulu's red-light district.

A Navy officer who had been billeted for a while in the
ramshackle hotel, had been there at the time that the mana-
geress, under mounting pressure from the indignant missionaries, had renamed the musty, run-down establishment the
Samoa House. The Holy Henrys had petitioned her to cease
flaunting the name of a brazen whore—even though fictitious
(sic!) —who had once upset the spiritual and moral decorum
of the peaceful naval base.

The officer, with an inherent superstition of the nautical
bad-luck in changing names of ships, felt that she was sim-

53

ilarly courting disaster by altering the name of the hotel. And he told her so on many occasions. But the part-Samoan lady had been brain-washed by the South Seas soul-savers and decided that *Samoa House* would be its permanent name. That is, until a tropical tempest roared up the bay, shattered an entire wall and ripped loose the roof—whereupon she hastily restored the former *Saddie Thompson Hotel* sign.

When advised of this incident, Maugham commented humorously:

"No doubt Sadie's indignant ghost putting on a tantrum. As long as she had had the game there she intended having the name."

It had occurred to writer Furnas, during his visit to Pago Pago, that the story-line of *Rain* had been employed by hundreds of writers long before Maugham had penned *Miss Thompson,* and that the triteness of the plot could have been set against a hundred backdrops other than Pago Pago.

However, the point that Mr. Furnas obviously overlooks is that not a single writer ever handled the hackneyed plot quite as adroitly as Willie Maugham, if one takes cognizance of its enormous accruement in royalties to its author for almost half a century.

Maugham had originally planned to by-pass Hawaii on his voyage into the South Seas, by taking a vessel direct to Tahiti from San Francisco. But a publisher in New York City had urged him to stop over in the Hawaiian group.

"They're delightful islands," he told him, "and they'll provide a suitable springboard for your voyage into the South Pacific." And he gave him a number of books to read on America's mid-Pacific island possessions.

"So I decided impulsively to visit Hawaii with Gerald Haxton. I was still convalescing from a lung ailment and two rigorous years of wartime duty of the First World War. It was winter-time and cold and damp in America—where I was visiting at the time—so I eagerly anticipated all the climatic benefits which the travel brochures promised chilblained visitors to these balmy sub-tropical isles, which your Mark Twain had sentimentally referred to as 'the loveliest fleet of islands that lies anchored in any ocean.'

"We boarded a large cruise ship at some port on the California coast, rather than taking the regular passenger-steamer between San Francisco and Honolulu, as we both felt that the food and accommodations would be superior. The service was adequate, but the almost 400 passengers aboard were a dreary, noisome, boring lot, the usual sort—a chamber of commerce delegation who had been promised a key to the city of Honolulu, made of special Hawaiian wood, and to be presented by the mayor, the usual complement of honeymooners, the decrepit bits and pieces of invalid humanity taking a sea-voyage upon their doctors' prescription, several flashy sea strumpets and a scruffy assortment of bounders clever with cards. But, in the majority, the passenger-list was composed of anonymous, faceless, sheep-like humanity.

"Gerald and I studiously avoided our fellow travellers—who somehow had been advised that there was a well-known writer aboard—kept to our cabin, played cards, read and rested. You can be sure that we were relieved when at long last, one morning, we raised the island's famous landmark of Diamond Head."

And it was most providential that Maugham had been persuaded to come to Hawaii. Otherwise the short story *Miss Thompson* could never have been conceived.

On the day that Maugham and Gerald Haxton walked down the gangway into Honolulu, a number of interesting events were to take place in widely separated places of the world and Honolulu.

The Allies of World War One had overwhelmed a five-mile stretch of German trenches on the Somme front, along the line of the river Ancre, capturing almost 4000 *boches* . . . Pancho Villa and his peasant rebels were resisting American forces near the city of Chihuahua in Mexico . . . one Un Pong Soon was still impatiently awaiting the return of his new bride, a Hawaiian lass of a fickle nature by the name of Mary Kua, following his visit to the Honolulu police station where he had lamented: "Mr. Policeman, prease you to find my wife who been lun away fo' we mally onry few hour! Whassa mattuh wit' Hawaii *kahuna pule* (*prayer-man*, minister), he not make good mally! *Wahine*[1] no stop long 'nough fo' me make her acquaint!" . . . at the Liberty Theatre in downtown Honolulu Pearl White, Creighton Hale and Warner Oland were appearing in Chapter 17 of the movie serial *The Iron Claw*; and film siren Theda Bara in *Gold and the Woman* was announced as the next super attraction at the nearby Hawaii Theatre . . . Jack London was seriously ailing from uremia at his home in the Valley of the Moon in northern California . . . Lai Duck was arrested for selling gold-plated nickels as genuine five-dollar gold coins on Hotel Street to soldiers from Honolulu's Fort Shafter . . . In America and the islands everyone was humming Irving Berlin's song: "I'm down in Honolulu looking them over." . . . Vice crusaders were regimenting their forces for an all-out war on the Iwilei red-light district in downtown Honolulu.

"Yes, the missionaries and the merchant princes of Honolulu had finally decided that it was time that the city became a bit more respectable now that pineapple and sugar were

---

[1] This is the Hawaiian spelling of the native word for *woman*. In Tahiti it is spelled *Vahine*. The *w* in Hawaiian converts to *v* in Tahitian, and vice versa.

bringing about economic changes," chuckled Maugham. "The clean-up groups had handed a petition to the foreman of the Grand Jury and the Sheriff of Honolulu, demanding that the notorious red-light district, known as Iwelei, where vice and violence were supposed to be rife, should be closed down once and for all. The subsequent investigation had started a week before my arrival in Honolulu, so I found myself right in the thick of it."

One night Maugham had made a visit to Iwilei, reached by one of the sidestreets near the harbor, over a precarious bridge, along a rutted road to a quarter of bars and barber shops in which Japanese women clipped hair. The red-light area was a wide road, with rows of tiny green-painted bungalows on either side.

"Iwelei is laid out like a garden city, and in its respectable regularity, its order and trimness, gives you an impression of sardonic horror; for never can the search for love have been so planned and systematised . . . there is a certain stir, an air of expectant agitation . . ."

Each prostitute's workshop was exactly alike, a small parlour containing chairs, a gramophone with a morning-glory flower horn, all blaring out the latest ragtime tunes, here and there some waiting customer picking out a one-finger melody on a dilapidated piano. The bedroom, with chest of drawers, a bar of coat-hooks on the wall, and a double canopied bed with curtains, was off the parlour, with a tiny kitchenette behind. Beer and bottles of gin and whisky were lined up on the sink; no food was in evidence. On the walls of the parlour and bedroom were pinned or pasted tear-out pages from magazines, of film actresses, scenes of Los Angeles or San Francisco, the home-towns no doubt of most of the inmates. A hawker of *September Morn* prints, depicting a nude woman in the shallow shore-water of a lake, had evidently passed through the infamous district, or had bawdily bartered or lost his entire supply of merchandise in one of the houses, because every bungalow parlour had this famous picture fixed to the wall, perhaps to titillate the sexual interest of a waiting client.

"Some of the houses had their blinds down, which meant that the prostitutes inside had a man in the bedroom and perhaps another waiting in the parlour drinking beer or whiskey. In others, in the open window, thickly rouged strumpets in gaudy attire sat reading, sewing, or just peering out vigilantly, like voracious hawks on the alert for prey, or they called out bawdy insinuations to passing seamen from ships in port, soldiers, American sailors from gunboats—mostly drunk—Chinese, Japanese, Negroes and Hawaiians. They wandered about in the night, and desire seemed to throb in the air.

"The prostitutes were all sizes, shapes and nationalities, and not many of them were young or attractive. It was a district of all races, Japanese, Chinese, Negresses, Germans, Spaniards, Portuguese, Hawaiian, Filipino and Spaniards and God-knows what else. Each house blared out the favorite tune of their country on a gramophone. It was bedlam.

"Of all the prostitutes in Iwelei, the Hawaiians appeared to be the prettiest and least ravaged and coarse; it was as if evilness couldn't contaminate their basically gentle and gay spirits."

As one writer observed:

"One feels that the Hawaiian *wahine,* however much she slept and drank with Jack ashore, however freely her husband or brother pimped for her, managed to be less shattered about it than her opposite number among the slack-jawed slatterns of the Barbary Coast. According to the natives' original moral standards, voluntary sexual intercourse with strangers was nothing to fret oneself about, and much of that attitude probably survived."

Maugham, out of curiosity, had decided to visit one of the women of Iwilei.

"She ceased her professional seductiveness when she learned I had come in only for a pleasant little chat. I refused a drink, in sharp awareness of the countless microbes no doubt incubated on the rims of the dirty glasses on her sink, and I didn't want my ear-drums rattled by the gramophone. She sat down, ill at ease, and studied me with increasing disfavor.

" 'You lookin' for a virgin, or a young boy?' she suddenly asked.

"I assured her, neither.

" 'Well, if you ain't in here to do nothin',' she informed me impatiently, 'then you'll have to pay double—which is two dollars. Bed-work is fast, talk is slow.' "

Maugham handed her two dollars, and walked out into the night.

"Bushwah!" the insulted whore shouted after him.

Maugham strolled along the line of bungalows, his route illumined by widely spaced street lamps or the occasional light from the open windows of the cribs.

"Men wander about, for the most part silently, looking at the women; now and then one makes up his mind and slinks up the three steps that lead into the parlour, is let in, and then the door and window are shut and the blind is pulled down."

Maugham, as with the other men who were just there to look, was taunted by the prostitutes; some exposed their breasts and called obscene suggestions to him, a few hooted

"Cake-eater!" as he passed their windows, and now and again one would rush out, take a hard grip on his arm, and try to drag him into the bungalow.

"It was all very sordid—and sad, too."

At one bungalow a line-up of "doughboys" extended in an uneven queue, fretful, muttering and foot-scuffing, for more than 75 feet. The blind of the bungalow was pulled down. And while they impatiently waited, they jingled the silver dollars in their pockets; it was a nerve-wracking medley.

"It was done, I suppose, to remind the woman inside that there were men standing outside under the stars with congested sexual energies, waiting to have their relief."

Suddenly, a harsh, strident voice grated through the thin wall. "Gawd damnit! Cud-oud that racket! You're drivin' me nuts!"

The tantalizing sound of waiting hard cash was slowly unnerving the harassed whore.

Maugham smiled thinly. "For all I know that popular prostitute could have been my Sadie. At least, it amuses me to think so. The tart of my *Miss Thompson* did come from Iwelei, you know."

Although one of the whores of Honolulu's red-light district was selling her body very cheaply, Maugham could not know at the time he made his excursion there that she would eventually, and incongruously, net *him* more than a half-million dollars!

A few nights later, at a dinner in the Alexander Young Hotel in downtown Honolulu, Maugham was introduced by Gerald Haxton to an elderly circuit court judge, whose duty it was to charge the Territorial Grand Jury to conduct an intensive examination of the evil of the Iwelei vice district.

"I think his name was Ashland,[2] and he seemed quite dedicated to eradicating the festering carbuncle from the lily-white rump of the fair city of Honolulu. No doubt his wife was on the clean-up committee."

Maugham who, as a medical student, had acquired considerable sympathy for the prostitutes he had encountered in the slums of Lambeth, argued with the judge that the closing down of the Honolulu red-light district would make it almost impossible to control the spread of venereal disease, and increase the potential of rape.

"The law must be upheld," retorted the judge, who had been severely jolted by the zeal of the vice crusaders. "We've had laws that date way back to the first penal code of the Kingdom of Hawaii in 1869, and the provisions concerning procurers and pimps and those penalizing owners and lessees of the houses used for prostitution and such were enacted in 1903. Iwilei, without consent from the city government, has been converted into a sordid red-light district, that has now become offensive to every decent, law-abiding man and woman of this community.

"As a result of the location of Iwilei, many hundreds of men constantly, and especially at night, frequent this red-light section, and it's apparent that much crime and disorder have attended, and still do attend, the presence of these disreputable females of Iwilei.

"In addition to our local and civilian population, there are now garrisoned on the Island of Oahu, from 8,000 to 10,000 men of the armed services, the vast majority of whom are in their early youth, unmarried and socially unattached, and with rather restricted means provided for their rational en-

---

[2] Judge Clarence W. Ashford.

tertainment, while off duty. And they're all garrisoned within easy access to Iwilei. Not only that but the red-light district adjoins our manufacturing establishments, such as the pineapple canneries, where young boys and girls are employed. These youths can be solicited by these hardened harlots, and the girls preyed upon by the pimps."[3]

"I've been told that the prostitutes have been making pay-offs to the police department," said Maugham. "And that the courts have been lenient, too."

"Not my court, sir, not my court—*never!*" protested the judge. "They've caught hell from me, I can assure you!"

"My observation has been," snapped Maugham, "that when moral reforms are instituted, the prostitutes are always the first to suffer the righteous wrath of the community, never the rascals in high places."

Judge Ashford didn't appreciate Maugham's attitude. He compressed his lips and held out his hand.

"Anyway, Mr. Maugham, if you're so inclined, sit in on the court trials that will follow the closing down of Iwilei. It might prove to be interesting for you. You'll see how I mete out justice to these shameless women. And, who knows, you might get a story or two out of it."

"That I doubt," said Maugham, turning on his heel. "The closing of a red-light district doesn't savour of originality or the unusual."

---

[3] It was also known that for some years callow youths of the Old St. Louis College—actually a high school—located on River Street, just off Beretania Street in downtown Honolulu, would sometimes play hookey and sneak over three blocks to the Iwilei red-light district to observe, in hiding, the amoral activities of the infamous quarter. And at graduation time it was a sort of ritualistic climax for the male students to converge in the late evening hours, after the graduation ceremonies, to lose their virginity, which the prostitutes obligingly acceded —for a bargain price, en masse.

But the fact remains that the flushing out of the prostitutes of Honolulu's Iwilei was to make possible Maugham's encounter with a blonde floosie whom he was to make famous all around the world.

And Maugham did keep an eye on the raids in Iwilei. The Federal Government joined forces with the city police, and charged the pimps of Iwilei with white slavery, and of the thirteen men picked up and served warrants by the U.S. Marshal of Honolulu, eight were of French nationality.

Maugham remarked: "Evidently, it suggests that the profession of pimping is peculiarly attractive to the citizens of France."

One hundred and eight prostitutes, on bench warrants, were herded into Judge Ashford's circuit court in Honolulu.

The judge saw that Maugham was a spectator in a rear seat, and he cleared his throat to make sure that his oratory would be heard by the British author.

"I wish you to know," he scolded the uneasy bawds, "that where pleas of guilty are made and a suspended sentence granted, it means that you are convicted of the offense of being common prostitutes for which the law provides a severe penalty.

"This prostitution has been winked at and tolerated so long that those who indulged in it have come to the conclusion that they are under the protection of the law. And so the prosecuting officials and the police, on indictments returned by the Grand Jury, have determined to attempt to stamp out this vice on this island.

"There are strong reasons for extending leniency to the women who have practiced vice in the past in consideration for pleas of guilty. But this leniency is taking the form of a suspension of sentence. During the next thirteen months this conviction will be hanging over you, and you are liable, in consequence, to be called in and have sentence pronounced because of this conviction. You must, therefore, behave yourself during the coming thirteen months."

The prostitutes exchanged baffled looks. How could they "behave" themselves and keep from starving? Maugham smiled rankly at Judge Ashford.

The judge rebukingly shook his finger at the stunned whores of Iwilei.

"So if you revert to the old practice of prostitution, or otherwise become disorderly persons, then you are liable to be brought into court and have sentence pronounced!"

It was noted in the court records of that day that there were six prostitutes against whom indictments were returned who had not been served with bench warrants for an appearance with the 108 disreputable women in Judge Ashland's court.

"My Sadie was fortunately among those six, because she definitely was not in court on the day I was there, otherwise I would have remembered her when I finally did see her aboard ship."

Maugham was highly amused at a sudden commotion in Judge Ashford's court when the whores, almost as one, turned their heads over their shoulders and glared at someone in the audience. Whereupon Sheriff Charley H. Rose of Honolulu and an enormous Irish captain-of-detectives, with the appropriate name of Arthur McDuffie, both heavily moustached, came forward and began to make an almost tearful plea for the expelled prostitutes of Iwilei. Would his honor, in his infinite mercy, considering the approach of Thanksgiving and Christmas, permit the ladies to return to Iwilei to "pursue their work" until after the first of the year, so as to earn getaway money to California?

"I should say not!" thundered the outraged judge. "The

sooner these women are off the island the better for all concerned!"

The prostitutes, in a state of panic, descended en masse on the steamship offices clamoring for space on the first available steamer for San Francisco.

Maugham made another excursion to Iwilei that night.

"Most of the houses were closed, and there was hardly anyone in the streets. Here and there little groups of three or four women discussed the news in undertones. The place was dark and silent. Iwelei had ceased to exist."

But somewhere in Honolulu, in hiding, a blonde escapee from Iwilei pondered her predicament, paced angrily, cursed, and tried to make up her mind if she should return to California, or travel in another direction. She didn't especially want to return to the mainland, and, fortunately, as she had never supported a pimp, she had a huge roll of bills in her purse, to take as long a trip anywhere as she wished.

That she eventually decided to take a steamer southward to Pago Pago was Willie Maugham's extraordinary good fortune.

5. On Hawaii and Hawaiians

"In case you might think that I spent all my time in Honolulu prowling about in disreputable districts, let me assure you that I did have an opportunity to see much of the Hawaiian islands, and to enjoy my visit thoroughly.

"I was, for the first time, on the threshold of the South Pacific, which, as I've said, I consider the most interesting ocean of the world. No waters wash the shores of so many varied isles and countries, no currents encompass the reefs and volcanic islands of so many different races. I had the thrilling expectancy that I was about to enter into an altogether new and exciting chapter of my life and career by setting forth on this Pacific voyage.

"Gerald and I were fond of having *apéritifs* on the high seaside verandah of the Moana Hotel, which was about three miles from downtown Honolulu. Seated in our rattan chairs, we could see people, white and *kanaka*, driving up in carriages in the huge courtyard below us which was shaded by a huge banyan tree. And out beyond the beach, bronzed Hawaiian sea-gods handsomely rode their heavy surf-boards in on the huge sunlit combers—all framed by coconut palms, the perennial pennants of Polynesia.

"I don't think that there is a more compatible growth that suits the tropics so well as the coconut palm, and the sight of it always arouses reflections of adventure and romance. Good luck surely attended the natives of tropical islands when the palm began to sprout along their sunny shores. The coconut palm supplies them with almost every necessity for shelter, food and drink. It is identical in its physical growth with man. From seed through infancy, childhood, virile youth, adult grandeur, into quiet old age, its span of years is remarkably the same. Although Mark Twain remarked that the coco palm reminded him of a feather duster struck by lightning, my enduring memory of Hawaii is of the coconut palms with their delicate tracery of fronds etched against a soft blue sky, framing the blue seas and surf-torn reefs beyond the beach at Waikiki."

Maugham had been fascinated by Hawaii and its people:

"Nothing had prepared me for Honolulu. It is so far away from Europe . . . so strange and so charming associations are attached to the name . . . along the streets crowd an unimaginable assortment of people . . . It is the meeting-place of East and West. The very new rubs shoulders with the immeasurably old. And if you have not found the romance you expected you have come upon something singularly intriguing. All these strange people live close to each other, with different languages and different thoughts; they believe in different gods and they have different values; two passions alone they share, love and hunger. And somehow as you watch them you have an impression of extraordinary vitality. Though the air is so soft and the sky so blue, you have, I know not why, a feeling of something hotly passionate that beats like a throbbing pulse through the crowd . . . It gives you just that thrill, with a little catch at the heart that you have when at night in the forest the silence trembles on a sudden with a low, insistent beating of a drum. You are all expectant of I know not what.

"The Hawaiians seem to be the happiest and most amiable. Their color ranges from copper almost to black. They are tall and well-made, their noses are flattish, their eyes are large and their lips full and sensual. Their hair is dark and crisply curling . . ."

Maugham was able to observe, compassionately, why the Hawaiians shied and ran away from humdrum labor devised by the white developers of the islands. Few, if any, of the financial adventurers who came to Hawaii from the mainland, and had an urgent need for unskilled laborers in their pineapple and sugar-cane fields or in their factories, held too high an opinion of the work-a-day diligence of the Hawaiians. The planters desperately needed native men and women to cultivate and harvest the "golden crops," but the proud, independent Hawaiians, who in former times had led an active life in their own culture, refused to toil from dawn to far past nightfall under a hot sun, with stinging sweat trickling into their eyes, draining their vitality, when they reasoned their time could be more enjoyably employed in dancing the *hula-hula,* singing and making love.

Regimented work was contrary to their Polynesian heritage. Many American, English, Austrian and Portuguese overseers of pineapple and sugar-cane plantations spoke bitterly of the "complete worthlessness" of the Hawaiian laborers, complaining that the islanders preferred to sleep and play while a "new civilization" engulfed and threatened to exterminate them, or relegated them to the refuse heap, as it passed them by. It was not calculated indolence that made the Hawaiians spurn work under the white man's regime. They simply had sufficient common sense not to be converted into plodding work-horses.

The Hawaiians were able to work diligently on jobs that they found interesting and that stimulated their imagination, particularly if the occupation was creative and artistic—but they refused to hack away with a sugar-cane knife in the thick, oppressive fields of fibrous fauna under a blazing sun merely because the world had acquired an insatiable sweet-tooth. If the Japanese, Chinese, Filipino and Koreans didn't mind slogging like automatons through forests of sugar-cane, monotonously hacking away at never-ending rows of plant-life, ruining their health, and moving like quadruped animals through long rows of pineapple, deforming their spines, then, the Hawaiians reasoned, intelligently and conveniently, let them have the work.

The Hawaiians certainly didn't lack in stamina or ambition for work. In fishing and tilling their own ground for edibles, in lifting and carrying heavy loads, in a test of endurance, one Hawaiian man could surpass five ordinary immigrants imported for indentured labor in Hawaii. When the rising tide of the "new progressive white man's civilization" breached his private lands, his fish-ponds and taro-patches, inundating and effacing thousands of his acres, washing away in land-tax erosions incalculable miles of valuable beach-front property, the Hawaiian shrugged his shoulder, sighed, and retreated to odd small corners of the islands with his fish and *poi,* where he could be healthy and happy.

One writer remarked: "How sad it is to think of the millions who have gone to their graves in this beautiful island and never knew there was a hell."

"I found the Hawaiians to be refreshingly lacking in inhibitions and pretenses," said Maugham. "They were sensualists in the purest form, and they saw no reason to subscribe to the moral restrictions that the deranged missionaries from New England tried to impose upon them. The Holy Hezekiahs and Hannahs from Massachusetts tried to stop the Hawaiians from performing their native dances, the *hula-hulas,* tried to expurgate their traditional gay songs, or replace them with an assortment of dreary, belly-moaning hymns. They stripped the men of their brief loin-cloths, and the women of their fresh *ti*-leaf skirts and bundled them into shapeless pants and jacket and the women into bulky, ankle-length night-gowns, or Mother Hubbards. The Hawaiians had magnificent bodies. Perhaps through envy, the scrawny missionaries couldn't support the contrast, and so covered with ugly vestments these Polynesian gods and goddesses.

"What the early missionaries to Hawaii couldn't know, try to understand, or want to believe, was that the Hawaiians were not by nature inherently debased or obscene. The *hula-hulas* had been made a part of their culture for a good reason. Frigid or barren native women, who could not normally conceive, entered into erotic dances and games and songs to stimulate the genital organs through sight, sound and emotional excitement, and most times their participation in sexual dances and play did accomplish fertilization of the barren wife and awakened potency in the husband. Only adult islanders took part in these sexual ceremonies, never under-age children.

"The missionaries deplored the wife-swapping among the Polynesians, but what they overlooked was that the exchange of women in sexual activities did produce children, of which the Polynesians have a consummate love, and which the opposing villages needed to keep their population in proper balance with other villages for necessary work and possible internecine warfare. So, if sexual excitement in their *hula-hulas*, songs and games, was aroused in a woman or man by someone other than his accustomed mate, then no one thought it wrong for the two to slip away into the darkness to copulate.

"Hawaiians had strict *kapus* (taboos) about incest, making exceptions only with the high-born, so that the noble strain could be preserved among the hereditary chiefs and chiefesses. The islanders had the system which they called *punalua*, whereby a husband inherited his wife's sisters and female cousins." Maugham smiled sardonically. "This, you will have to agree, must have eventually been a step in the right direction toward monogamy.

"Rape was unheard of in Hawaii, until the white missionaries, sea-rogues and traders arrived. The missionaries could never comprehend why the Hawaiians were so casual about sex, making it a part of ceremonial speeches, common conversation, games and amusement. They were forever joking and laughing about sex; they gave pet names to one another's genitals. One man-hungry queen had her vagina nicknamed 'the lively one,' because of her uncontrollable nymphomania.

"Certainly, one must concede that the Hawaiians had infinitely more fun with sex than the soul-warped missionaries, who, either through envy or ignorance, tried to reform them. The missionaries, in their writings, constantly refer to the Hawaiians as 'benighted children,' but it's clearly apparent that the missionaries were the ones living in darkness and stupidity. When they made little or no headway with the Hawaiians, their only soul-salving recourse was to flop down on their knees, raise their pious eyes heavenward and groan: 'Forgive them, Father, for they know not what they do!'

"The missionaries accused the Hawaiians of being 'drunken pigs,' but the early navigator, Otto von Kotzebue, reported in 1816 that an inebriated Hawaiian was always 'most cheerful and affectionate, not murderously quarrelsome like white seamen.'

"Make no mistake about it but that the early missionaries to Hawaii were not very intelligent or educated men. They had not even the slightest comprehension of anthropology, sociology, native Polynesian cultures, traditions and taboos, and certainly not hygiene. The early missionaries were physically careless, and infected the pure-blooded Hawaiians, who were without anti-toxins in their blood, with God-knows how many insidious microbes and bacteria. Most of them were deeply disturbed men and women, suffering from sexual aberrations; certainly they were congenital neurotics, because they had come from small villages in New England governed by zealots and fanatics. You couldn't call any of them well-born gentlemen. One sea-captain who had skippered a boatload of missionaries into the Pacific, had, after days of observation, called them 'overzealous, fanatical, stupid, crude, inhuman, intolerant, all of them low-born sectarians.'

"Missionary work, in those years, did not attract men of substance or intellect, or just ordinary common sense. They were hardly the proper religious emissaries to bring 'spiritual light' into the dark corners of the Pacific."

The Reverend Henry T. Cheever had written in 1850: "None need be sorry for the occasion that has called forth . . . so convincing a success, which will be none the less real and true though, in the mysterious providence of God, the whole native race expires just as it is Christianized."

Another of the early missionaries, the Reverend Hiram

Bingham, reported that "Honolulu . . . has long been familiar with demonstrations of puerile excitement and folly."
Still, with such an unattractive prospect for him, Bingham
was shortly called "King Hiram" by the Hawaiians because
of his business acumen, which eventually was to make him
immensely rich. He had said: "Can these (the Hawaiians) be
human beings? How dark and comfortless their state of mind
and heart! How imminent the danger to the immortal soul,
shrouded in this deep pagan gloom! Can such beings be
civilized? Can they be Christianized? Can we throw ourselves
upon these rude shores, and take up our abode, for life,
among such people, for the purpose of training them for
heaven?"

Nevertheless, with such a harrowing prospect, the Reverend Bingham and his colleagues entered into business enterprises, accumulating vast personal fortunes, that paved the
way for the forming of the Big Five monopolistic financiers
of Hawaii. It's a long-standing joke in Hawaii. The Hawaiians say: "Missionaries tell us look always up to God, but
when we lower our eyes we standing in sea up to knees, and
we have no more land."

Returning to the subject of the Hawaiian himself,
Maugham said:

"My impression of the Hawaiian was that he was a very
thorough-going fellow. He didn't like to talk big, if he made
a statement he meant it, and he didn't like to be lied to, or
be made promises by the *haoles* (whites), who most times
had no intention of keeping their word with him. If a Hawaiian invited you to visit him at his home, he saw to it
that you were treated royally, your every wish granted; his
hospitality was perfect. Some of the Hawaiians, it is true,
were a bit thin-skinned and carried a chip on their shoulder,

74

resenting the merest slights or hints of insult, which a *haole* might otherwise ignore. But this was because the Hawaiian had been long subjected to so much social ostracism and criticism by the early missionaries.

"The early missionaries considered it low to speak the Hawaiian language, because they were fearful that they, or, more seriously, their children would innocently acquire phrases in the native tongue that could hardly be used in polite society. Yet, ironically, when a Hawaiian lad was sent to America for schooling and acquired a fluent knowledge of English, he was shocked at the obscene conversation of his schoolmates. Therefore, because the early missionaries scorned the so-called 'crudities' of the Hawaiian language, few had the academic background or the easy facility with the tongue to convey any sensible or practical ideas to the Hawaiians."

Critics of the Hawaiians have constantly accused them, in the "new civilization," of the lack of incentive and drive to establish for themselves their rightful position and to take any interest in national affairs, or to care too much what happened to their cultural heritage.

"The only thing that they could possibly be proud of was their lost, magnificently barbaric civilization," said Maugham. "One needs to make only a cursory study of the history of Hawaii to see that the Hawaiians had been callously dispossessed of their ancient birthright and racial independence. They were tossed into the huge Pot of Races, and stirred up with God knows what other human vegetables, from the syphilitic seamen off the sailing-ships to Chinese from Kwangtung Province. I might add that it didn't hurt the Hawaiian to get some Chinese blood, as it made him a sharper fellow than he was, and softened the heavy bones and facial structure. It's a miracle, with such a careless ethnic pot-boiling, that today even a vestige remains of the original happy, friendly, handsome Hawaiian."

The ancient civilization that had developed in the Hawaiian islands was founded on an autocracy, with feudal and priestly controls, that was not too different from the old countries of Europe. Kings held the power of life and death over their subjects; the *kahunas,* or priests, influenced every system of tribal life. A *kahuna* of old Hawaii was a hereditary and esteemed professor of sorts, and there were many different grades of *kahunas:* one was a priest of the pagan rituals, one could direct canoe-building and the Polynesian secrets of ocean navigation through their knowledge of simple astronomy, another supervised the construction of village dwellings and the chief's council long-house, and still another had a remarkable knowledge of medicine, surgery and pharmacy, with nature's herbs and medicinal leaves growing wild right in his own backyard. Then there was the *kahuna anaana,* the sinister priest possessing the dark secrets of witchcraft, of placing death-curses on victims. Even today it is not unheard of for a modern, self-appointed *kahuna* to threaten to "pray to death" someone who has incurred his disfavor.

"Their form of government, the conduct of the rulers, and the rigid customs of the royal Hawaiian court of ancient times, could conform with the kingdoms of Europe," explained Maugham. "And even the style of garments designated for royalty, chiefs, *kahunas* and the commoners, was quite similar to that of the Old World—yet they, apparently, had had no contact with the early civilization of Europe.

"I saw some ancient cloaks and helmets worn by the Hawaiian chiefs during my visit to Honolulu, at the Bishop Museum, and they appeared to be made of the tiny yellow and red feathers of birds. They were breathtakingly handsome, and the Hawaiian nobility must have looked very regal in such attire; they reminded me of the royal vestments of the ancient Greeks and Phoenicians."

While at the museum, Maugham had the opportunity to inspect some relic wooden food-bowls of the early Hawaiians. Trunks and branches of the *koa*-tree were used for fashioning highly polished utensils, all of varying sizes and shapes, in which the food was to be served. There were special round bowls for *poi,* the staple *taro*-pudding of the Hawaiians, which they always had to have with their fish and pork. There were long trough-like receptacles for pigs roasted in the *imu,* or ground-oven. Fish were laid upon green leaves on carved flat platters; calabashes and gourds contained sauces, special condiments, and sea-salt crystals. And they had bowls for desserts. Between each diner was a large bowl, in which aromatic leaves or ferns floated, used to cleanse the fingers at regular intervals.

"You couldn't deny the fact that the Hawaiians had as handsome a set of dishes for their ground-table of fern leaves as could be found in any palace or manor-house of Europe or the Orient, even if one wanted to compare them with the finest Chinaware. And all anthropologists were in agreement that their eating-habits were far superior to the banquet halls of medieval Europe. There was no vulgar display of gluttony, of wrenching and gnawing savagely at fowl or roast pig. The Hawaiians, from king to commoner, exercised strict etiquette in dining. The customary position was for them to recline on one elbow or hand, leaving the other free to choose and pick apart the food, and bringing the morsels to the mouth with grace and relaxed savour. Early Roman and Greek frescoes and murals show a similar scene of eating. And the finger-bowls of *koa*-wood were constantly used.

"I don't think that such refinement in eating could be attributed to the Europeans of this period in Hawaiian history; even the British kings, as late as King Henry VIII, were the most repulsive hogs imaginable, and the swizzling, chomping and belching nobility in the courts of the Louis would have been banished as barbaric gluttons from the Hawaiian banquet table."

Maugham had made some other revealing discoveries about the Hawaiians:

"It was very interesting for me, with the short time afforded me in Honolulu, to learn that the rituals of the Hawiian *kahunas* were rather close to those of the Jews of ancient Palestine. Even the way in which the Hawaiians constructed their *heiaus,* or temples, was rather similar. The Hawaiians, on the Big Island of Hawaii, had a *kapu* City of Refuge,[1] where those fleeing from a crime against a person or having violated a tribal law, or women and children, escaping a battle scene, could find immediate and inviolable sanctuary, or asylum, receive shelter and food, and care from any physical injuries suffered. In the case of an alleged wrongdoer, he could remain in the City while his case was examined by a tribunal of high chiefs, and his guilt or innocence determined.[2]

"The ancient Hawaiians also purified their temples with sea-water, or salt itself, the same as in ancient Palestine and

---

[1] The City of Refuge, at Honaunau, Big Hawaii, is today in a splendid state of restoration.

[2] In September of 1957, a Hawaiian attorney, Bernard Kaukaohu Trask, envoked the ancient law of sanctuary of the City of Refuge, by sending one of his clients, charged with a criminal offense, into this abandoned temple site, until extraditon proceedings against him could be settled. The maneuver halted court action, as it was learned that the ancient law of sanctuary of the City of Refuge at Honaunau had never been revoked. But the fugitive, weary of confinement under primitive conditions in the ruined *heiau* fortress, and suffering from loneliness, ventured out, and waiting police promptly arrested him.

in Japan and elsewhere; they rigidly adhered to the Jewish practice of circumcision; and they, believe it or not, had their sackcloth and ashes.

"The Hawaiian *kahunas* influenced the autocratic government of the islands in the same manner that the priests of the Holy Land directed the affairs of the kingdom."

Hawaii even had its Caesar and Napoleon in the person of Kamehameha the First, who, by brilliant conquest and unification, welded the kingdom of Hawaii under one ruler. As the supreme king of Hawaii, Kamehameha the Great became a legendary figure in Hawaiian history, born years ahead of his time. He died in 1819, just a year before the arrival of the missionaries.

"This Hawaiian warrior, Kamehameha, was also a maker of laws, good laws, apart from his brilliant generalship and conquests," said Maugham. "One of his laws, held in strict observance today in our modern society, compares favorably with our laws governing safety of travel and one's right to walk unmolested in any street in any city or hamlet. His law, literally translated, proclaimed: 'Know ye and reverence your god. Have an understanding heart that you may regard the small as you would the big man. Love one another, lest your affections go . . . Let the old man and the woman, and the little child, travelling, sleep unmolested on the King's Highway. Let none disturb or harm them as they walk or sleep. The Penalty is Death.' "

This proclamation of Kamehameha's, a law to protect the weak, became a strict *kapu,* or edict, of Hawaii, because of his own injustice in making a personal attack upon two fishermen of his foes.

He had been travelling in an outrigger-canoe along the coast of Big Hawaii at Keaau, when he sighted two fishermen of the village of his enemy, Keoua. Kamehameha ordered his men to land him on the beach, and he took off in pursuit of the fishermen. He caught one and tried to wrench away the casting-net that he was carrying. The King was a stalwart man, but he could not subdue him. In the struggle Kamehameha's foot slipped into a crevice and became securely wedged, trapping him. The other fisherman, seeing that the King was helpless, turned back, raised his paddle and brought it down heavily upon his head, the impact splintering the blade. The fisherman did not attempt another blow, but fled after his companion. Kamehameha's canoemen, seeing their King's predicament, came to his aid, releasing his foot and attending to the severe head wound.

He ordered special investigators to find the two fishermen and bring them before him. They were captured, and thrown on the ground in front of Kamehameha. The King asked the trembling native who had struck him with the paddle: "Why did you hit me only once? I was helpless. You could have shattered my skull if you had wanted to."

"One blow satisfied me," replied the fisherman. "I am not a violent man, and I do not like to harm anyone who is not capable of defending himself."

Kamehameha stared at the fisherman for a long time, then his otherwise stern face relaxed into a slow smile. "Fisherman, I was wrong in attacking you in the first place. My priests have always told me that brutality and thievery are evil and should be punished by death. I now will make a law to protect the weak from the strong. Anyone who violates it will be put to death."

The two fishermen were freed, received many gifts from Kamehameha, and were escorted back in safety to their village.

From this incident involving the two fishermen, Kamehameha drafted the edict of non-violence against the weak, and to assure the safety of defenseless travellers. The year was 1797. He called the law *Kanawai Mamalahoe,* "The Law of the Splintered Paddle,"[3] in reference to his illuminating experience with the two fishermen.

"The royal court of Kamehameha the First had all the pomp and circumstance of that of Caesar or Napoleon," said Maugham. "He was in constant conference, either in war or peace, with his high chiefs and his fighting generals. And, later, he brought into his court British and American advisers, upon whom he conferred high titles.

"The court ceremonies must have been very impressive and colorful. All the chiefs had to be garbed in their feathered helmets and capes, and each understood his role and activity in the pageantry. The unique standards of Hawaiian royalty, the *kahilis,* rose high above the heads of the assembled, and they were moved in accordance with every move that Kamehameha made, or any position that he designated for them. The *kahilis* were as important as the standards of Caesar, or the battleflags of any great general: when Kamehameha rose to his feet they were shifted, when he sat quietly listening to the oratory of a high chief they were moved accordingly, when he sat in judgment and imposed penalties they were ever-present; and they lined the route along which conquered chiefs tread in surrender. The *kahilis* were sacred and omnipotent; none dared to ignore or discredit them.

"I am sure that the Court of Kamehameha under the open

---

[3] In Hawaii today, *The Order of the Splintered Paddle Award* is given to persons who have distinguished themselves in national and international humanitarian acts, or in special instances of outstanding accomplishments. There have been 21 awards of *The Splintered Paddle,* the first being made to former President Dwight Eisenhower, September 15th, 1955.

Hawaiian sky was as sophisticated in its own way as Napoleon's rococo court at Versailles. Napoleon marched all across Europe with his armies, winning victory after victory, vanquishing rulers and princes. Kamehameha had done the same thing in the Hawaiian islands.

"I wondered what had happened after Kamehameha's death, so I spent an afternoon in the Bishop Museum of Honolulu, looking into some old volumes of the reliable historians. He died on May 8, 1819, and his son, Liholiho, of no particular merit, became Kamehameha the Second. It was a sad day for the Hawaiians, one that was to start them down the long trail to almost complete effacement.

"Kamehameha the Second's wife, Keopuolani, from all reports a contrary, rebellious, stupid bitch, brazenly sat down one day with her son Kauikeaouli to eat. She definitely understood by doing so that she was breaking the strongest *kapu* of Hawaii. The act, as she had so planned, was witnessed by a large multitude, and it almost caused a civil war. The damage it caused can never be adequately measured. Women, since earliest times, had never dared to sit down and eat with a male, no matter how young, under penalty of death. But as nothing happened to this Hawaiian suffragette, either through their pagan gods or man, it was decided that women were the equals of men. Centuries of restrictions against women were shattered. So, therefore, the ancient *kapus* lost their power, and the heathen religion, the *heiaus* (temples) and the idols of basalt and wood held lesser value and discipline for the Hawaiians. And at last, the son of Kamehameha the Great gave the order to destroy these symbols of their ancient way of life.

"The renouncement of their gods and religion couldn't have been timed better. To these green mid-Pacific islands sailed the first missionaries from New England. The first voracious band arrived March 30, 1820, and they were over-joyed and relieved to find a bewildered Polynesian race with-out a religion.

"What Hawaii must have been like before the first mission-aries made their unsolicited visit is not hard to visualize. Even at the time of my visit, much of the charm of old Hawaii could still be found in isolated areas among the old native folk.

"Yes, I fell in love with Hawaii and its people, and I can understand why Mark Twain, Robert Louis Stevenson, Charles Warren Stoddard, and Jack London wrote such glow-ing tributes to these mid-Pacific islands."

He recalled what Mark Twain had written about Hawaii:

"No alien land in all the world has any deep, strong charm for me but that one; no other land could so longingly and beseechingly haunt me sleeping and waking, through half a lifetime, as that one has done. Other things leave me, but it abides; other things change, but it remains the same. For me its balmy airs are always blowing, its summer seas flashing in the sun; the pulsing of its surf-beat is in my ears; I can see its garlanded crags, its leaping cascades, its plumy palms drowsing by the shore, its remote summits floating like islands above the cloudrack; I can feel the spirit of its wood-land solitudes; I can hear the splash of its brooks; in my nos-trils still lives the breath of flowers that perished twenty years ago."

Hawaii proved to be a veritable treasure-house for William Somerset Maugham.

6. A Drinking Monarch—and a Volcano

Maugham, while on a short stroll with Gerald Haxton in downtown Honolulu, was to discover a famous bar, in which one of Hawaii's kings had sat, brooded, and drunk.

It was the Union Saloon.

They had reached it, quite by accident, in a narrow alley-way off King Street. Cunha Alley split a portion of the business section, where financier and clerk could, in transit presumably to an appointment in another office, step through one of the three entrances for a quick gin, whiskey or beer. And it was so close to the docks and shipping offices that skippers, first mates and engineers of vessels flying the flags of every nation could sit with agents and chandlers, discuss manifests, cargoes, and then plan their evening's roistering.

There were three entrances, as noted, to the huge square room, and one of these entrances was reserved for a special customer, who occupied a private booth. Across from the heavy dark-wood bar, shining and mellowed from years of elbow polishings and rag-wipings, the corners of the room were divided off into small booths. And in one of these private cubicles, the last King of Hawaii, David Kalakaua, a very Merry Monarch, indeed, had come here with Robert Louis Stevenson to drink, unseen by his admiring subjects.

Stevenson and Kalakaua Rex had had many spirited discussions in this isolated booth, on a subject that was a well-gnawed bone of contention between these two friends—the missionaries.

Kalakaua would bang the table with his heavy fist, curse roundly, and threaten a general massacre of the cadaverous, black-browed ghouls from New England, who were leading his gentle people down the dark path to extinction.

Patiently, Stevenson would restrain him in his mounting rage. "Now, now, David, force is not the answer. Your people must just resist peacefully, and you must lead the way by returning to your old gods."

"Too late, too late," Kalakaua would mumble. "The damn missionaries now have warships to support them."

And the drinking would continue.

Stevenson was always astounded at Kalakaua's capacity for spirits in the Union Saloon:

"My spasm of activity has been chequered with champagne parties . . . Kalakaua is a terrible companion . . . a bottle of fizz (champagne) is like a glass of sherry to him; he thinks nothing of five or six in an afternoon as a whet for dinner. You should see a photograph of our party after an afternoon with H.H.M. (Kalakaua) : my! what a crew!"

And after an expensive session in the Union Saloon, Kalakaua would perhaps turn calmly to someone in the party that he didn't like too well, and order him: "You pay the bill."

Sometimes the King would play poker here with Claus

Spreckels, who later became the Sugar King of Hawaii. One game in particular Spreckels was to remember. He had put down four aces and was reaching for the winnings, when Kalakaua grabbed his wrist. "Not so fast, Claus!" "Vat's wrong?" demanded the other. "You lose!" chuckled the King. "But . . . but four aces, your Highness . . .!" "Well, I have four kings!" Kalakaua retorted, turning them up, and, jabbing himself in the chest with a thumb, he added: "And I'm the *fifth* king. Five kings beat four aces—right?" Spreckels, who was playing for higher stakes, grinned weakly and sat back, as the King gathered in the pot.

Maugham was to learn more about Hawaii and its people in the Union Saloon than he did on his numerous tours around Oahu and excursions to the outer islands: It was the perfect milieu for an inquisitive and observant writer such as Maugham. "The *ambiance* was conducive to the fine art of conversation. No women were about, and the men could talk freely. After a few drinks one was in the proper mood of speaking, or listening to long-neglected topics. I've felt that way in so many odd places about the world. You come into a street, an alleyway, a *piazza*, a hotel, a bar, look about, and you say to yourself: 'The right time, and in the right place.' An ideal combination."

The Union Saloon could be considered a sort of oasis in the center of a heavily trafficked commercial district, where clerk and sea-captain, if they were of a mind, could silently weigh the benefits of the other's role in the scheme of life— one yearning for an escape from his sedentary existence behind a desk, the other envying the landlubber his permanent anchor to land—until drink moved them to conviviality and conversation.

The room was panelled in dark wood almost six feet from the floor, and above this were pasted, tacked, or hung a conglomeration of pictures: a study of Queen Victoria, a pair of magnificent caribou horns, some efforts in oil paintings left by itinerant artists and sailors, a striking portrait in a gold frame of a truculent-looking King Kalakaua, etchings, tear-outs from the *Illustrated London News* of a quarter century ago, lurid inducements to drink special brands of whiskey, gin and beer. There were yellowed photographs of baseball teams that had played in another decade, boxers and athletes; Hawaiian trios and *hula* dancers. Two gargantuan part-Hawaiians in white starched pants and shirts moved indolently up and down the bar, serving, effacing beer rings with an effortless swab, maintaining a steady stream of lyrical chatter, with the bonus of a spiralling Polynesian laugh, and the innate hospitality that only a Hawaiian is capable of dispensing.

Maugham's primary impression of the bar was that of the creative writer: "The place had a vaguely mysterious air, and you can imagine that it would be a fit scene for shady transactions."

Maugham's attention to Kalakaua had first been directed to the painting of the Hawaiian king that hung on the wall of the old Union Saloon.

"I was constantly reminded what a heavy drinker the king was," said Maugham. "I suppose the painting was on the wall of the saloon to honor one of their most dehydrated customers."

Robert Louis Stevenson, a confidante of the king for a time, never overlooked the opportunity of recording his extraordinary capacity for spirits:

"A very fine, intelligent fellow, but . . . what a crop for the drink! He carries it, too, like a mountain with a sparrow on its shoulders. We calculated five bottles of champagne in three hours and a half (afternoon) and the sovereign quite presentable, although perceptibly more dignified at the end."

Kalakaua had been elected king of the Hawaiian islands February 13, 1874, largely with the support of the American government, which knew that he was favorable to a Treaty of Commercial Reciprocity and to granting use of the present Pearl Harbor as a base for American warships in the Pacific. But against him he had Queen Emma, of the Kamehameha clan, widow of the recently deceased Kamehameha the Fifth, who had hoped to ascend the throne; the British community; the Reform Party of businessmen of Honolulu; and the newspapers. But despite the opposition he ruled from 1874 to 1891.

"His friends called him 'Rex,' and the hangers-on at his court dubbed him 'The Merry Monarch,' " said Maugham. "But he was not the complete profligate and drunkard as some historians described him. He liked a good time, was a notorious satyr, and he loved to laugh, sing, dance and drink. Nevertheless, he did have some very sober ideas about white missionaries and avaricious *haole* business-men. He intended the best for the Hawaiian people, but he had too many obstructionists surrounding him."

Two of the most unscrupulous members of his court were Walter Murray Gibson, who controlled the ministers, and a shrewd lobbyist by the name of Celso Caesar Moreno, from California, who persuaded the king to guarantee him a stupendous sum of money to establish a steamship line between Honolulu and China and a trans-Pacific cable.

"Kalakaua did eventually 'clean house' and send Gibson and Moreno packing, but the harm had been done. Moreno went off to Europe with three Hawaiian young men under his guardianship, who were supposed to be tutored in military strategy, and Gibson ended up in San Francisco, where he died. With a new Cabinet, Kalakaua did try to make amends, but he didn't have strong enough support. Apparently his head began to clear of alcoholic fumes, and his political acumen started coming into sharper focus. He suddenly realized that the United States had designs on the islands, and would eventually try to annex them, either peaceably or by force. So, while on a world trip, he stopped off in Japan and tried to make a bargain with the Emperor to marry his lovely young niece, Princess Kaiulani, heiress to the throne, to an imperial prince of the Mikado's court. Kalahaua reasoned that if Hawaii became a co-kingdom of Japan, America would not be able to make Hawaii an outpost of California. The Emperor refused, knowing that in time, with immigration and contract-labor, Hawaii would become a settlement for many of his people[1] without the hazards of a questionable oriental-Polynesian marriage."

Kalakaua, disappointed, continued his world trip, accompanied by his Chamberlain, Colonel C. H. Judd and his Attorney-General, William N. Armstrong. Although he was royally received by the potentates of many countries, the tour had all the ludicrous aspects of a comic opera. In Kalakaua's entourage was an Austrian or German valet, who was constantly in an intoxicated condition, and who on several occasions purloined the King's royal feather cape to parade in the streets of foreign capitals, compelling passersby to bow down before him.

In Italy Moreno appointed himself the official guide to the King, leading him into one riotous adventure after another.

"Kalakaua turfed Moreno out when he learned that the fellow was telling everyone that the three Hawaiian cadets under his chaperonage in Italy were actually royal bastards of the King, living in exile."

Another of Kalakaua's canny plans, in the interest of Hawaii's security against being taken over by the United States,

---

[1] Today there are more Japanese in Hawaii than any other nationality.

was his dream of the Kingdom of the Pacific, over which he would rule as Emperor of Oceania. He had bought a 171-ton English vessel, combining steam and sail, for $20,000, renamed it the *Kamiloa* and sent it to Samoa, with a crew of inmates from Honolulu's reform school, to try and scare out the Germans who were trying to administer the Samoan islands. Tonga, Samoa, the Gilberts and the Carolines had not been taken over at this time by any white power, and Kalakaua felt that the rulers of these archipelagoes would be agreeable to an alliance to form a single Oceanic Republic.

"But Kalakaua had made the wrong choice of his ambassador to Western Samoa. His name was Bush, and instead of attending to business and arranging a treaty with King Malietoa, he spent his days and nights in the bush, drinking 'bush-liquor,' and chasing the wild *fafines* (women). He was well-named—*Bush*. The *Kamiloa* only by a miracle made it back to the port of Honolulu with its seasick, wretched crew.

"Nevertheless, despite his mistakes, during Kalakaua's reign, Hawaii made its most rapid progress, if you care to measure progress by industry and commerce. Honolulu became known as an interesting and attractive city; the social life was pleasant, gay and diversified. Artists and writers translated the islands in complimentary terms. Kalakaua built a new Iolani Palace and an opera house. He encouraged musicians from abroad to visit the islands. He was a music lover, and was constantly surrounded by musicians and dancers. He himself composed *Hawaii Ponoi*, the national anthem of the islands, and one of the most delightful melodies I heard while in Hawaii was his *Sweet Lei Lehua*. It is lamentable, really, that King Kalakaua was abused by historians. In my opinion he was the most colorful king who had ever sat on the throne of Hawaii. The more I heard and read about him, the more I was moved to write his biography —which, of course, I never found the time to do."

Kalakaua had always held missionaries in disfavor. And in Robert Louis Stevenson he had found another anti-missionary zealot. They had held long, bitter discourses, in complete agreement, on the harm wrought by the New England missionaries in Hawaii and elsewhere in the South Pacific.

"One of Stevenson's nannies, Alison Cunningham, whom he affectionately called 'Cummy,' had, in his youth, frightened the poor consumptive nipper half to death with her rabid bible blather and hymn-howling. At an early age he began to associate places near his home with readings from the Bible. *Death's dark vale* of the metrical Twenty-third Psalm became the long, gloomy railroad passageway that traversed the family property, and when he came across the phrase 'Resurrection-men,' he translated them as ghouls, committing foul deeds in the closeby cemetery."

Stevenson had written almost hysterically, as a boy, of his fears engendered by a fanatical religion: "I remember repeatedly awaking from a dream of Hell, clinging to the horizontal bar of my bed, with my knees and chin together, my soul shaken, my body convulsed with agony . . . I piped and snivelled over the Bible, with an earnestness that had been talked into me . . . Had I died in those years, I fancy I might perhaps have figured in a tract."

And he had later penned some extremely antagonistic verse about men of the cloth:

> "Stand on your putrid ruins—stand,
>> White neck-clothed bigot, fixedly the same,
> Cruel with all things but the hand,
>> Inquisitor in all things but the name . . ."

Most of the missionaries in Hawaii had at some time conspired against Kalakaua. And he was to take his revenge upon them.

The King had always been fascinated by Masonry, and so he revived, to the utter mortification of the missionaries, the pagan *Hale Naua* cult, named for the secret society of ancient chiefs, with rituals of *Kahuna* witchcraft. The fraternal order convened every Sunday evening after nightfall under a huge tree in the Palace grounds. There were fifteen carefully selected Hawaiian men and thirty-six *wahines*, of outstanding beauty, shapeliness and passion, who sat on the ground in a double circle, with a floral vine draped attractively across their bare shoulders. Before each *wahine* was a stone god with erect phallus, and in front of each male a female idol of fertility.

When it was time for King Kalakaua to make his appearance, a conch shell was blown, and then nose-flutes and small drums were played and struck softly, and the members of the *Hale Naua* bowed low from the hips, their faces almost touching the grass. Kalakaua regally approached the altar, upon which burned a torch. Above was an unfurled banner with a field of yellow edged with scarlet, bearing the symbol of a sun on a cross and the name *Hale Naua* beneath.

Then Kalakaua divested himself of his garments, and the female priestess sprinkled his huge naked body with the sacred waters of Kane. An attendant then quickly fastened Kalakaua's royal loincloth about his hips, and the ancient yellow-and-red hereditary feather cloak of royalty was adjusted across his massive shoulders, and finally the feathered helmet placed on his head.

Slowly, accompanied by chanting from the members, Kalakaua sat down upon his improvised garden throne. Beside him was a huge sacred gourd, inside of which were neatly packed six balls of *olona* twine.[2]

---

[2] One can be viewed today in the collections at the Bishop Museum of Honolulu.

Then Kalakaua spoke:

"*Aloha,* members of the *Hale Naua.* The meaning of love, as it was given to me by my Polynesian god-ancestors, I will now explain.

"Man's desire is kindled in his sight. The eyes are attracted to the female face and form, and this causes the strength of the *Halala* [Penis]. Likewise, the woman's sight of the male phallus causes her desire to flame.

"And so desire is transmitted from the eyes to the brain, and from there the pleasurable fever is conveyed to the belly, the arms, the legs, and finally it concentrates in testicles and ovaries.

"Thus love becomes the sacred motivation through sight."

The seated male members then withdrew from the circle, moving far back into the deep shadows of the Palace wall. Thereupon, while nose-flutes subtly carried an ancient love melody and drums pulsated faintly, Kalakaua reached down and picked up a ball of *olona* twine and casually tossed it toward the circle of *wahines* facing him. The girl that the ball touched picked it up, started reeling in the cord, moving gracefully toward the King until she was embraced in his arms. Then they walked off toward the Palace for a night of sexuality.

As soon as Kalakaua had left with his woman, the other fifteen men came back to the circle, and the sex-game of "rolling the *olona* twine" was repeated, until the remaining thirty-five *wahines* had each made love with a male member.

"Kalakaua had too many black marks against him," said Maugham. "Time was running out for him. He became ill, either through his excesses in vice, or from despair and frustration, and left for San Francisco to regain his health. He never returned, in life, to Hawaii."[3]

---

[3] Kalakaua died in the Palace Hotel in San Francisco, January 20th, 1891, at the age of 54 years.

Kalakaua's sister, Liliuokalani, she who composed the imperishable *Aloha Oe* farewell-song of Hawaii, took over the throne, determined to rule with the absolute power of her ancestors, not under the restraining provisos of a constitutional monarchy. "I am the State!" she announced. But American intervention pushed her from the throne, deciding that the time was at hand to establish a solid, progressive government. Alfred Thayer Mahan, an American naval commander, irascible, egotistical and arrogant, had counselled Secretary of the Navy, Theodore Roosevelt:

"Do nothing unrighteous, but as regards the (Hawaiian) problem, take the island first and solve the problem afterwards."

A republic was formed by Americans in Honolulu. The Pineapple Kingdom had replaced the Kingdom of Hawaii!

"The Spaniards impulsively blew up an American warship in Manila Bay, in 1898. 'Remember the *Maine*' became a battlecry, and the American naval commander sent word to his president: 'Send troops!' Hawaii, in mid-Pacific, became the 'Crossroads of the Pacific' and because Hawaii was playing mid-Pacific hostess to soldiers who were on their way to fight Spain in the Philippines, the United States, to protect Hawaii, formally annexed the Hawaiian islands,"[4] Maugham said.

After a brief silence, he added:

"It was too bad that the Hawaiian monarchy was abolished. But I suppose it was inevitable, because the heirs and heiresses to the throne were quarrelling too bitterly among themselves. There was no unity among them. Had they joined in a common cause, the monarchy could have been saved. Today it might have served as a symbol of prestige and honor for the rather discouraged and ill-used Hawaiian people. But,

---

[4] The Congress of the United States passed a Joint Resolution of Annexation, July 6th, 1898.

as I say, there were just too many plotters within the monarchy, blinded by their own selfish interests. The Hawaiian monarchy was doomed."

Maugham visited Kilauea Volcano on the Big Island of Hawaii, which was in eruption during his visit. He and Gerald Haxton made the trip from Honolulu to Hilo aboard a vessel of the Inter-island Steamship Company. A car was provided in the port and they drove up through sugarcane and rice fields, finally ascending to the extensive forests of tree-fern. Maugham called the giant ferns "weird and strange like the imaginations of some draughtsman of the horrible."

The fiery devastation of the volcano was in evidence long before they reached its rim, stumps of trees charred and splintered, with hardened grey-black oceans of lava, as if suddenly frozen in undulant surge, bleak and hushed as the dark face of the moon. Not a living green plant was in evidence, nothing in motion, not even the silent wing-beat of a hovering bird. It was like a dead planet.

Here Maugham and Gerald were compelled to alight and proceed by foot the rest of the distance to the safe rim of Kilauea Volcano. Lava cinders crunched under their precarious tread. Fissures in the frozen lava flow released spirals of sulphurous smoke.

"With my weak lungs I did a lot of coughing," reflected Maugham. "The lava fields reminded me of a half-cooled section of hell."

Finally they reached, with others, the narrow rim of the crater.

Maugham was overawed.

"Nothing has prepared you for the sight. It is stupendous and alarming. You look down upon a vast sea of lava. It is black and heavy. It is in perpetual movement. The lava is only a thin crust, and it is broken at irregular intervals by gashes of red fire, and here and there are geysers of flame rising into the air, thirty, or forty, or fifty feet."

The active fountains appeared heavy and viscous. A lava pond was overflowing in a ribbon torrent about 100 feet long and eight feet wide, which raced down the slope to the wall where it spread right and left in a glowing mass. The heaving lake of molten lava appeared crusted and a line of spears of blue flames, shaped like the teeth of a saw, burst through the splits in the crust. Then a huge fountain would explode and mushroom up, to relieve the gas pressure. There was a constant rumbling.

"The two most impressive things are the roar: it is like the roar of surf on a gloomy day, as unceasing, or like the roar of a cataract, as formidable; and secondly the movement: the lava moves on, on, all the time, with stealthy movement in which you may almost see the purpose of a living thing. There is something strangely determined about its quiet progress, it has a malign tenacity; and yet it transcends anything living, it has the inevitableness of fate and the ruthlessness of time."

Overflows began in wide floods across the bench, immediately filling the hollow to the wall and spreading right and left, so that the flood, moving westward, passed beneath the south station and beyond. Seven fountains broke out with bombardments of lava east, southeast and southwest. The spatter reached almost to the rim.

Contemplating this fury of subterranean fiery violence, Maugham had likened it to a monster slowly unleashed from its lair:

"The lava is like some huge formless creature born of primeval slime, crawling slowly in pursuit of some loathsome prey. The lava comes forward steadily towards a fiery gap and then seems to fall into a bottomless cavern of flame. You see vast holes of fire, great caves of flame.

"A man standing near said: 'Gosh, it's like hell!'

"But a priest beside him turned and said: 'No, it is like the face of God.' "

When the time was at hand for Maugham to leave Honolulu for Pago Pago, he succinctly summarized the port of departure:

"Honolulu . . . a civilization which, if not very distinguished, is certainly very elaborate."

But of the actual ship's sailing, he was somewhat sentimentally affected:

"When your ship leaves Honolulu they hang *leis* around your neck, garlands of sweet smelling flowers. The wharf is crowded and the band plays a melting Hawaiian tune. The people on board throw colored streamers to those standing below, and the side of the ship is gay with thin lines of paper, red and green and yellow and blue. When the ship moves slowly away the streamers break softly, and it is like the breaking of human ties. Men and women are joined together for a moment by a gaily colored strip of paper, and then life separates them and the paper is sundered, so easily, with a little sharp snap. For an hour the fragments trail down the hull and then blow away."

Now Maugham and Haxton were southward bound.

III

SAMOA

7. On
Reading, Sadie, and the Samoans

For Maugham the voyage southward from Hawaii was a pleasant, restful one. He found time now to resume his reading. Maugham had always been an avid reader.

"Every decent, inspiring and worthwhile event in my life has somehow had a relationship with books and reading. I suppose, primarily, from a person's reading habits, he develops the urge to get out into the world to find the places and peoples of fact and fiction. Very early in life I found the beauty in the written word, in all manner of subjects.

"At eighteen I knew French, German and some Italian, but I was extremely uneducated and I was deeply conscious of my ignorance. I read everything that came my way. My curiosity was such that I was as willing to read a history of Peru or the reminiscences of a cowboy, as a treatise on Provençal poetry or the *Confessions* of St. Augustine. I suppose it gained me a certain amount of general knowledge which is useful for the novelist to have. One never knows when an out-of-the-way bit of information will come in handy . . . I read a lot of history, a little philosophy, and a good deal of science. My curiosity was too great to allow me to give much time to reflect upon what I read; I could hardly wait to finish one book, so eager was I to begin another. This was always an adventure, and I would start upon a famous work as excitedly as a reasonable young man would go in to bat for his side, or a nice girl go to a dance.

"Now and then journalists in search of copy ask me what is the most thrilling moment of my life. If I were not ashamed to, I might answer that it is the moment when I began to read Goethe's *Faust*. I have never quite lost this feeling, and even now the first pages of a book sometimes send the blood racing through my veins. To me reading is a rest as to other people conversation or a game of cards is. It is more than that; it is a necessity, and if I am deprived of it for a little while I find myself as irritable as the addict deprived of his drug.

"I have put books aside only because I was conscious that time was passing and that it was my business to live. I have gone into the world because I thought it was necessary in order to get the experience without which I could not write, but I have gone into it also because I wanted experience for its own sake. It did not seem to me enough only to be a writer. The pattern I had designed for myself insisted that I should take the utmost part I could in this fantastic affair of being a man. I desired to feel the common pains and enjoy the common pleasures that are part of the common human lot. I saw no reason to subordinate the claims of sense to the tempting lure of spirit, and I was determined to get whatever fulfilment I could out of social intercourse and human relations, out of food, drink and fornication, luxury, sport, art, travel . . . But it was an effort and I have always returned to my books and my own company with relief.

"And yet, though I have read so much, I am a bad reader. I read slowly and I am a poor skipper. I find it difficult to leave a book, however bad and however much it bores me, unfinished. I could count on my fingers the number of books that I have not read from cover to cover. On the other hand there are few books that I have read twice. I know very well that there are many of which I cannot get the full value on a single reading, but in that they have given me all I was capable of getting at the time, this, though I may forget their details, remains a permanent enrichment. I know people who read the same book over and over again. It can only be that they read with their eyes and not with their sensibility. It is a mechanical exercise like the Tibetan's turning of a praying-wheel. It is doubtless a harmless occupation, but they are wrong if they think it is an an intelligent one.

"Through books, I acquired an intense preoccupation with human nature. And because of this interest, I suppose you could say that my reading originally launched me upon a writing career, and the only way for me to translate my study of human nature was to start putting my observations down on paper.

"I have been attached, deeply attached, to a few people; but I have been interested in man in general not for his own sake, but for the sake of my work. I have not, as Kant enjoined, regarded each man as an end in himself, but as material that might be useful to me as a writer."

So Maugham, with a valise crammed with books, made his first voyage into the tropics.

And the South Pacific Ocean was all he had anticipated.

"On some days it offers all your fancy pictured. The sea is calm and under the blue sky brilliantly blue. On the horizon are fleecy clouds and at sunset they take strange shapes so that it is almost impossible not to believe you see a range of mountains. The nights then are lovely, the stars very bright, and later when the moon rises, it is dazzling in its brilliancy . . . The most wonderful thing about the Pacific is its solitariness. You pass day after day without seeing a ship. Now and then a few seabirds suggest that land is not far distant, one of those islands lost in a wilderness of waters; but not a tramp, not a sailing vessel, not a fishing-boat . . ."

Aboard ship Maugham kept mostly to himself reading, briefly sun-bathing on deck, or having a game of cards with Gerald Haxton.

"Gerald mentioned from time to time about some gossip aboard the ship concerning a single blonde woman, who was conducting herself in an uncommon and brazen manner. Once he pointed her out standing at the rail. My opinion was that she was a rather common person, badly dressed and rouged. The fact that there was a missionary and his wife aboard, too, caught my fancy. I'm sure he was a Mormon missionary, because many of them were spreading out into the Pacific during those years. I can't remember which year it was now, but it had to be one of the First World War years, because we had lifeboat drills almost every day. Anyway, I thought: what would happen if that prostitute and the missionary came into sexual conflict. The more I thought about it, the more powerful it became as a theme.

"This blonde strumpet, whose real name I don't remember now, started raising a rumpus the first night out of Honolulu, according to Gerald. She had a gramophone with a trumpet-flower horn, and an inexhaustible supply of discs, most of them Hawaiian melodies, which, no doubt, had been for entertaining her former customers in Iwelei, and she kept the infernal machine going up to a late hour, until passengers in adjacent cabins complained to the Chief Steward. She had a man in her cabin, and a bottle of whiskey, and they were really knocking them back. When ordered to quiet down, and have her guest leave, she kicked up a devil of a row, cursing and slamming things all about.

"I think she was drunk for the entire trip to Pago Pago. All day long that confounded gramophone kept blaring out ragtime tunes and Hawaiian bedlam. She sang, danced, laughed her head off, and kept open house for anyone in a party mood. I think some of the ship's officers had a go at her, but at the end of the voyage she wound up with the quartermaster.

"Gerald had a few words with her, and she invited him down to the cabin, but he politely declined. He was convinced that she had sailed on the boat to escape arrest, that there was a warrant out for her. However, the charge couldn't have been serious, otherwise she never could have left Honolulu so easily. I think the authorities just wanted to make sure she left the island.

"You can imagine my chagrin when, arriving at the boardinghouse on the outskirts of Pago Pago, I found that she had the room next to mine. I had planned to continue on to Apia, in Western Samoa, but a bad storm blew up, and there was the rumor of a measles and a small-pox scare in Pago Pago, so all travel temporarily was under an embargo. So there Gerald and I were, marooned in a dilapidated lodging-house, upon whose corrugated iron roof the heavy tropical rain beat incessantly. The partitions of the rooms did not come flush with the ceiling, affording an air-space for ventilation, and the hellish din of that blonde floosie's gramophone. And she shortly had visitors, mostly husky Samoan sailors of the Pago Pago naval station. Although we were only in the place for several days, Gerald and I almost went out of our minds. But there was nothing we could do, because it was the only lodging-house on the island.

"The missionary and his wife who came down on the same boat, and were also staying there, had their quarters on the other side of her, and they were shocked with what went on in her room. She had taken on a Samoan lover, and he sneaked out of the barracks and into her room when things quieted down a bit. So if it wasn't the gramophone driving everyone insane, it was the rusty bed-springs creating a horrid disturbance. I asked the part-Samoan woman who ran the wretched establishment if she couldn't do something about the noisy bed, but it only set her off laughing steadily for a long time. I didn't much care for that!

"I don't know how long she remained in Pago Pago after I left. But there was sufficient recommendation in the naval port that she be deported. And I knew that the missionary had been having some talks with the governor concerning her brazen conduct. My Sadie had purposely gone out of her way to annoy the missionary and his wife. I suppose she held a grudge against all missionaries as being responsible for forcing her out of the easy money of Iwelei. And it was obvious that the naval administration in Pago Pago must have been staggered by the monstrous effrontery of a young white woman fornicating with a brown-skinned Samoan man, although it didn't seem to be improper for the naval officers and ratings to surreptitiously fornicate with the brown-skinned Samoan women.

"The weather cleared at last, the embargo on travel was lifted, and Gerald and I finally boarded the inter-island schooner for Apia in Western Samoa, an overnight voyage to the west.[1]

"While the vessel was being readied for the trip, Gerald called my attention to the floosie standing quite forlornly under the overhang of the dock shed, a rather pitiful object, watching with an odd, soft expression the natives embracing, kissing and weeping over departing friends and family. I think she knew that her time in Pago Pago had just about run out, and that when she left there would be no one, except perhaps a policeman, to see her off, no one to place a fragrant flower-wreath around her neck, or shed any tears over her departure. Her face was in repose, and I was able to watch her for a while. The coarse and sullen mien was quite altered; she looked lonely and frightened.

"My contempt and aversion to women of her tawdry profession have always been tempered by the belief that many of them have become prostitutes through a strange, almost masochistic serf-obsession. And I suppose there is some foundation in the philosophical verse: 'that if weak women went astray, their stars were more in fault than they.'

"So with my Sadie, circumstances of one kind or another, had forced her out into a rather hostile world, at a time when a girl should be enjoying a normal family life, having beaux, going out to dances, thinking of a husband and children. On the surface she presented a coarse, flippant and vulgar personality, but underneath she was, as with most prostitutes, suspicious, skeptical and insecure in her crushing loneliness. Her life had been that of a harried transient, with no steadying ties or emotional involvements. A few months here, a

---

[1] Maugham based his short story *Red*, which has a setting of Samoa, on the factual notes that he kept on this voyage between Pago Pago and Apia, even to using the real-life skipper as one of the principal characters of this fiction piece.

few months there, earning quick money, but, out of sheer boredom and restlessness, throwing it as quickly away. When she left a place it was usually under cover of darkness, with the police breathing down her neck, and all her worldly possessions crammed hurriedly into a cheap valise. She had perhaps assayed a few pimp-lovers now and again, out of sheer desperation, which had to end in shattering disillusionment for her kind. Love had always come to her in the guise of a furtive, self-conscious or drunken man pulling down his trousers. She was just one of the many weary wayfarers through life.

"I suppose that Sadie's lewd calling gave her many a bad quarter of an hour. And Gerald's opinion was that, in coming down to the dock, she was just taking five minutes out to feel sorry for herself, that before the schooner was half-way down the bay she'd be back in her room with a bottle of whiskey, the gramophone going full blast, waiting for her Samoan lover to tussle her down on the bed. One like my Sadie you had to give up as a bad job.

"Notwithstanding, as the boat pulled away from the dock at Pago Pago, I gave considerable thought to the blonde prostitute from Honolulu. I realized that, using such a bawdy female in a story with a man-of-God was going to be rather strong meat to place before my readers and critics, particularly at that time. Anyway, I intended using my imagination to have Sadie and the missionary experience an emotional collision that would be as shocking in print as censorship at the time would permit." He smiled slightly in reminiscence.

"In the meantime, I intended having a look at the islands of Western Samoa, only two years before taken over from the Germans by the New Zealand Government. I had read a considerable amount of literature about these islands, chiefly of Rupert Brooke, Robert Louis Stevenson, and his stepson Lloyd Osbourne. Stevenson had retired to Upolu Island to write and die, and had finally been carried by strong Samoan men up a road they had made to honor him, 'the Road of the Loving Heart.' He now was entombed in a native-made sepulchre in his private mountain-top cemetery of Vaea that overlooked the broad green valley that swept down to Apia.

"And Rupert Brooke had preceded me by only a few years to Apia, to fall in love with these remote islands and people, whom he described as 'the loveliest people in the world, moving and dancing like gods and goddesses, very quietly and mysteriously, and utterly content.'

"So off Gerald and I sailed for Apia. I must say that I was relieved to quit Pago Pago. The village had been stupidly located at the far end of the bay, completely landlocked, cut off from the trades, in the direct path of the heavy tropical downpours that regularly descended from Rainmaker Mountain. It was oppressively hot, humid and sticky, with the eternal stench of wet rot and mildew. I acquired a stubborn rash, no doubt fungus, while in the filthy hotel in Pago Pago, and it took weeks to cure it.

"The natives of American Samoa were, in my judgment, lazy, thieving and worthless. Perhaps it was not their fault. They had become charity cases of a benevolent naval government, who spoiled them by initiating them to tinned foods, the cast-off clothes of white men, and the avarice attendant to the American dollar. While living in the hotel my baggage had been rifled by some of the chambermaids, and a pair of gold sleeve-links and a silver hair-brush were missing.

"It was an old story, such an island as American Samoa, where, upon the white man's occupation of the island, the natives had been converted into whining, conniving beggars for handouts. I can't say that it was the deliberate fault of the American naval administration; they made regular inspections of the native villages, instituted hygienic measures and tried to keep everything shipshape and disciplined. It was just that the Samoans of Tutuila Island took it for granted that a nation of such obvious affluence as the United States could well afford to take care of their Samoan wards, while they, the adopted islanders, reverted to the sensual indulgence of 'how beautiful to do nothing all day, and then rest up afterwards.'

"So even though the 70-ton, battered schooner was a filthy scow, her hull gouged and her paint blistered, both Gerald and myself suffered the discomforts of the voyage to reach the islands of which we had read so many enthusiastic reports. Now I wonder how we endured that wretched trip. The *Manua* leaked, and crawled with huge cockroaches, who fought you for every mouthful of food. The lamps and the auxiliary engine were fueled with paraffin, and the sickening stench, combined with the constant rolling, once we got out to sea, made us deathly ill for a while.

"The skipper, an American in his thirties, heavy-set and florid of face, with a shock of blond hair, had, through drink and debauchery, compounded by losing a ship through outright negligence, drifted down to the islands. But he seemed happy and satisfied with his sorry craft."

"I'm not a worried man anymore," he told Maugham at suppertime, washing down Hamburger steak, potatoes and canned apricots with tumblers of warm flat beer. "Too much responsibility and worrying can kill a man off, you know. Now I eat and drink and sleep fine. This schooner more or less sails herself, even though she was built for calm, shallow sailing. You can tell how she rolls all the time that her bottom's too round, and I wouldn't be surprised if sometime, in a squall, she flips right over and takes a header. Well, I just hope I'm ashore, if that does happen, snoring beside my girlie. My crew, a half-dozen good-natured Samoans, as you can see, don't give me no trouble. I make damn little money, but I ain't broke, and I don't owe no one a lousy cent, and I run a tight boat."

The skipper inquired of Maugham the latest news of "the white hooker at the hotel," and was told there was the official word that she would be deported back to Honolulu.

"Yeah," grunted the skipper, "so I figgered. But I guess she was asking for it. I had a drink with her, and she told me that they were riding her. I tried to talk her into coming on the *Manua* over to Apia and taking a job as a bartender. But I think she was stuck on a Samoan boy and didn't want to leave, at least not right then. Over in Apia she'd have done real well with 'the Beach,' a blonde with her sensational frame and gift of gab." He winked salaciously at Maugham. "As for me I'm strictly a *kanaka*-woman man. They're easy and obliging and soft-spoken, not a mean bone in their body. They ain't gold-diggers, neither. All they expect and want is what you give them out in the bushes. And that's just the way I like it, no fuss or nonsense like you get from white bitches.

"I lost track long ago of the native cuties, young and pretty, too, that I've taken to the sleeping-mat since I've been down here. I guess you might think I'm a gone-native beach-comber, or something. Well, maybe I am in your eyes. But I don't feel no shame or regret if I am a kind of white bum and chase the native women. All I know is that I'm damned happy with the life I'm living. In some of the villages I've got bastard kids, but no one picks on them, because these Samoans love kids, no matter where they come from. I can tell you one thing, once you've slept with a Samoan *fafine,* you wouldn't even spit on a white woman. These Samoan women try their best to please a man—in *every* way."

Maugham abruptly asked him his opinion of the Samoans of Western Samoa, as compared to those of American Samoa.

"The Samoans over in Apia are a helluva lot better than in Pago," he told him. "They have a lot more self-respect and gumption, and their village life is run more along the old times. The native chiefs are still in control, and they run the whole show, even to when and what the natives will eat, and how long they'll work, and how much each one is to kick into the village fund. And it works fine, otherwise they'd just sit around on their asses, like they do back there in Pago. The *matai*-system [rule of hereditary chiefs] is okay in my book.

"The women in Western Samoa are better looking than in Pago. You must have seen for yourself how ugly the women are in American Samoa. But over in Apia it's different. When the Germans were running the islands, they had to import a gang of Chinks to work in the coconut plantations, because the Samoans just wouldn't work, and some of them got to the native women. And I can tell you that a Samoan girl with a little Chinee blood in her is really something! Gives her upturned cat-eyes, not quite so hefty a butt, slenders her down all over. The skin and hair are better, too. I've got a Samoan-Chinee gal in Fagali'i Village, and she's the wildest . . ."

Maugham interrupted to ask him if he knew what was the opinion of the old residents, European and Samoan, who had known Stevenson when he was living at Vailima.

"Oh, yeah, that limey-writer who wrote *Treasure Island,*" he replied indifferently. "A good enough book. I ain't read his history books on Western Samoa, about the battles between the high chiefs which is supposed to be the straight dope,[2] but I think he was considered a good enough feller by the whites and the Samoans. They built a long road with their hands, just to have a way to lug his body up to the top of that mountain where they put him in that cement or brick tomb. I went up there once. It was a good enough place, with a swell view. No man would gripe about being put away in such a nifty spot. But it was sure one helluva hike up to the top of that mountain, or hill it should be called, and it was hot as hell and I really sweat. A young Samoan cutie showed me the way up, and when the going got tough she got behind me and pushed on my bum to help me up the steep, muddy places. I brought along some beer, and when I had cooled off a bit, I took her into the bushes. So the trip wasn't exactly wasted, if you get what I mean. But I wouldn't make that hike again, just to see a guy's grave."

Maugham, after an early supper of tea and bread, which was all he could hold on his stomach, went on deck for fresh air. The schooner, with all sails set, was not rolling so violently and he felt somewhat recovered from his *mal de mer*, even though there was a heavy swell running. The twilight is always brief in the tropics, and night closed down abruptly over sea and schooner.

"It was not unpleasant sitting on deck, with the riding-lights of the schooner casting a radiance over the cut-water at the bow and the crested waves that flowed away from her flanks on either side," said Maugham. "Tutuila Island was arear, a dark mass superimposed against the heavier shade of night. Far down upon the horizon I found the Southern Cross, making a very bright display."

Later some of the crew had come on deck to smoke and

---

[2] Stevenson's *A Footnote to History (1897)*.

talk, and after a while the skipper came on deck and asked them to play and sing. A banjo, ukulele, guitar and concertina were handed up through the hatch, and the Samoans started to entertain. Two of the Samoan seamen were urged to dance, and they sprang to their feet commencing movements and gyrations that intrigued Maugham.

He had written: "It was a strange, barbaric dance, in which there was something savage and primeval, a rapid dance, with quick movements of hands and feet and strange contortions of the body; it was sensual, sexual even, but sexual without passion; it was animal, naive, weird without mystery, natural in short, and one might almost say childlike.

"It was a curious emotion to sail through this silent sea under the stars and the passionate sky, while the *kanakas* played and sang and danced. At last they grew tired and stretched themselves out on the deck and slept, and all was silence."

For Maugham, there were many impressions on which to reflect.

8. A View of Robert Louis Stevenson — and Moetotolo

Maugham sat alone on deck, wrapped in thought, reflecting on his war duties in Switzerland; his promise to the British War Office to go to Russia on a secret mission when this trip of convalescence was over; whether or not to marry Syrie Barnado; how he could effectively utilize the personality of the blonde prostitute from Honolulu in a story; what Western Samoa would offer for observation and impressions; and if the voyage to Tahiti, the ultimate destination, would prove to be a fruitful one on the Gauguin writing project.

Someone came up the companionway, walked to the side and spat into the sea. He turned and Maugham recognized him as the supercargo of the *Manua*, a small sparrow-like man, tense, but of good cheer, with a close-shaved head. He offered Maugham a drink which he refused, and then sat down on deck beside him.

"I've read some of your books, Mr. Maugham," he informed him. "I liked the *Magician* book, but best of all *Of Human Bondage*. I've read it twice, a great book, indeed, if I may say so."

Maugham thanked him.

"When you were talking to the skipper I wanted to come over and say something," he continued, "but I thought it was best to keep my trap shut. The skipper is a good man, and we get along okay, but he's not a thinker, at least not a very educated man. Now, I've had a bit of schooling, and I'm a self-educated man, too. I read a lot.

"But, getting back to the skipper, I knew you wanted to hear some solid facts about the Samoans, but I'm not a buttinsky, so I waited until now to have a talk with you, if you don't mind."

"By all means do let me have your opinions," said Maugham. "I'm interested."

"Well, first, the skipper doesn't have any intellectual pursuits, he doesn't read any worthwhile books. So what he tells you about the islands is hearsay, or somehow mixed up with his boozing and messing around the native women. There's more to these Samoan islands than that, you've got to agree."

Maugham acquiesced on this point.

"I heard you ask him about Robert Louis Stevenson, and that was when I was itching to jump in and really give you the facts about him. First, Stevenson wasn't the big man that he liked to believe he was in Apia. He lived up there in that big house at Vailima with all his family, and from what I've heard it was a kind of mad-house. His woman was a real spitfire, I hear, arguments and rows all the time. I don't see how he got any writing done.

"And he went around in boots and white pants and a kind of Russian shirt. The Samoans liked him, but most of them thought he was a little peculiar. He made a lot of friends with the high chiefs, and he was always having them up to his place for eating and drinking. One thing I can tell you, if he hadn't put out a fortune for food and booze, they wouldn't have bothered going up to see him.[1] Polynesians are that way, they just judge a man by what he gives them or what they can get out of him, so Stevenson, being a good host, always had his verandah jam-packed with hungry islanders. So he got a reputation in Samoa of being a real good sport when it came to hand-outs, or putting on lavish parties. Most of the chiefs just came to get their bellies full of good food and liquor, nothing more. They didn't savvy half what he talked to them about, just pretending to, sitting there politely, but their minds too peanut-sized to grasp much of what he was spouting, and figuring out a way to leave now that their guts were filled.

"As for that road they built for him to carry his body along, they needed the road anyway, and today it's kept up by the prison gangs in Apia, not the original natives who built it. Stevenson today is quite forgotten in Western Samoa, at least by most of the natives. He's no longer there to throw parties for them, so they've just forgotten about him. That's the way it is, no matter what they say about people eating their hearts out when someone dies. Sad, but true.

"As for the Samoans themselves, they aren't the 'children of nature,' unspoiled and gentle, that some writers try to picture them. The Samoan is a rough type of Polynesian. One thing I notice is that they don't have any record of their ancient gods. This is funny to me, because most Polynesian races have stories and legends of their pagan idols and gods of the sea and heaven. That's where my education and read-

---

[1] The first name of honor that Stevenson was given by the Samoans was "The Rich Man."

ing comes in. I've figured out that the Samoans were, long ago, perhaps, kicked out of some other group of islands, and most likely in disgrace, because they didn't bring any gods with them to set up. When the Tahitians came up to Hawaii on their migration, they brought their gods in the double-canoes. But, as far as I can find out, not the Samoans. If you'll notice, the Samoan has a rougher face than the other Polynesian races, heavier boned, and he is ruder and more quarrelsome.

"One thing I can tell you to watch out for when you're in Western Samoa is their *malaga* procession. That's when the natives take off from their village to visit another village. They carry big, long, sharp axes, and only men make the march. Their faces are streaked with colored paint, and most of them are wild on bush-liquor. If anything happens along the way to rile them up, they use those axes on anyone who gets in their path. In the in-wars they were always chopping the heads off their enemies, especially young children and women.

"You've maybe seen those photographs that were taken up at Stevenson's home at Vailima, showing the Samoans grouped around him with their long axes. Well, they weren't there to clear his property or chop him fire-wood. Those were their weapons, which they carried all the time, in case they got into fights along the way. A Samoan is an ugly customer if he's drunk and annoyed about something." He pointed aft and then forward where the native passengers were bedded down with their baskets of green coconut leaves, and bundles of personal effects tied up into colorful sarongs, or *lava-lavas*. "They're quiet, friendly and docile now, but just let any of them, man or woman, get into an argument, and before it's over there'll be one helluva riot; someone is bound to get hurt or killed."

He shrugged his shoulders, walked over to the rail again, spat, and then came back.

"A white man who lives with a native woman down here is asking for trouble. He loses the respect of the white officials and residents. And where the Samoans themselves are concerned, if he doesn't let his woman's relatives borrow or steal from him all the time, they start sneering at him, and laughing behind his back, making faces and insulting gestures; they show him about as much respect as they would the crumbiest beachcomber. And if you don't take up with one of their women, they think that you're a queer one, that there's something wrong with you sexually.

"There are some quite all right native women down here, but these are the ones who have a little German blood in them, makes them more sensible and honest.

"Well, that's my little speech about the Samoans, and I hope it might be of some value to you."

He uncorked his bottle of whiskey, tilted it to his mouth, and took a long swig. He gave a dry hacking cough, wiped his mouth with the back of his hand, nodded goodnight to Maugham, and went below.

Almost immediately the engineer in oil-stained dark pants, faded flannel shirt stiff with dried perspiration and paraffin spatterings, and ragged tweed cap, came from aft and spoke, almost sullenly:

"You won't take to heart, sir, too much of his blather now. He's soured on the Samoans for one reason or another. That's why he boozes all the time, always getting up with a headache and upset stomach. The truth is that he's had bad luck with his native women. They're always running out on him, or laying up with someone else when he's between ports. One stole a bit of his savings once. But he doesn't know how to treat these native women. He's always treating them too politely, taking their arm to help them out of a buggy, letting them walk ahead of him, even doing most of the housework. I think he's keeping company with a Samoan-German girl in Apia now.

"Then I hear he tries to educate them, get them interested in his piles of books. *Kerist!* they don't want to exercise their brain, they're only interested in exercising one thing. Instead of trying to make them smart, he oughta just make babies with them. That's the ticket with Samoan women—keep them barefoot and pregnant, as they say.

"One thing I will say for the Super, he's always even tempered, laughing and clowning and cracking jokes, no matter how bad with a skinfull he feels in the morning.

"As I say, I just want to set you right about the Samoans. You're new to these islands, and it's best to go ashore with an open mind." He laid a friendly hand on Maugham's shoulder. "So just don't let them confuse you. What I'm telling you is the God's truth. Goodnight and pleasant dreams, sir."

Maugham, as the *Manua* sailed toward Apia, remained on deck most of the night, rather than hazard the communal sleeping-cabin below, which was noxious with paraffin fumes and the vomit of seasick passengers, and where enormous and voracious cockroaches "awaited the unwary voyager with cannibalistic intent."

The tropical port of Apia, which Maugham saw in the early morning from the deck of the *Manua,* was little changed from the waterfront of today. The commercial section of the town, with its trading-stores of red sheet-iron roofs, sheds and government buildings trailed straight across the scene, from the brief promontory of Matautu to Mulinuu Point, with the sometimes clustered structures separated, as if by quarantine, by the alabaster-white mission churches, Catholic and Protestant, almost side-by-side, shielded at intervals from the blazing sunshine by huge plane-trees and coconut palms.

The town lay somnolent, yet aware of its hazardous exposure to the open sea that thundered on the protective barrier-reefs. The port faced an unprotected roadstead, providing only a precarious anchorage for vessels that had to discharge their cargo into lighters for unloading at the small jetty that jutted out from shore beyond the center of the waterfront. Only a narrow channel, bristling on either side with treacherous shelving coral-ledges, admitted the ships into the reef-enclosed basin. A high surf roared incessantly on the outer and inner ramparts.

Not far from shore, on an apron of coral, lay the rusting hulk of the German gunboat *Adler*, far over on her shattered side, just as the hurricane of March 16, 1889 had cast her, along with six other frigates, cruisers and corvettes, German, British and American, now far below the surface, who had refused to leave the roadstead because of the hotly contested wrangle over control of Western Samoa. The *Adler* had been on the same reef grave-mound all these years.

The Central Hotel, on the waterfront of Apia, where Maugham stayed on his visit, was a ramshackle frame building, three storeys high, with comfortable wicker chairs and potted plants on the encircling verandahs, from any of which one had an unparalleled view of the waterfront, the harbour and the reefs, milky-white with the shattered combers of the South Pacific. On the ground floor was a bar, popular with the white guests and residents, and a dining-room. The bedrooms on each floor were separated by central corridors, terminating in toilets and showers. Outside in the large yard there were quarters for the Chinese help, and stables and space for the two-wheeled traps and buggies in which the planters travelled from the outlying districts.

"The accommodations were limited, a little primitive," said Maugham, "but the bar made up for whatever discomforts one suffered from concave, mildewed mattress, varied crawling insects, and brazen Samoan chambermaids who didn't need any overtures to crawl, unbidden, under your mosquito-net. Into the bar, at sundown, came the only interesting whites on the island. If it hadn't been for the Central Bar, I would have been bitterly disappointed in Apia."[2]

The owner of the Central Hotel, a short, stocky man, with thinning grey hair, ragged moustache, florid complexion, and small broken-veined nose, was a Britisher, who, through the chemistry acquired as a dentist's assistant, had learned to brew beer. When he was not absent in some secret part of the hotel, decanting the fermented concoction from huge earthen crocks into bottles, he could be found in the bar, engaging one and all in verbose arguments, or imparting all the gossip of the islands.

"One night he made the mistake of picking a row with Gerald, who was a remarkably athletic man, fast on his feet and a master of defense with his hands," recalled Maugham. "It had to do with Gerald being an American, a citizen of a country not actively engaged in the war. He, the proprietor, was forever threatening to close the hotel and go off to the trenches to 'do his bit.' On this occasion, he all but accused Gerald of being a 'slacker,' indulging himself with travel and plush living rather than doing his patriotic duty.

"Gerald, who had had a few drinks, reached across the

---

[2] Maugham again used his South Seas diary pertaining to his visit to this hotel, its owner, and the characters he met in the Central Bar, for his most famous Samoan background novelette, *The Pool.*

bar, took him by his black tie, and gave it a few tremendous jerks, which almost snapped the other's head off. 'That'll do now,' Gerald cautioned him in a quiet voice. 'I've carried more wounded and dead soldiers in a Red Cross ambulance than you've carried beer bottles down to this bar. And anytime you want to pack up and take off for the front lines, just go ahead, and I'll be only too happy to take your place behind the bar, and try to improve on the lousy bitter beer you make from dirty old socks, assorted garbage, or horse manure.' That settled the matter. But a few minutes later, his rawboned wife, quite an imposing white woman of about fifty, who seemed to have some occult sense when her husband was drinking too much or making a nuisance of himself, put her head into the room. 'What the devil are you up to?' she snapped at him, and crooked an index finger for him to follow her. A few minutes later, in an upstairs room, we heard a devil of a row, of furniture being bumped, a body hitting against a wall, all accompanied by her strident, accusing tirade. Some of the guests told me that she frequently used her fists and even her feet on him, when the transgression merited it.

"But he was not entirely a bad sort, despite his weakness for alcohol and argument, and appeared pleased that I had selected his hotel for my stay in Apia. 'I've read your books, Mr. Maugham,' he informed me. 'I'm writing a book too, about what I see and hear in this hotel, and my opinions of human nature. All you have to do is just sit here in the bar, and you'll get all the stories you need.'

"Frequently he would disappear, and when I would inquire of him, the chambermaids would grin and jerk a thumb to an upper floor of the hotel. It meant that his tyrant of a wife had locked him in his room, and that his only commerce with friends was to hail them from his small private verandah, asking for the gossip of the port, conveying greetings, and bartering for varied merchandise. He would attribute his confinement to a liver complaint rather than the belligerence of his jailer-wife, of whom he seemed terrified."

One of the more interesting characters that Maugham met in the Central Bar was a small, thin man with close-cropped dark hair, black bow-tie and wide-brimmed crushed felt hat with a fanciful band around it, and tussore silk suit, beneath which a looped watchchain held his waistcoat together loosely.

His name was Charlie Roberts, and he was the Chief Judge of the Court of Samoa.

Charlie Roberts, for Maugham, proved to be a very valuable informant on Samoan life and the foibles of the European community, particularly the sexual intrigues between the whites and the native women. Gerald Haxton and Maugham made a number of excursions around Upolu with him. Without Charlie Roberts' assistance and knowledge of Samoan culture Maugham could never have acquired in so short a time such an astonishing insight into island customs and lore.

Yet it is strange that Maugham alluded just briefly to Charlie Roberts in his factual notes on this trip:

"C. He trains horses for the local races. He is an Australian . . . so dark that you might take him for a half-caste; his features look a little too big for his face, but in his white riding breeches, spurs and gaiters, he is a trim, handsome and upstanding figure . . ."

Maugham, with Charlie Roberts for a guide, visited the Samoan villages outside Apia. He was impressed with the orderliness of the thatched, conical-shaped *fales,* or huts,

with their sugar-cane roofs. He had examined the *fales* carefully, marvelled at the intricate thatchwork in the under-
roof that supported the layers of sugar-cane leaves and the
lashings of coconut cord that held the heavy beams, all constructed without a nail or bolt. Scrupulous attention to detail was Maugham's greatest asset as a writer. Later he was
to describe a *fale* with authority in his short-story *Mackintosh*:

"The Samoan huts are formed in this way: trunks of slender trees are placed in a circle at intervals of perhaps five
or six feet; a tall tree is set in the middle and from this down-
wards slopes the thatched roof. Venetian blinds of coconut
leaves can be pulled down at night or when it is raining.
Ordinarily the hut is open all round so that the breeze can
blow through freely."

The centuries-old patriarchal system of village-rule was
vested in the high chiefs and talking-chiefs, the latter skilled
in oratory and genealogy. Obedience and discipline were
maintained in the villages.

"I saw that the basic food was boiled green bananas, breadfruit, taro and fish, a very nutritious diet indeed, the proof
being in their well-formed limbs and beautiful white teeth.
Even the old men and women had all their teeth, ground
down a bit, but, nevertheless, sound and without cavities.
I saw no Samoan wearing glasses, except a few native missionaries, who had ruined their eyes on the badly printed,
microscopic words of their prayer books, hymn books and
tracts.

"The hospitality and dignity of the chiefs were perfect.
They received a guest in their large meeting-house *fale,* and
you sat on finely woven mats, with your back against one
of the smooth upright posts of the structure; a cooling breeze
blew continually through from the sea, and there was no

discomfort. Beautiful young girls, bare to the waist, their bodies shining with coconut oil, sat before huge carved bowls of a milky liquid which they prepared, the celebrated *kava* of Samoa and Fiji. It was made from an indigenous root, pounded and then crushed, mixed with water and finally strained. Each guest, in order of importance, is served a coconut half-shell of *kava*, as the talking-chief calls out his name and recites his genealogy and talents. It had a slightly herbal taste, a bit peppery on the tongue, but not unpleasant.

"Charlie Roberts said that the effect was a little insidious, more narcotic than alcoholic. One's limbs, if a large quantity was taken, became a little unmanageable, but the brain remained clear and with increased perception.

"He also explained to me that the girls who prepared the *kava* were *taupos,* or virgins, usually the daughters of the high chiefs or talking-chiefs. And the virginity of these specially selected girls was closely guarded. Earlier, ignorant seamen who had landed in Samoa, thought it great sport to waylay a *taupo* and violate her. These rapists, if they didn't leave the island, were shortly found beheaded.

"At the time I was in Samoa the virginity of a *taupo* was still under a strict taboo.[3] The daughter of a chief had to go to the sleeping-mat of her groom, a young chief, with her hymen intact. Death was not unusual to be dealt to a *taupo* who had slyly lost her virginity and tried to carry out a deception."

It was not too many years ago that the examination and rupturing of the hymen of a *taupo* was conducted in public. She was led into a huge *fale*, with all her family, the family of her future husband, and special invited guests seated in a circle. Two old women led her naked around the circle,

---

[3] And still is today, where chiefs' daughters are concerned.

while talking-chiefs chanted her genealogy and praised her physical attributes. Then at a given signal, she was brought before the high chief, compelled to kneel before him, whereupon he inserted two fingers, wrapped in pure-white *tapa*-cloth, into the vaginal canal. The audience waited with hushed tension for the proof of her virginity. If the *tapa*-cloth was withdrawn stained with blood, a great sigh of relief would come from the *taupo's* family, and a shout of happiness from the groom's. Then the deflowered *taupo* was led around the circle by the old women, while the assembled villagers shouted her praises.[4]

But if a *taupo* was found to be a spurious one, she was quickly seized by the old women, even her own family, and strangled; her name was erased from the genealogy of the village, and none mentioned it again.

Maugham was also to hear about the charming Samoan sex custom of *moetotolo*, or *sleep-crawling-seduction*[5] a traditional form of courtship for young people not bound to virginity—as in the case of chiefs' daughters—wherein, under cover of darkness, a youth would crawl into a girl's *fale*, while her family were sprawled snoring all around her on sleeping mats, pretending to be unaware of the intrusion and ravishment of the teen-age daughter. If she had been attracted previously, in meetings in daytime, to the youth, she cooperated quietly, but if she was expecting another admirer to her sleeping-mat, she might raise a hysterical outcry that would arouse her family and send them with curses and clubs after the would-be seducer.

Samoan fathers and mothers of nubile maidens have even

---

[4] In 1960, in Apia, a modern part-Samoan woman proudly showed the author an heirloom "fine mat," stained with blood, which had been the sleeping-mat of her virginal daughter married in that year.

[5] A detailed account of *moetotolo*, and Samoan sexual customs, can be found in Margaret Mead's *Coming of Age in Samoa*.

trained fierce male dogs to drive off these roving night-crawl-
ing seducers, but the youths countered by bringing along
bitch-dogs in heat to pacify the ferocious watch-dogs. Families then employed castrated dogs as sentries, but the young
Samoan lechers countered this challenge by tossing chunks
of fish, impregnated with a strong herbal sedative, to put
the vigilant canines to sleep. Today, for the most part
parents shrug their shoulders, and, for peace of mind and
unbroken sleep, assume a what-can-you-do-about-it attitude
concerning the concupiscent crawlers.

"Chastity, except in instances of *taupos,* was not a virtue
of much esteem in Western Samoa when I visited there,"
said Maugham. "Sex was discussed, joked about, danced,
sung, and enjoyed with great relish. No Samoan girl, married or otherwise, had the least hesitancy in telling her suitor
or husband of her numerous lovers. Nor did he hesitate to
tell her of his conquests as a virile seducer. While spending
a few days in a native village, especially on my trip to the
adjoining larger island of Savaii, I witnessed many scenes
of *moetotolo.*

"Charlie Roberts told me about an amusing case of a
young man who crept into a young girl's hut, but instead of
finding the teen-ager of his choice, found himself seized and
violently ravished by the maiden's mother, who had taken a
fancy to her daughter's suitor. I venture to claim that the
young Samoan night-crawler learned a thing or two before
he was able to creep weakly out under the *fale* again.

"He also told me of the guileless attitude of Samoan girls
toward sexual relations. A pretty girl of fifteen, filling out
a form at a mission school, pondered seriously the word *SEX*
on the entrance application. The blank space opposite it
provided for a write-in of *male or female,* and she finally
decided to use her own interpretation of the word. She

wrote candidly: 'Yes, many times in a banana grove in Mulifanua.'

"Anyway, that *moetotolo* custom, or night-creeping-seduction, sounded like a lot of fun for everybody, even if it ended in a 'run-sheep-run' chase after the young Samoan Casanovas.

"Roberts called our attention now and again to women who appeared to have suffered serious damage to their ears, as if mutilated by accident or by some infection. Sometimes the ear-lobe would be missing, and in some instances the entire ear. He explained to me that a married Samoan woman becomes vindictive if she finds that a promiscuous girl of the village has lured her husband to her sleeping-mat, and then boasts about it afterwards, ridiculing the wife's proficiency in coition. She awaits her opportunity to waylay her, wrestles her to the ground and, with savage efficiency, sinks her molars and bicuspids into the flirt's ear, *biting off* as much as she is capable of doing in the brief, but fierce struggle, forever branding her as a 'husband-stealer,' or marital meddler."[6]

Stevenson had written: "In Samoa perpetual song and dance, perpetual games, journeys, and pleasures make an animated and smiling picture of island life . . . The importance of this can scarcely be exaggerated. In a climate and upon a soil where a livelihood can be had for the stooping, entertainment is a prime necessity."

And the meaning of "entertainment" to the Samoans was —*Sex!* At least, that was Maugham's observation.

---

[6] A few years ago, the author witnessed an ear-severing assault on the dock at Pago Pago, American Samoa, when a revengeful Samoan wife grappled with a prostitute of the Pago Pago Bar, slicing off her right ear with a sharp knife, in retaliation for impudently continuing sexual relations with her husband—which compelled the bar-girl forever afterwards to rearrange her hair to hide the unsightly mutilation.

"Whenever Gerald and I would take a stroll after dark along the roadways leading out of Apia, we would frequently come upon young Samoan men and women scarcely concealed by the bushes, some lying in open grassy culverts under the stars, making love. In the Samoan *fales,* which had no partitions, and in the villages' immediate vicinity too many children frolicked about in play, so the young people had to steal away to less trafficked places for sexual relations.

"Sometimes we came upon scenes of violent altercation, when a youth discovered that a girl, who had only just left his embrace, had continued down the dark path less than a hundred yards to keep an assignation with his rival. This exposed the cuckolded lover to the taunts of his friends who questioned his virility in being unable to satisfy the girl sexually.

"A favourite after-dark playground for the sexually precocious young Samoan men and women of Apia was Mulinuu Point, which formed the extreme westerly peninsula of Apia Bay. There were some sandy beaches covered with trailing ground-vines, grassy areas and coconut palms, and when sexual excesses stimulated their appetites, they could wade out into the lagoon to search for shell-fish.

"They would take their *fa'amafu* and beer, guitars, banjoes, ukuleles and concertinas, and they would spend the entire night there until the first light of dawn, drinking, singing, dancing and copulating. In some of my early morning walks, I would come upon couples, still locked in each other's arms, blissfully snoring, their bare feet in the shallow shore-water of the rising tide. Gerald had joined some of these saturnalias on a few occasions, and he had described the orgies under the moonlight as 'bacchanalian scenes of an almost vanished era of Samoan paganism.'

"Long after midnight most of the revelers out at Mulinuu

Point would start coming back into town, among them some of the errant daughters and sons of the upper-class part-Samoan merchants of Apia. They walked slowly, listlessly, exhausted by their frenzied play on moonlit beaches, the once pristine, starched gowns of the young women wrinkled and torn, the young men disheveled and staggering. Now and again traps and buggies, on their way back to nearby villages, would be loaded down with happy natives, still playing their ukuleles and concertinas, but with less vigor than out at Mulinuu, because now their animal spirits had been soothed with their sensual indulgences. It was all charming, innocent and gratifying."

The Mulinuu Point of Maugham's time has not changed. It is still the rendezvous for the predatory young Samoan women of Apia. But instead of reaching it by foot and horse-drawn carriage, they bring their boy-friends, off the Union Line vessels, out in taxi-cabs. The play is of the same pattern: Beer and singing, and dancing and venery. When a vessel is in port, the small peninsula is overcrowded, with briefly spaced clusters of seamen and *fafines,* separated only by darkness and discretion, with some desperate couple even forced to seek the shadows inside the fence of the tomb of a Samoan patriot that now marks the end of the promontory. It was still, as Maugham opined, "charming, innocent and gratifying."

One white visitor had become so obsessed with the riotous merrymaking on this peninsula orgy-ground that he soon became known as "Mulinuu Point Willie." Another American visitor, caught in *flagrante delicto* with the young part-Samoan wife of a businessman of Apia, was chased down the moonlit beach by the irate husband, clad only in his T-shirt, crouched low, his buttocks arched high into the lunar brilliance, busy bare feet wildly scattering the coral rubble. The revelers cheered lustily when the culprit made good his escape into the night sea. Thereafter, the Samoans honored his agility by giving him a native name. He was proud of the appellation, that is until I gave him a literal translation: the islanders, to commemorate the ruckus, had dubbed him "Bare-behind Barney."

9. Tales of Samoa

When one reads Maugham's fiction of Samoan background, it is evident that he had the rare faculty of rapidly absorbing and cataloguing the most minute detail of white and native deportment. His knowledge of anthropology, sociology and ethnology was sound, and I found few instances of mistakes in his familiarity with Polynesian culture, or lore. Possibly the mountainous stacks of books that he had read had prepared him for Samoa and Tahiti and the Far East. His visit to Western Samoa was brief, far too brief for the ordinary writer to have gained such an astonishing reserve of incidents, characters and authentic scenery.

I don't think that any old-time white resident of Samoa could find much fault with the verisimilitude of Maugham's short story *Red, The Pool, Mackintosh,* and *Miss Thompson,* or *Rain,* all with Samoan settings.[1]

---

[1] These are all included in his *The Trembling of a Leaf.*

Almost everyone is familiar with *Sadie Thompson*, because of the many times it has been filmed by Hollywood.

The tale *Red* is in the familiar Maugham vein of cynicism: An American sailor with red hair deserts his ship in Apia harbor at the turn of the century and runs off into the bush with a beautiful young Samoan girl. Some critics maintain that Maugham described *"Red"* with almost homosexual enthusiasm: "He was tall, six feet and an inch or two—and he was made like a Greek god, broad in the shoulders and thin in the flanks; he was like Apollo, with just that soft roundness which Praxiteles gave him, and that suave, feminine grace which has in it something troubling and mysterious. His skin was dazzling white, milky, like satin; his skin was like a woman's . . . And his face was just as beautiful as his body. He had large blue eyes, very dark, so that some say they were black, and unlike most red-haired people he had dark eyebrows and long dark lashes. His features were perfectly regular and his mouth was like a scarlet wound. He was twenty. . . . He was unique. There never was anyone more beautiful. There was no more reason for him than for a wonderful blossom to flower on a wild plant. He was a happy accident of nature."

The Samoan girl, whom Red called Sally, was equally attractive, and their love for each other, as Maugham wrote, was "the real love, not the love that comes from sympathy, common interests, or intellectual community, but love pure and simple . . . the love that draws the beasts to one another, and the Gods."

Maugham kept Red in true character, as with all seamen, by having him desert Sally and sailing away. The native girl, grief-stricken, refused to eat, became ill. But in time another white man came along, and she went to live with him, never forgetting, however, her first lover. The spectre of Red haunted this man, Neilson, convalescing from tuberculosis. He knew that he was ugly as Red was handsome. "She had yielded to him, through weariness, but she had only yielded what she set no store on." They lived on the site of the hut that she and Red had shared, and which she had burned down the day she agreed to become Neilson's mistress. The years passed, and finally the torment of his unrequited love lessened. "She was an old woman, for the women of the islands age quickly, and if he had no love for her any more he had tolerance."

It is at this point, actually the opening of the tale, that an old schooner captain, a man of gross obesity, extraordinarily repellent, finds his way to Neilson's house, and tells him, in flashbacks, of the romance of Red and Sally. It is not until the end, when an elderly native woman in a black Mother Hubbard shuffles into the room, speaks briefly with Neilson, glances without interest at the skipper and then leaves, that one senses that it is not just an aimless stroll that has brought the seafarer to this place. "What is your name?" Neilson asks him. And the other tells him, as he leaves, chuckling maliciously, that for thirty years in the islands he had been known as—*Red!*

The cynicism of Maugham is heavy in this story, especially when he has Neilson make this observation: "The tragedy of love is not death or separation . . . Oh, it is dreadfully bitter to look at a woman whom you have loved with all your heart and soul, so that you felt you could not bear to let her out of your sight, and realise that you would not mind if you never saw her again. The tragedy of love is indifference."

Maugham's philosophy on love can be found in almost all of his essays on women.

His short-story *Mackintosh*, with a setting of Savaii, the largest island of the Western Samoan archipelago, is a powerful tale of a despotic Irish administrator by the name of Walker and his scholarly assistant Mackintosh. Here is one of Maugham's best character delineations, coupled with a story-line of mounting tension. Hating his superior for his vulgarity and apparent brutal treatment of the natives, Mackintosh cleverly arranges for a young native chief, who has been degraded by Walker, to steal his pistol and assassinate the loathsome administrator. But at the end, fatally wounded, Walker in a death bed talk with Mackintosh reveals his true character: "You must say it was an accident. No one's to blame. Promise me that . . . They're children. I'm their father. A father don't let his children get into trouble if he can help it."

Then Mackintosh pulls his hand from the dead man's fingers, takes the pistol that has been returned to his desk, walks out into the lagoon, and blows his brains out.

An old resident of Apia, who had known the real-life Walker intimately, told me:

"Dick Williams would have been all for suing Maugham for slander and libel up to a point in that story. Dick did do a lot of shouting and ass-kicking at the natives over on Savaii, particularly when he wanted a road constructed clear around the island, which is Walker's pet project in the story. And don't think that Dick wasn't above playing tricks on the natives, working one village against the other, to gain his point, particularly in short-changing them for wages, as Maugham's administrator Walker did in *Mackintosh*.

"But when Dick got to the part when he's going to die, and tells how much he likes his assistant, how no one must be punished for his murder, and how he dearly loves all his Samoan charges like his own kids, and entrusting them into Mackintosh's care—well, you can be sure that Dick bawled his eyes out to think that Maugham would have had such an insight into his lily-white soul. So he naturally didn't sue Maugham for damages."

True to the suggestion of the owner of the Central Hotel in Apia, who told Maugham he could "get all the stories you need," by just sitting and drinking in the bar, the characters of his novelette, *The Pool,* did come within his range of study in the hotel's ground-floor pub.

In this dramatic story, Maugham once again served as its fictional narrator, and it was based on fact.

The Pool treated a subject that had occupied Maugham's attention and interest from time-to-time while visiting in Hawaii, Pago Pago, and now Apia—the true aspects of the sexual and marital relationships between whites and Polynesians. He obviously didn't condone or hold much brief for such liaisons, in the instance that a white man invariably succumbed to the torpor of the tropics, losing all ambitions of career, and, eventually, sinking to the apathetic level of the islanders, wherein mental or physical deterioration at last destroyed him, or rendered him unfit for a place of respect in society or commercial enterprise.

His fictional portrait of the true case-history of "Lawson" of *The Pool* is as sharply drawn as the debauchee in Oscar Wilde's *The Picture of Dorian Gray*. Maugham, in the factual chronicles that he kept of his South Seas voyage, had made a note of this man, as follows:

"L. He was an estate agent in London and came to Samoa originally for his health. He is a little thin man, with a long face and a narrow, weak chin, a prominent nose, large and bony, and good, dark brown eyes. He is married to a half-caste and has a small son, but she lives with her parents and he at the hotel. He has rather a cunning, shifty look and does not impress you as honest or scrupulous; but he is anxious to be thought a good sport and is full of surface jollity. He is quite intelligent. He drinks a great deal and is dead drunk three or four days a week, often by mid-afternoon. Then he is quarrelsome and wants to fight people. He is sullen and vindictive. He lies about stupefied, and when obliged to walk waddles on bent knees."

This is almost a word-for-word description of the Lawson of *The Pool*, manager of a branch bank in Apia, who becomes enamored of a pretty part-Samoan girl of sixteen, whom he meets at a deep swimming pool not far out of Apia.

The pool becomes a place of inexorable destiny for Lawson:

"But the spot that entranced him was a pool a mile or two away from Apia to which in the evenings he often went to bathe. There was a little river that bubbled over the rocks in a swift stream, and then, after forming the deep pool, ran on, shallow and crystalline, past a ford made by great stones where the natives came sometimes to bathe or to wash their clothes. The coconut trees, with their frivolous elegance, grew thickly on the banks, all clad with trailing plants, and they were reflected in the green water. It was just such a scene as you might see in Devonshire among the hills, and yet with a difference, for it had a tropical richness, a passion, a scented languor which seemed to melt the heart. The water was fresh, but not cold; and it was delicious after the heat of the day. To bathe there refreshed not only the body but the soul. . . ."

And then there was his fateful meeting with the part-Samoan girl Ethel Brevald, daughter of a shiftless Norwegian and a Samoan mother: "A girl was sitting there. She glanced around as he came and noiselessly slid into the water. She vanished like a naiad startled by the approach of a mortal . . ." And he found her there again: "She took no notice of him. She did not even glance in his direction. She swam about the green pool. She dived, she rested on the bank, as though she were quite alone: he had a queer feeling that he was invisible. Scraps of poetry, half forgotten, floated across his memory, and vague recollections of the Greece he had negligently studied in his school days. When she had changed her wet clothes for dry ones and sauntered away he found a scarlet hibiscus where she had been. It was a flower that she had worn in her hair when she came to bathe and, having taken it out on getting into the water, had forgotten or not cared to put in again. He took it in his hands and looked at it with a singular emotion. He had an instinct to keep it, but his sentimentality irritated him, and he flung it away. It gave him quite a little pang to see it float down the stream . . . He wondered what strangeness it was in her nature that urged her to go down to this hidden pool when there was no likelihood that anyone should be there. The natives of the islands are devoted to the water. They bathe, somewhere or other, every day, once always, and often twice; but they bathe in bands . . . It looked as though there was in this pool some secret which attracted Ethel against her will."

Thereafter, Lawson met her there regularly, and at last overcame her shyness with him, and decided to marry her.

He is warned by his business associates that old Brevald, the father, is anxious to get rid of his many daughters by four Samoan wives, and that the daughter Ethel has purposely set a trap for him, knowing of his respected position as a banker in Apia. One remarks: "I'm all for having a good time with the girls out here, but when it comes to marrying them . . ."

Nevertheless, Lawson does marry Ethel. And from the moment he takes her into his bungalow on the sea his troubles commence: the white community of Apia snubs him, only the part-Samoans accept him; the girl's relatives move into his home to eat him into debt and distraction; the son born to them is more Samoan than white.

It is then that Lawson makes up his mind to take his wife and son to Scotland, so that the boy will have the opportunity of a good education, and so escape the humiliations and restrictions of a half-caste, who is scorned by the pure-blooded Samoans and rejected by the whites. A part-Samoan girl could marry a white man if she were attractive and shapely, but a part-Samoan boy was compelled to marry his own kind.

But the wife is bitterly unhappy in Scotland, so far away from her island-home, and she finally takes her son and runs away, returning to Apia. Lawson follows her back and, destitute, is forced to resume married life in the littered plantation home of the rum-swizzling white father. Here Lawson's conversion to a drunken, quarrelsome, and scorned white man commences. Native members of the household sneer at him, his wife has only contempt for the broken man, and she begins to disappear at nights on secret visits, which he suspects is to a gross German-American importer of Apia by the name of Miller. He beats her with a riding-whip, and when later he crawls back to her, whining for forgiveness, she had "the native woman's disdain of a man who abased himself before a woman." She kicks at him scornfully.

Lawson goes looking for Miller to accuse him of infidelity with his wife, finds him in the British Club on the evening of Christmas Day, and lunges at him with a billiard cue. But Miller, a stronger man, knocks him down.

Maugham, as the narrator, has the last meeting with Lawson, and tells him that he is leaving Apia within a week for Sydney. The wretched man sighs: "It would be jolly to go home once more . . ." And then he adds flatly: "I've made an awful hash of things. That's obvious, isn't it? I'm right down at the bottom of the pit and there's no getting out for me." Maugham was deeply moved, and he reflected: "To me there is nothing more awe-inspiring than when a man discovers to you the nakedness of his soul."

Maugham is the last one to see Lawson alive.

When Miller and his friends, after an all-night poker game at the club, decide to take a swim in the famous pool—they find that someone had preceded them. One of the swimmers, diving deeply into the pool, finds Lawson standing upright at the bottom, fully clothed, "with a great stone tied up in his coat and bound to his feet . . ."

Maugham has Miller make the final sardonic remark of the tale:

"He was set on making a good job of it."

The incredible license that Maugham took with this story and the characters is without parallel. Practically everyone in the novelette *was* a real person in Apia.

Chaplin, the owner of the "Metropole Hotel" in *The Pool*, who first introduces Lawson to Maugham, was actually the proprietor of the Central Hotel, previously mentioned, where he and Gerald Haxton stayed in Apia.

The pretty part-Samoan girl Ethel was the actual daughter of a wizened, conniving plantation owner, whose real name was Swan, which he used for the scrawny dirty quartermaster of *Rain*, but in *The Pool* Maugham called him *Brevald*.

Miller, the lover of Lawson's wife Ethel, Maugham described under his real name in his South Seas travel notes:

"Gardner is a German American who has changed his name from Kärtner, a fat, bald-headed big man, always in very clean white ducks; he has a round, clean-shaven face and he looks at you benignly through gold-rimmed spectacles . . . He drinks heavily, and though fifty is always willing to stay up all night with the 'boys,' but he never gets drunk. He is jolly and affable, but very shrewd; nothing interferes with his business, and his good fellowship is part of his stock in trade. He plays cards with the young men and gradually takes all their money from them."

For a minor character in *The Pool*, Maugham uses the name of Nelson, who presumably was Oscar Nelson, owner of a large trading store in Apia and other islands of the Samoan group, still operating today.

But in the notes on his South Pacific travels, he refers to him as "Gus": "He is a half-caste, son of a Danish father and a Samoan, and owns an important store dealing in copra, canned and dry goods; he has several white men in his service. He is fat and smooth and quietly smiling; he reminds you of the eunuchs you see in Constantinople; he has an ingratiating way and a suave, oily politeness."

Clearly, *The Pool* is not a figment of Maugham's imagination, but a story based on solid fact.

And it is amazing that Maugham escaped unscathed on this story. Any of the real-life persons that he used in *The Pool* could have brought serious charges in court against him. All they needed to do was to communicate with a London barrister, who would have found substantial grounds on which to institute an important case of slander, criminal libel, invasion of privacy, grievous mental suffering, etc., etc. *ad infinitum*.

Why they didn't is only too apparent: the rest of the skeletons which Maugham had danced so gleefully out of so many closets in Apia would have to be paraded in court—to substantiate again that truth is, indeed, stranger than fiction.

Maugham had his memory of Ethel of *The Pool*:

"She was a most attractive half-caste, and her manners were those of a refined gentlewoman. She was much too good for her husband. I received a letter from her, years afterwards, when the story appeared with my other tales of the Pacific, in *The Trembling of a Leaf*, and she scolded me for using living persons so cruelly in my stories. In reply, I pointed out to her that I felt I had used her with exceptional kindness in *The Pool*, considering the circumstances, but I don't think she appreciated the innuendo."

Maugham had described his first meeting with her in *The Pool*:

"And a few days later I met his wife. I knew they had been married for five or six years, and I was surprised to see that she was still extremely young. When he married her she could not have been more than sixteen. She was adorably pretty. She was no darker than a Spaniard, small and very beautifully made, with tiny hands and feet, and a slight, lithe figure. Her features were lovely; but I think what struck me most was the delicacy of her appearance; the half-caste as a rule have a certain coarseness, they seem a little roughly formed, but she had an exquisite daintiness which took your breath away. There was something extremely civilised about her, so that it surprised you to see her in those surroundings . . . She must have been ravishing when Lawson first saw her."

While Maugham was in Apia, he remembered to make a pilgrimage to the tomb of Stevenson on the top of Mount Vaea.

"He had provided me many days and weeks of delightful reading," said Maugham, "and so I felt it proper to pay my respects to him before leaving Samoa.

"A Samoan drove us in a buggy to Vailima, and as an

intervening stream swollen by heavy rainfall prevented our reaching the trail that ascended the rear of the steep hillside, this obliging fellow carried us singly on his broad back across the torrent. On the other side two comely young native girls awaited us, to 'guide' us to the tomb of Tusitala (The Storyteller). They were attired in tightly wrapped *lava-lavas* and wore only the sheerest of muslin blouses, which left nothing to the imagination as to the perfection of their anatomy.

"The hike was difficult, made for the most part up a muddy path that was frequently blocked by a fallen tree or landslide; mosquitoes plagued us every foot of the ascent. Gerald and I were soon out of breath and perspiring in every pore. Had not Stevenson been at the top, I'm afraid we would have turned back. And the girls were forever urging us on, saying that the summit was only a 'little ways.' On the difficult climbs, they got behind us and pushed with their hands on our buttocks, their bare toes finding amazing traction in the thick mud. Gerald's 'pusher,' the prettier of the two, sang as she laboured, and once he confided to me that her hands sometimes wandered afield from the center of propulsion. Without their gay banter and play the climb would have been a wretched one.

"We finally reached the top, and it was only when the Samoan girls called our attention to the tomb that we saw it. It was a disappointment. We had expected something more imposing, monumental, grandiose. I had somehow imagined Stevenson interred in an enormous Grecian style sarcophagus surrounded by fluted pillars and marble urns. The low round drab-colored tomb deflated us. Yet, when we reflected, we realized that in view of the steep hill and narrow path built by the Samoans, wherein they had been compelled to carry on their shoulders every pound of material for his entombment, the tomb, small though it was, was a remarkable accomplishment."

Rupert Brooke had also made the pilgrimage to Stevenson's tomb on Mount Vaea, and had made this comment:

"I went up the steep hill above Valima, where the grave is. It's a high and lonely spot. I took a Samoan of about 20 to guide me. He was much impressed by Stevenson's fame. 'That fellow,' he said, 'I think every fellow in world know him.' Then he looked perplexed. 'But my father say,' he went on, 'Stevenson no big man—small man.' That a slight man of medium height should be so famous, puzzled him altogether. If he had been seven feet high, now! Fame is a curious thing. . . ."

"It was, in truth, a magnificent hill for his grave," Maugham went on. "One looked down the wide green valley to the port and the shimmering sea, with the white clouds on the horizon. Only the song of birds broke the silence, and all about were flowering bushes. His spirit was at rest here.

"The Samoan girls had picked some hibiscus flowers along the way, and Gerald and I placed some of them on the apron of the tomb. We read the familiar words on the brass plaque;[2] and then we again looked down the long valley to the sea. A few minutes later we started the long difficult descent to Vailima, the Samoan girls in front, like faithful llamas, to prevent a slip into oblivion. And at last we reached the bottom, where the girls disappeared, but to

---

[2] Under the wide and starry sky
Dig the grave and let me die.
Gladly did I live and gladly die,
And I laid me down with a will.
This be the verse you grave for me:
Here he lies where he longed to be;
Home is the sailor, home from sea,
And the hunter home from the hill.

return a few minutes later bearing two drinking-coconuts, brimming with the most refreshing wine of nature's choicest vintage, the clear, chilled liquid of the green nut. They invited us to rest in their *fale* on a mat, adding flirtatiously that their parents were away in a distant grove cutting bananas. We thanked them, and gave them some money. I think it only amounted to a few shillings. They romped off, laughing like happy sprites. I think Gerald regretted not having accepted the invitation to repose on his girl's sleeping-mat."

Maugham and Gerald Haxton left Apia a week or so after Christmas (the year he could not recall), with brief stops at Fiji and Tonga.

"All the time my thoughts were on the blonde prostitute from Honolulu, on temporary refuge in Pago Pago. I wondered what the outcome had been of the missionary's campaign against her. I knew I should settle definitely in my mind how I would use her in a story. Once I was in Tahiti my mind would be occupied with a novel on the life of Paul Gauguin. I wrote a few pages, but they did not satisfy me. I decided to forget her for a while. I had some notes on the girl from Iwelei, and these would have to suffice until I felt able to settle down to the chore."

There was no doubt that the prostitute from Pago Pago had gripped Maugham's imagination.

IV
INTERLUDE

IV

INTERLUDE

10. "RAIN"—
and an Attack on Maugham

Maugham did not write his short story, *Miss Thompson*, until 1920, when he was over forty. He sent it to a number of magazines, but they turned it down. The editors reasoned that their readers would be offended by a man of God, Reverend Davidson, having sexual relations with a blonde whore. At last Henry Mencken, editor of the controversial *Smart Set Magazine*, accepted it, ("the blue-noses be damned!") and published it in the April 1921 issue. *Rain*, as Maugham later called *Miss Thompson*, was the first story that he wrote from his South Seas notes.

And how John Colton and Clemence Randolph adapted the short story as a play is interesting, and has something to do with psychological timing.

Maugham was staying in a hotel in Hollywood in 1921, considering movie offers and making plans for a trip to Australia, Borneo and Malaya. His first six short stories, *Rain* among them, were already in galley-proofs for the book, and he had only received them that week. He hadn't even looked at them. If he had taken the time, and had not been so diverted by another South Pacific itinerary, he might have taken a second look at *Rain* and reserved it for his own play-writing skill. But, as it happened, Maugham was bored with conferences with studio story-heads and producers, and restless to be aboard ship again, to roam lazily among tropical islands.

One night, John Colton, whom he had previously met, and who had a room across the hall from him, knocked on his door.

"I'm having a devil of a time sleeping," he said. "Do you have anything I can read? Fiction, if you have it."

Maugham had no magazines or detective stories. Then his eyes fell upon the still wrapped bundle of galley-proofs of *The Trembling of a Leaf*. He picked it up and handed it to Colton. "This is all I have."

The next morning, early, Colton was hammering excitedly on Maugham's door. "I want to make a stage play out of *Miss Thompson,* that is, if you don't plan to!"

"The idea hadn't occurred to me," Maugham informed him coldly, annoyed at being awakened two hours before his usual time.

"Then, please, let me do it!"

"Well . . . I . . . Oh, hell, if you want to, go ahead. You have my permission."

Maugham sealed the bargain with a handshake and went back to bed. But when *The Trembling of a Leaf* was published, many playwrights immediately saw the dramatic possibilities of *Rain,* and Maugham was besieged with offers, some even guaranteeing large sums of option-money for the

privilege. And among them were eminently successful drama-
tists, of a higher professional standing than John Colton, who
now was worried, realizing he only had a handshake as a
contract-claim to the short-story.

But Maugham had a high code of ethics. He assured a very
disturbed Colton that he still had sole rights to the stage
adaptation of *Miss Thompson.*

The rest is theater history. *Rain* became one of the most
successful plays ever presented in America. It opened in New
York City, on November 7, 1922, with the incomparable
Jeanne Eagels as its star.

"I went to see it with John Colton for the first time, and
when it was over I felt it had been a mistake to turn my
short story into a play," said Maugham. "John Colton and
the co-author, Clemence Randolph, had made a lot of
changes. Stage-wise I suppose they were commercially sound.
But when John turned to me at the final curtain and asked:
'Well, what's your opinion now?', I had to tell him honestly:
'I still think *Miss Thompson* is better as a short story.'"

I'm inclined to think that Maugham was deeply embarrassed by the tremendous success of *Rain* as a stage play. It
perhaps wounded his pride that he hadn't seen its dramatic
potentials and authored the play himself. Even at our meeting, long years after *Rain's* demise, he stubbornly dispar-
aged the stage presentation, I suppose in the defensive
reaction, as the orientals are inclined, "to save face."

But *Rain* was too solid a hit for Maugham to ignore.
Apart from its long run on Broadway with Jeanne Eagels,
there were the London engagements, and sundry roadshows.
And when Jeanne Eagels gave her last performance, Hollywood picked up the bawdy Sadie Thompson, producing over
the ensuing three or four decades three movie versions of
her equatorial escapades: the original with Gloria Swanson

in 1928, the next with Joan Crawford in 1932, and the third with Rita Hayworth in 1953. And to keep Sadie alive in the minds of the present generation, Kim Novak, in 1957, enacted a dramatic scene from *Rain* in the film *The Jeanne Eagels Story.*

A few other capable actresses, in between, have given their interpretations of Sadie. Tallulah Bankhead attempted a 1935 Broadway revival, but was personally rejected by Maugham when she went over to London for its production there, for which she never forgave him; Lenore Ulric played it in Flatbush; June Havoc sang and danced in the 1944 musical version; Bette Davis portrayed Sadie in a sketch in her 1952 revue *Two's Company;* Juliet Prowse not too long ago performed the *Sadie Thompson* dance on television, and the late Marilyn Monroe, just before her suicide, was signed to play Sadie in a lengthy TV spectacular. Even bubble-dancer Sally Rand has played it in drafty barns on the straw-hat circuit.

And although Maugham was piqued when *Rain* became a huge success, certainly it helped to mitigate the chagrin when he shared equally with John Colton and Clemence Randolph more than a million dollars in royalties. For a change, brassy, slutty Sadie had been the one who had paid off!

Maugham, in his *Miss Thompson,* provided a perfect example of how closely the author utilized real-life characters and their emotional problems in his short stories, novels and plays. With Sadie he didn't have to borrow too heavily on his imagination.

Why Maugham has never been soundly thrashed, maimed, or had pot-shots taken at him by enraged white hosts and hostesses throughout the South Seas and Far East, in particular, where communities are small and gossip is rife, and where an original character is more readily identified, even though presented in a work of fiction, can only be explained by the possibility of Maugham living a charmed life. I know of at least a dozen of his stories wherein the prototypes had full legal grounds to drag him into court and sue him for slander and libel, defamation of character, and invasion of privacy. But Maugham was a shrewd and skilled literary slanderer. Before he peeked into his hosts' or hostesses' scandal-closet of skeletons, he made doubly certain that the offended parties, guilty as sin, just couldn't chance a showdown in an open court.

Maugham, however, was himself neurotically thin-skinned. A misquote in an interview could send him into a trembling, white-faced, screaming fury. Not too long ago, he sent a letter to all of his friends and acquaintances asking them to burn any of his letters,[1] in case, after his death, a biographer started collecting them. He has refused to cooperate with biographers, and has given tacit instructions to his executors to offer no help, after his death, to anyone contemplating a biography. He rarely read a newspaper or magazine account of his literary activities or travels, because his indignation and effrontery over the merest sly innuendo or flippancy of a journalist could upset his writing program for an entire week.

He savored lampooning or exposing real-life men and women in his fiction—as evidenced in his *Cakes and Ale*— but he suffered deeply when he found that he had been caricatured. When the *Cakes and Ale* castigation of Thomas

---

[1] In 1957 he and Alan Searle burned all of his unpublished manuscripts and all of his letters.

Hardy and Hugh Walpole was published in England, a hue and cry arose against Maugham for the malicious attack upon two of England's most respected authors.

One writer was so outraged that she decided to retaliate with a devastating and vindictive fictional biography of Maugham. Her name was Elinor Mordaunt, and her *Gin and Bitters* was published in America in 1931 under the pseudonym of A. Riposte, and in England under the title of *Full Circle*. It was a sadistic stripping of the flesh off the bones of one *Leverson Hurle*, an itinerant lecherous novelist with a penchant for the South Pacific islands and Malaya, a literary monster whose perverted pastime was writing despicable novels about beloved novelists, and betraying his hosts and hostesses by pillorying them as swine and adulteresses purely on the basis of vicious gossip he picked up in ship's bars, hotel lobbies and white men's clubs in Polynesia and the Far East. The British authoress let it be known from the offset what she thought about Maugham's physical appearance. "Leverson Hurle was a small dark man, proud of his smallness; rather sallow; showing, even then, yellow pouches under his dark eyes: eyes as sad and disillusioned as those of a sick monkey."

And she kept chastising him for the manner in which he so callously and savagely attacked "superior writers": "Towards the end, in his decadence, he lost all sense of decency. In particular he took to lambasting his fellow writers, alive and dead: placing the private lives of the living under a sort of microscope, deliberately shifting the slide, so that it became distorted in its aspect while what he did to the dead will scarcely bear speaking of . . . He sucked his new impressions, his new friends, as he might suck an orange: then moved on, to other islands, other continents, both actual and mental."

Miss Mordaunt kept alluding to his erosion as the years passed, in his travels through the Pacific and the Far East:

"It seemed as though the crust of self-esteem and satisfaction which each year grew thicker, would now and then break through: precipitating him into a depth of despair from which there seemed no hope of rescue. Not that he wanted to be rescued: not that he cared what became of him. All he wanted was to die, so long as he could tread a few people under foot, squelch them, first: pay them out for being so uninteresting, banal, sheep-like."

It is surprising that Miss Mordaunt wrote such a third-rate novel about Maugham, because she actually did travel to Tahiti and other places in the Pacific and Far East which Maugham had visited, and had she been less vituperative and revengeful and more astute in her research,[2] she certainly could have found many people in these colorful places who would have supplied her with first-rate anecdotes about Maugham. As it was she appeared to be constantly carried away by her own personal loathing of Maugham.

It was a merciless literary attack on him, and Elinor Mordaunt dogged his footsteps through Tahiti and Malaysia, involving him in one monstrous circumstance after another. She used every adjective in the dictionary to degrade him: he was a doddering egotist without grace or humility, a crashing snob, a snivelling coward, an objectionable boor, a disgusting poseur, an insufferable ingrate, a character-assassin, a conceited ass, and an arrogant bully. Miss Mordaunt left no doubt that she considered him an utterly

---

[2] As a minor example she gives a name to a Tahitian that never could be Tahitian, in the case of the owner of the place where *Leverson Hurle* lodged in the country district of Tahiti (Papeari). She called him *Philau*. The *Ph* is never used in the Tahitian language, nor is there an *L*.

worthless human, and saw to it that he died in obscurity, without friends or spiritual salvation, a wretched and bitter literary ghoul. She wrote of his demise as follows:

"For there was a wry smile upon Leverson Hurle's face when it was all over, and Harris [Gerald Haxton] shaved him for the last time . . . There may be a place where the mirror is held up . . . to punish a man by allowing himself to see himself as he really was in life. As everyone else—even his valet and secretary—saw him."

Her consecrated butchery of Maugham was in defense of her favourite authors, Thomas Hardy and Hugh Walpole, and she alluded to them in this novel. Walpole was thinly disguised as *Mr. Polehue*.

Many readers thought that Hugh Walpole had written the book, and he was shocked, not so much by the insinuation that he would stoop to such a folly, as by the assumption that anyone would credit him with the authorship of such an inferior and maliciously written work. Walpole surprisingly assisted Maugham in suppressing the book in England. There were those who suspected that his philanthropy, in defending Maugham, was merely a public disavowal that he had ever for a single moment considered that Maugham had him in mind as the character of Alroy Kear in *Cakes and Ale*, otherwise he never would have rallied to Maugham's side in belting down *Gin and Bitters*, which, as a result, sold a mere trickle of less than three thousand copies.

"If *Cakes and Ale* caused a storm of protest with many readers, my novel on Paul Gauguin, *The Moon and Sixpence*, brought in a flood of vitriolic letters from admirers of the painter," said Maugham. "Some damned me for making him British instead of French, which they insisted was completely out of keeping with the strong character and unusual talent of Gauguin. A considerable number even

hinted that I had changed his nationality to British, so that
I could indulge myself in the luxury of drawing a parallel
between Charles Strickland's philosophy of life and my own,
mine being, they declared, one of ruthlessness, a contempt
of social laws, and a relentless scorn for women.

"And while browsing in Tahiti for material on Gauguin's
life in French Oceania for my *The Moon and Sixpence,* I
quite by accident discovered an original Gauguin on the
glass panes of a door in a native's dwelling. I bought the
door very cheaply, giving the Tahitian double what he
asked. Immediately a hue and cry went up around the
world: I had cheated the poor ignorant native out of a fortune, had robbed him of his rightful legacy."

Maugham expelled his breath wearily.

"One thing a successful writer must acquire early in life
is the thick hide of a rhinoceros."

I had known for some years of Maugham's ownership of
the unusual Gauguin-on-glass, which he had installed in a
window opening of his study on the roof of the Villa Mauresque on Cap Ferrat. And twenty years previous to my meeting with Maugham, I had in the mid-Thirties, at the age of
14 or 15, visited Tahiti for the first time with my father.
Born in Normandy, France, he had always evidenced an
interest in Gauguin's neo-impressionistic work and his life
in French Oceania, and so the trip to Tahiti had been inspired by Gauguin's art and writings. I had accompanied my
father on his many excursions around the island in search
of Gauguin lore. Eventually we learned that Gauguin's native
son, Emile, was living in the country district of Punaauia,
on the island's west coast. Emile's mother, Tahura, was still
alive at this time. She was Gauguin's former teen-aged
mistress, of whom he had written so fondly in his volume
Noa-Noa, and who had posed for many of his now famous

Polynesian canvases, including the figure on the glass door that Maugham had discovered in Tahiti in 1917.

Now, at the Beerbohm *villino*, with Maugham about to leave for the French Riviera, I hastily mentioned my Tahiti visit and its relation to Gauguin and the glass door.

His reaction was what I had hoped for. "You must come along to Villa Mauresque and see my Gauguin-on-glass!" he exclaimed. "And you can tell me all about Gauguin's native woman and the son."

A day, several weeks later, was mutually set.

Then, taking courage, I inquired if I might bring along a young, attractive French-English girl from Nice, whom I had met at the Beerbohm party, and who had offered, on my departure, to drive me to Monte Carlo.

Maugham's face tightened slightly and the hoods of his eyes lowered in annoyance.

"No," he said, with finality. "I think we'll have a more interesting conversation about Gauguin without a woman about, interrupting, chattering like a magpie. Most women are just curious to poke about in my villa and see what I have there."

On the drive along the Mediterranean coast road toward Monte Carlo, Mlle. B— became increasingly incensed over Maugham's rejection of her.

"The unmitigated bastard!" she growled. "The dreary woman-hater! He treats women as he does in his stories, as if they were all whores, or afflicted with leprosy! He has no time for women, unless they are good bridge-players! To hell with him!"

11. Maugham, Women—and Villa Mauresque

It is obvious in his writings that Maugham does hold an intractable and acrimonious attitude toward women. And, privately, he seems to have his justifiable reasons. No male is a born misogynist.

For Maugham there were extenuating circumstances. His mother had died early in his life, leaving him in the care of indifferent nannies and, later, the guardianship of his austere and humorless vicar-uncle in Whitstable and a severe and bleak German wife. While a medical student at St. Thomas' Medical School in London, his first sexual experience with a woman, a prostitute of Piccadilly, resulted, according to his own published admission, in an infection of gonorrhea, a mild experience with most young men, but for the stuttering, deeply disturbed Maugham, one of shattering disillusionment and distress.

When he abandoned the medical profession and began writing plays, which by 1908 earned him acclaim and financial independence, he fell in love with an attractive actress whom he identified only by her first name of Nan, and whom two decades later, as a revenge-catharsis because of her rejection of him as a husband, he portrayed as the nymphomaniac Rosie in his *Cakes and Ale*.

From his references to Nan, it is apparent that he was deeply in love with her, perhaps the only woman in his entire lifetime that he had ever loved. He described her in his *Looking Back*: "She had pale golden hair and blue eyes . . . she reminded one of one of Renoir's luscious nudes . . . She had the most beautiful smile I had ever seen on a human being." He was her lover for eight years. But he had no illusions about her: "I knew that all my friends had been to bed with her . . . There was no vice in her. It just happened that she enjoyed copulation and took it for granted that when she dined with a man sexual congress would follow."

When she went to America to appear in a play, he followed her to Chicago with an engagement ring, but she flatly turned down his proposal of marriage. Her prospective groom was already with her in Chicago—an earl's son, whom she married a few weeks later.

Although Maugham spoke objectively about this love-affair, in his late eighties, the loss of Nan did affect him adversely, strengthening his misogynous attitude. He ended his reference to her on a sardonic note: "I took the engagement ring back to the jeweler who had sold it to me and he gave me the money it had cost, less ten percent."

His one and only wife, Gwendolen Syrie Barnado, daughter of Dr. Thomas John Barnado, Irish humanitarian and founder of the famous Barnado Homes for children in England, was at the time Maugham met her, in 1913, married, but separated from her Wisconsin-born husband, Henry Wellcome. He was a noted scientist, twenty years her senior, and a rich partner in the firm of Burroughs and Wellcome in London.

Maugham described their first meeting at a dinner-theatre party at the home of mutual friends: "She had lovely brown eyes and a beautiful skin. She was very nicely dressed in the height of fashion and wore on her fingers large cabochon emeralds. I did not then know that they were false."

Maugham was told by the hostess that Syrie's husband had treated her brutally, which was why she had separated from him, leaving her young son in his custody. Syrie needed more money than her husband had settled upon her for the separation, two hundred pounds a month, to maintain her scale of living. Maugham was unattached and an affluent playwright, so she set about acquiring him as a lover, although at the time she was being kept by another lover, Gordon Selfridge. She had two pregnancies, of which she accused Maugham, and although the first one resulted in a miscarriage, the second produced a daughter in Rome, out of wedlock, whom they named Elizabeth, or Liza, after the heroine of his first novel, *Liza of Lambeth*.

Later, when they returned to London, Henry Wellcome, thoroughly outraged over Syrie's promiscuity and her flaunting of conventions by having a child out of wedlock, decided to divorce her for adultery with a considerable number of men. But, because Gordon Selfridge was married, and Maugham was a well-to-do bachelor, he was named as co-respondent.

A short time later Syrie attempted suicide by taking a large number of veronal cachets, not in shock over the imminent divorce, but to scare Maugham into marrying her. Maugham, in great agitation, summoned a doctor friend and

Syrie's mother, and within forty-eight hours Syrie was quite recovered.

Maugham was taken aback by Mrs. Barnado's attitude: "She was as usual calm and composed, as though Syrie's attempt to commit suicide was just one of those things that people do." He learned that Syrie was somewhat suicide-prone: there was also the time, because she had been abandoned by a French lover, when she had thrown herself out of a mezzanine window in Cannes, but had broken only her wrists.

Maugham didn't want to marry her, but he was chiefly concerned with the baby Liza, whom he was not certain he had sired, but, as he wrote: "I could not bear to think what its future would be if I didn't marry its mother." He married her in New Jersey in 1917.

Maugham spent very little time with Syrie after the marriage; they lived in separate homes, and he was away on trips most of the time. Because of her loose morals, he had very little respect for her.

He wrote her a long letter, explaining his aversion to her: "I was forty-three when I married you. I was too old to be treated in that way. I am too sensitive. You have lived all your life among people who say the most awful things to one another, but I haven't . . . You have driven me to talk to you practically about nothing but frocks and furniture . . . You see, you have no resources of your own. It seems to me tragic. I am very sorry, but how can I help it. I often thought that your attitude towards life is shown by the way you take a man's arm. Most women just rest their hand on it and the gesture is pleasant and friendly, but you throw your whole weight on the man so that in a little while he grows tired and releases himself. Because you have no resources of your own you want to adopt mine, but how can one do that? It is impossible . . . When it comes down to brass tacks about all you do is sit about in beautiful clothes and look picturesque. It isn't very much, is it?"

Syrie was almost arrested and jailed on several occasions in her profession as an interior decorator, for fraud, and pawning an expensive jade necklace, with which Maugham had gifted her, and then attempting to claim theft-insurance on it.

In 1927, when they finally divorced, Syrie relieved Maugham of exactly one million dollars. She died of a heart attack in London in August of 1955, at the age of 76.

And the daughter Liza, Lady John Hope, was to give Maugham no respite. She sued him for $648,900 in May of 1962, claiming this amount as her share of the $720,000 realized from an auction of part of his paintings and objects of art at Sotheby's in London, and which, at her solicitors' legal maneuvers, two British courts had impounded, declaring that nine of the paintings sold rightfully belonged to her.

Maugham was incoherent with rage when informed of her action.

"It's an act of ingratitude! My daughter never cared a ha'penny for me!"

He petitioned the High Court in Nice, France, in December of 1962 to prevent his daughter from sharing in any of his fortune when he died. At the same time he invoked Articles 590 and 955 of the French Civil Code, to recover $2-million in gifts he said he had lavished on her, which was, essentially, a legal technicality to eliminate her as a beneficiary in his multi-million-dollar estate, so he could leave it all to his secretary-companion, Alan Frank Searle, 52 (1964), whom he has now adopted as his son and heir.[1] Maugham's

---

[1] Alan Searle, an old friend of Maugham's, started work as his companion-secretary, in December of 1945. Maugham used Searle as a character, Ned Preston, in *Episode* and *The Kite,* the latter included in the movie *Quartet.*

contention was that Liza was legally someone else's daughter and was conceived while the mother, Syrie, was still married to Henry Wellcome.

But in July of 1963 the French Court in Nice, employing both French and English precepts,[2] ruled against Maugham's attempts to disinherit Liza in favor of Alan Searle. In early 1964, the case was settled out of court, in Liza's favor. She received $280,000 in cash for the paintings auctioned off at Sotheby's, future royalties from some of Maugham's books, in addition to a majority interest in Villa Mauresque on Cap Ferrat. All told, she won a judgment of almost a million-and-a-half dollars.

Maugham could only mumble gloomily: "As far as I can judge, with women it is all take and no give. Most women are liars."

It is quite obvious that Maugham had a rancorous association with the wrong assortment of women, who disgusted, repelled and tried his patience. Although he could handle them capably, to his satisfaction, in fiction, he couldn't get them to behave properly in real life. And, reviewing his private grievances with women, it's understandable why he treated them so shabbily in fiction and alluded to them with so much sarcasm and cynicism in his essays.

His *Writer's Notebook* (1949), a condensation of about fifteen of his notebooks which he kept most of his life, from 1892 to well into the 1940s, and that recorded his observations, philosophies, character sketches, and ideas for stories,

---

[2] Because both parties were British subjects, the Court had to arrive at its decision on the basis of British law, which clearly states that a child born out of wedlock to a couple, who eventually marry, is *not* illegitimate. And, because Maugham lives in France, he became subject to French law on this issue, which holds that a legitimate child cannot be disinherited.

there is an entry under the date of 1894, when only twenty years of age, which expresses his antipathy concerning the female sex—a note taken down in the lecture room of St. Thomas's Medical School:

"The Professor of Gynaecology. He began his course of lectures as follows: 'Gentlemen, woman is an animal that micturates once a day, defecates once a week, menstruates once a month, parturates once a year, and copulates whenever she has the opportunity.' I thought it a prettily balanced sentence."

And other attitudes, later on in his life:

"A woman may be as wicked as she likes, but if she isn't pretty it won't do her much good."

"If women exhibit less emotion at pain, it does not prove that they bear it better, but rather that they feel it less."

"No man in his heart is quite so cynical as a well-bred woman."

"As soon as the instinct of propagation has been satisfied, the madness which blinded the lover disappears and leaves him with a wife to whom he is indifferent."

"A married couple. She adored him with a selfish, passionate devotion, and their life was a struggle on his part to secure his soul and on hers to get possession of it. Then it was discovered that he had T.B. They both knew that this was her triumph, for thenceforward he would never escape her. He killed himself."

"She was successful, well-off, admired; she had a host of friends. She should have been a very happy woman, but she wasn't, she was miserable, nervous and discontented. Psychoanalysts could do nothing for her. She couldn't tell them what ailed her, because she didn't know herself. She was in search of her tragedy. Then she fell in love with a young airman, many years younger than herself, and became his mistress. He was a test-pilot, and one day, when he was trying a machine, something went wrong, and he crashed. He was killed before her eyes. Her friends were afraid she would commit suicide. Not at all. She became happy, fat and contented. She had had her tragedy."

"Women's friendships everywhere are unstable. They can never give their confidence in its entirety, and their closest intimacy is tempered with reserve, misgiving and suppression of the truth."

"American women expect to find in their husbands a perfection that English women only hope to find in their butlers."

"For centuries satirists have been holding up to ridicule the ageing woman who pursues a reluctant youth; the ageing woman continues indefatigably to pursue the reluctant youth."

Once, overhearing two women comment sympathetically about the death of the daughter of a friend—one observed that the bereft mother's hair had become streaked with grey overnight from the shock—Maugham grunted sourly: "No doubt, she must have missed a trip to the beauty parlor!"

Maugham was a close friend of H. G. Wells, and particularly admired his no-nonsense attitude on women, and relished quoting him on the subject: "H.G. had strong sexual instincts and he said to me more than once that the need to satisfy these instincts had nothing to do with love. It was a purely physiological matter. He said: 'You know, women often mistake possessiveness for passion and when they are left it is not so much that their heart is broken as that their claim to property is repudiated.' . . . He was fat and homely. I once asked one of his mistresses what especially attracted her in him. I expected her to say his acute mind and his sense of fun, not at all; she said that his body smelt of honey."

When Wells was occupied with his writings, women never interested him, and he deeply wounded or enraged many of his mistresses, when he isolated himself from them, or rebuffed them when they attempted to intrude upon his occupations. Of his sometimes callous indifference to his female admirers, he had written: "There comes a moment in the day when you have written your pages in the morning, attended to your correspondence in the afternoon, and have nothing further to do. Then comes that hour when you are bored; that's the time for sex."

He relished relating incidents when women were placed in ignominious positions. His favourite one concerned H. G. Wells and a haughty grand-dame visiting Villa Mauresque at the same time. The lady, suffering with what Maugham called "incontinence of the bowels," had to make a desperate dash for the bedroom bath on the first floor, only to find H.G. soaking in the bath-tub next to the w.c. Her emergency, as Maugham described it, "brooked no delay," and she icily ignored H.G. who continued sponging himself. Then she arose, touched at her hair, and made a regal exit. Later, both were formally acquainted in the drawing-room, and acknowledged graciously their first proper introduction.

In his novel *Theatre,* published in 1937, and later produced as a successful stage play, Maugham indulged himself generously in analyzing women, by telling the story through the principal of Julia Lambert, the accomplished British stage actress of the story. As he said: "I have sought to worm myself into a woman's heart and see life through her eyes and feel emotion through her sensibilities. No one but a woman can tell if I have succeeded."

He portrayed Julia exactly as he saw women, ruthless, selfish, cruel, sexually precocious and predatory. Her amoral adventures follow the Maugham formula. She adores her lover Michael, until she marries him, then accepts him as she would a requisite stage prop, with a bored tolerance, while carrying on with a youthful lover.

She considers the world and acquaintances, friends, lovers, husband, even her son, as if she were in the wings and about to make a startling entrance in Act Two and they were all on stage awaiting her entrance-cue. She constantly strikes exaggerated calisthenic poses, as if conscious of always being down-stage center, her conversation is generously laced with effective bits of dialogue from plays; her emotional displays are always borrowed from a dramatic stage role. Her sincerity is no thicker than her stage make-up. She is a woman incapable of normal, sincere, human reactions. When crises occur it is the actress who confronts them. She succeeds in assuring herself that the real Julia is always on stage, merely a ghost off.

In the end, triumphing over a rival-actress who has stolen the affections of her lover and a stage role she wanted, and having settled with her husband, she feels that she has earned the right to celebrate her victories, which have momentarily freed her of the emotional fetters of love and diet. She sits down determinedly to a supper of beer, steak, fried onions and potatoes. "What is love beside steak and onions?" she cynically observes with dramatic conviction. "It was an amusing experience."

This was Maugham at his best.

I recall that he had mentioned to me, at the Beerbohm meeting, his summation of his relations with women:

"I've had my love affairs with a number of women in different countries of the world," he had said, with a slightly deprecatory smile. "But I was customarily in the role of the lover, rarely the loved one. Well, I suppose that the love that lasts the longest is the love that is never returned.

"A marriage, at the best, is the most abnormal of relationships between man and woman. I refuse to believe that it was ever intended for man and woman to be bound together by a legal contract under one roof. It constitutes an invasion of privacy, an encroachment on individuality, the shattering of peace-of-mind, the interruption of independent thought and action, and the engulfment of an innocent human into the bog of boredom. John Dryden, the eminent British dramatist and poet, more than three hundred years ago, suggested this epitaph: 'Here lies my wife: here let her lie! Now she's at rest, and so am I!'

"There are men who desperately crave and seek affection. These are the lonely, unoccupied men and women who are unable to be alone, who cannot be content to spend an evening with a book, with good music and art. They must have someone near them to listen to their problems and stupid chatter, and to reassure them, by caresses and copulation, of their sex. They are really quite sad humans."

He had given a cynical chuckle, adding: "True love, as my favorite French writer and moralist, La Rochefoucauld, maintained, is like ghosts, which everybody talks about and few have seen."

Maugham honestly appeared to have little need of company or affection. He liked stimulating, intelligent, humorous persons to spend week-ends at his Villa Mauresque, but a time came of satiation, when he would peremptorily send them packing. No guest ever dared interfere with his morning's labor at writing in his study atop the villa.

There are men, such as Maugham, who are quite sufficient unto themselves, who are not bothered by individual or public opinion, who rarely back-water on an issue, or alter their decisions, or change their evaluation of a friend, an enemy, or a principle. Some call this breed cynics and eccentrics. Maugham has been called a wretched, lonely man. This is not true. He has had the best of two worlds. He has been extremely happy, productive, and at peace with himself.

"My cynicism toward women some construe as my outlook on life in general, which is erroneous," he told me. "Unfortunately, my cynicism about women was too obvious. Women always anticipated from me a certain hostility, suspicion, perhaps an amused tolerance, an expectancy of being stripped of their pretenses, no doubt the likelihood of ending up as an odious female in one of my stories.

"However, where women are concerned, I can't honestly says that I was ever an overly affectionate man, or even a patient one, to put up with the stupid whims and temperaments of a restless, vacuous woman; I could never, for seduction purposes, bring myself to disarm them with maudlin sentiments or platitudes. I've found that the great lovers of history were usually of low intellect, because if they had been interested in cultural pursuits they never would have had so much time to waste in women's boudoirs.

"As for the great beauties and sirens, most of them, too, were of inferior mentality; they ended up eventually in some stupid circumstance. I remember travelling in 1916 from Liverpool to New York on the same boat with the international beauty, Lily Langtry, this when she was over sixty, with only a warm smile left. In New York City I learned that she haunted dance-halls, paying men fifty cents a dance to trip the light fantastic; and she, who once had had the crowned heads of Europe at her feet, felt no shame about it.

"La Rochefoucauld was right when he said: 'In their first passion women love their lovers, in all the others they love love.' From an early age I shied away from the 'battle of the sexes.' I didn't care to embroil myself in a senseless ruckus in which psychotic males and females mutilated and murdered each other with all the weapons in the arsenal of amour.

"I know that I wasn't even likable as a boy, and I can understand now why my vicar-uncle was happy to pack me off to school, to be rid of me. I was withdrawn and unhappy, I brooded, and rejected most overtures of sympathy over my stuttering and shyness. It didn't take me long, in young adulthood, to realize that a tall, handsome man has the opportunities of moulding a more charming character than a man of middle stature; that suffering and self-sacrifice destroy self-respect rather than strengthening it; that physical deprivation has ruined many creative talents. I've felt more productive in my writing after finishing a sumptuous meal of pheasant and vintage wine than one of cheese and crackers."

As he once wrote: "I have long known that there is something in me that antagonizes some persons; I think it is very natural, no one can like everyone; and their ill will interests rather than discomposes me. I am only curious to know what it is in me that is antipathetic to them.

"No, I was never what is known as a 'ladies man.' I didn't have the looks or the disposition, or, I might add, the time to play at it. In my company I found most women uncomfortable and somewhat contentious, somehow sensing that I found them transparent and was quite aware of all their grubby little tricks. I think that most women went to bed with me out of curiosity, or accepted me as a temporary lover to maintain their standard of copulating only with well-known and well-to-do gentlemen, or for personal gain."

But in Maugham's writings there appear now and again references of resentment that he was not a "ladies man" or well-liked by his fellowmen:

"My soul would have been quite different if I had not stammered, or if I had been four or five inches taller; I am slightly prognathous; in my childhood they did not know that this could be remedied by a gold band worn while the jaw is still malleable; if they had, my countenance would have borne a different cast, the reaction toward me of my fellows would have been different and therefore my disposition, my attitude toward them, would have been different too.

"For consolation, in what it's worth, to a number of women, still living, with whom I have had affairs, I most certainly don't intend to leave behind any manuscripts to be published after my death, telling of my dalliances, as did Frank Harris in his *My Life and Loves,* which Sinclair Lewis called 'a senile and lip-wetting giggle of an old man about his far distant filthiness.' I have been working on a 'last book,' an essay-autobiographical sort of thing, called *Ragbag,* which will be about my earlier years, and which will be published after my death. No one need be alarmed concerning its contents."

He had made this last pronouncement with a sardonic smile.

Some weeks after our meeting, Mlle. B—— drove me in her sports-roadster from the Hotel de Paris in Monte Carlo through the fishing-village of St. Jean and along the shoreline of Cap Ferrat peninsula to Maugham's estate, fronted by a double grilled iron-gate, with the famous Moorish insignia on the right wall, and the name *Villa Mauresque* below it. It was a brilliant day of sunshine and the Mediterranean was very blue. A French gardener, trimming the foliage overhanging the encircling white wall, opened the gate for us, and we drove up through the terraced garden of orange, avocado, rare shrubs and flowering bushes in which several laborers were at work weeding and pruning.

As we neared the entrance to the huge, white square-shaped villa, tall double green doors with a duplication of the Moorish symbol above it, we saw Maugham, dressed in baggy slacks, tweed jacket and open-neck shirt, standing outside talking to a gardener.

Mlle. B—— gave a disparaging sniff through her finely cut nostrils. "Well, there's your precious Mister Mawg-ham, as the French call him, his baronial majesty giving orders to one of his vassals. He reminds me of the head mummy of a mausoleum!"

Maugham, as we approached, turned and strolled back to the doorway and waited with a rather frozen smile as I got out of the car and walked up to him.

He shook my hand, rather formally, and murmured politely: "Nice of you to get here punctually. My secretary is off to post some mail and do some shopping, so we'll be able to have a few hours to ourselves."

He nodded courteously to Mlle. B——, in the process of turning the car around, but she made no acknowledgment, other than to gun her sleek sports-car and roar off down the driveway.

Maugham observed her angry departure with a faintly amused smile. "It's apparent that she's very provoked at me. But I just can't have my home over-run with curious sight-seers. And I have to classify *her* as a sightseer.

"My secretary and staff, and the gardeners, have explicit orders to turf out the curious who try to trespass. You should see them, particularly in summer-time, babbling schoolteachers, buck-toothed librarians, literary groups from America and Great Britain, even scruffy, bearded existentialists, or beatniks as you call them, with their dirty-neck, stringy-haired girl-friends. Some of these girls have invaded my estate in nothing more than a strip of cloth about their thighs, just the flimsiest *cache-sexe*."

Maugham took me on a brief tour of the villa, the upper terraces and the gardens. His property embraced approximately 14 acres on the side of the hill of Cap Ferrat, with a superb view to the west of the Esterel Mountains, Nice, Antibes and Cannes; to the north the former pirate port and stronghold of Villefranche, with the snow-mantled French Alps far arear; to the east Cap d'Ail, Menton and Italy's Riviera-of-Flowers; and straight out the infinite expanse of the shimmering Mediterranean, with the island of Corsica silhouetted on the horizon on a clear day.

The site of his villa was formerly the property of an elderly Bishop from Algeria. The land had been presented to him by King Leopold The Second of Belgium, who had a constant fear of dying without the proximity of an ecclesiastic to give him the Sacrament of Extreme Unction. Maugham purchased the property in 1928, and spent hundreds of thousands of dollars over the ensuing years remodelling and landscaping the hideous hybrid pile of Moorish and Renaissance architecture into one of the most habitable and attractive estates on the French Riviera.

High up on the hill, on a terrace, he constructed a palatial swimming pool, patterned from an Eighteenth Century original, and in Florence he found a marble mask by Bernini, out of which gushes water down the blue-tiled pool's stairway.

Over the years he has filled his home with antique furniture, priceless *objets d'art*, and originals by Matisse, Picasso,

Renoir, Toulouse-Lautrec, Pissarro, Lepine, Utrillo, Monet, Rouault and Siseley.

In an upper hallway I saw a portrait of Maugham by Marie Laurencin, and as I considered it for a short while I was struck by a resemblance: with swastika armband and a little heavier moustache it could have been a thirtyish Hitler.

There were Chinese bronzes, and jade horses, and a jade statue of the Chinese Goddess of Mercy, Kuan Yin, on the table in the entrance-hall. No matter where one glanced there were relic articles and decor of many years of travel, blended with a taste for the ornate of Africa, the Orient, England, France and Italy. There was a tendency, also, to the heraldic, as if to include in the ascetic domicile of an eastern potentate the sober tempering-influence of a member of King Arthur's Knights-of-the-Round-Table. And there were books everywhere, closely packed in book-cases, on any available shelf, on tables, on chairs, some even in corners of the room on the floor, wherever they could be stored for easy access.

The cabalistic symbol, familiar on the dustcovers of Maugham's books, was in evidence wherever one glanced. On the entrance wall, on ash-trays, stationery paper, cigarette cases, matchboxes, fireplaces and radiator grillwork, it appeared as a talisman-insignia to ward off evil. His father had brought it back from one of his trips to French Morocco, having discovered it in the Blue Atlas Mountains beyond Marrakech. As far as I could ascertain it was a Moorish representation of the human hand, of a taboo-design, to protect, as might the Christian Crucifix, its possessor from harm of every category. Leonard Lyons, who had visited Maugham, described it as "a TV aerial capped by a pronged nose cone, but it has no relation to the century's twin threats, television and missiles."

During World War II, although his secretary-companion, Gerald Haxton, with the aid of French neighbors, had concealed most of Maugham's valuable collections, his paintings, cars, and yacht, vandals had caused considerable damage. The Italians carried off most of his furniture, the Germans cleaned out his wine-cellar and mined the gardens, and a British warship, attempting to knock over a semaphore on the crest of the hill, missed and hit the villa a shattering blow.[1] And the post-war occupation of Villa Mauresque as a rest-home for British and American troops completed the wrecking job. But, undeterred, Maugham returned in mid-1946, from America, and had the villa restored and the fabulous furnishings and art collection re-installed. And the gracious living at Villa Mauresque was reinstated.

The pre-war *soirées at* Villa Mauresque must have been a little on the spectacular side. Maugham insisted on formal attire at dinner, which was usually served on the terrace just off the drawing-room, with a lofty, moonlighted view of the Mediterranean. The dinners were attended by elegant footmen in full livery, serving a gourmet's cuisine on silver platters.

His week-end guest list for the summer season, on different occasions, might have included H. G. Wells, the Aga and Begum Khan, his neighbor Jean Cocteau, G. B. Stern, the King of Sweden, Sir Winston Churchill, the Maharanee of Baroda, the ex-Queen of Spain, another neighbor, the King of Siam, and the Duke and Duchess of Windsor; and, of course, many writers: Rudyard Kipling, Arnold Bennett, Michael Arlen, Noël Coward, J.B. Priestley, S.J. Perelman, Moss Hart, Samuel N. Behrman, Glenway Wescott,

---

[1] Some anonymous neighbors, with a more profound love of nourishment than love of domesticated canines, roasted and ate his pet dogs.

Sir Desmond McCarthy, Elizabeth Russell—which is only a partial list of the many friends and celebrities who enjoyed his hospitality for short or long visits. Most of them were good bridge-players or story-tellers.

It was at Maugham's villa where the Duchess of Windsor first delivered her famous pun about the Duke. Maugham was her partner at bridge, and when he took the bid, she dropped her cards, remarking with mock contriteness: "Too bad, Willie, but I have very little for you."

"Oh, to the contrary, I see you have a couple of kings."

To which the Duchess came back instantly with the quip: "But of what value are kings? They occasionally abdicate, you know."

Maugham's estimation of the Duke of Windsor was slightly condescending. "I can't say too much for his intelligence. However, one must bear in mind that he is *bien élevé*."

Maugham, the eternal snob, entertained many rogues in his villa, but he insisted that they be of substantial family background.

Maugham was an excellent host, and although he disappeared in the morning for a few hours of serious writing in his penthouse study—which no one dared to enter, or even approach within sight—he always left explicit orders with his large staff of servants that the slightest requests of the guests were to be fulfilled. There were the tennis court and the palatial pool for exercise, and the *Sara*, registered under the American flag to Gerald Haxton, in the yacht basin at adjacent Villefranche, aboard which the guests could sail out upon the Mediterranean for a swim, to fish, or to enjoy a nautical picnic, with hampers of delicacies and chilled bottles of vintage wines.

But as the years passed, Maugham became less tolerant of his guests. "One can't run a Grand Hotel forever. Besides, it took too much time away from my writing."

In his cynical, impatient attitude, with the irascibility of advancing years, he began to take a bilious attitude on guests in general: "In the last twenty-five years I have had a lot of people staying with me and sometimes I am tempted to write an essay on guests. There are the guests who never shut a door after them and never turn out the light when they leave their room. There are the guests who throw themselves on their bed in muddy boots to have a nap after lunch, so that the counterpane has to be cleaned on their departure. There are the guests who smoke in bed and burn holes in your sheets. There are the guests who are on a regimen and have to have special food cooked for them, and there are the guests who wait till their glass is filled with a vintage claret and then say: 'I won't have any, thank you.' There are the guests who never put back a book in the place from which they took it, and there are the guests who take away a volume from a set and never return it. There are the guests who borrow money from you when they are leaving and do not pay it back. There are the guests who can never be alone for a minute and there are the guests who are seized with a desire to talk the moment that they see you glancing at a paper. There are the guests who, wherever they are, want to be doing something from the time they get up in the morning till the time they go to bed at night. There are the guests who treat you as though they were gauleiters in a conquered province. There are the guests who bring three weeks' laundry with them to have washed at your expense and there are the guests who send their clothes to the cleaners and leave you to pay the bill. There are the guests who telephone London, Paris, Rome, Madrid and New York, and never think of inquiring how much it costs. There are the guests who take all they can get and offer nothing in return."

But, of course, Maugham did enjoy some of his guests.

"There are also the guests who are happy just to be with you, who seek to please, who have resources of their own, who amuse you, whose conversation is delightful, whose interests are varied, who exhilarate and excite you, who, in short, give you far more than you can ever hope to give them and whose visits are only too brief. Such a guest was H. G. Wells. He had a social sense. When there was a party he wanted to make it go."

He led me to his private study on the top of the villa, reached by a transit of the flat roof, where he could be isolated and work in quiet when the villa was filled with guests, and I felt a mounting excitement as I realized I would shortly see the famous Gauguin-on-glass, which he had discovered in Tahiti so long ago.

The study is not large, almost bare, lined partly with bookshelves, with a familiar lectern for a reference-volume or two. His writing-table was bare except for his horned-rimmed reading-glasses, knitted gauntlets to permit smoother movement of his arms when writing with the fountain pen which he had specially designed with a thick collar for a tighter hold and added weight. There were just those few items and a stack of unlined manuscript paper.

Then he touched my arm, and I glanced in the direction he had inclined his head. There in a window opening was the rare Gauguin on glass panes, the first sight that greeted his eyes whenever he sat down to write. Although thinly painted, it was a superior example of Gauguin's neo-impressionism.

"A Tahitian Eve in the Polynesian Garden of Eden, holding the fatal apple in her hand,"[3] he said gently. "As you can see, I unfortunately was compelled to brick up the window opening, because the strong Mediterranean sun was destroying the true colors."

I noted that there was a white rabbit in the painting, which Gauguin curiously introduced into many of his works.

"The events leading to my finding that Gauguin on the glass panes of the door are interesting," he murmured, gazing at it raptly.

And he sat down and told me of his early interest in Gauguin and the eventual trip to Tahiti to research for his *The Moon and Sixpence.*

---

[3] As an appropriate substitution for the apple of an orthodox Eden, the Tahitian girl Tahura, who posed for this painting, is holding an indigenous fruit of the island—*breadfruit!*

V

TAHITI

SOMERSET MAUGHAM at work   (BALKIN-PIX)

SIR MAX BEERBOHM
at his home in Rapallo,
Italy, where Sir Max
introduced the author to
Somerset Maugham.
(CAMERA PRESS BLAU-PIX)

LOUVAINA CHAPMAN,
the "Tiare Johnson" of THE
MOON AND SIXPENCE,
taken in the garden of
Hotel Tiare, Papeete, the
"Hotel de la Fleur"
of the novel.

SOMERSET MAUGHAM
and GERALD HAXTON,
his secretary-companion
for many years.
(SCHALL-PIX)

SOMERSET
MAUGHAM with his
nephew, Lord Maugham.
(CAMERA PRESS-PIX)

SOMERSET MAUGHAM on the steps of the home built for
him by his publisher, Nelson P. Doubleday, in Yemasee,
South Carolina. Mr. Maugham lived there during his
stay in America.
(PIX)

SOMERSET MAUGHAM reading on the beach at
Gray Head, Martha's Vineyard
(ALFRED EISENSTAEDT-PIX)

SOMERSET MAUGHAM
in the doorway of Villa
Mauresque. Above the
entrance is the Moorish
sign that "brings luck".
It can be found on the
title pages of all of
Mr. Maugham's books.
(BLAU-PIX)

SOMERSET MAUGHAM and WINSTON CHURCHILL
in the garden of Villa Mauresque.
(DALMAS-PIX)

SOMERSET MAUGHAM
in the grounds of
Villa Mauresque.
(HENRI DE CHATILLON-
BLACK STAR)

LADY JOHN HOPE, daughter
of SOMERSET MAUGHAM
by his marriage to Syrie Barnado.
(CAMERA PRESS-PIX)

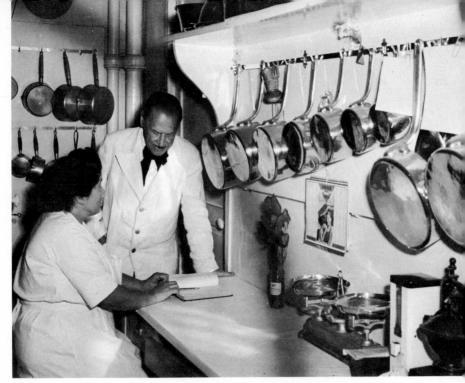

SOMERSET MAUGHAM in conference with his cook,
Annette, in the kitchen of Villa Mauresque.
(ILLUSTRATED-COULTER-BLACK STAR)

MAUGHAM'S hands in a "calming position". He often holds
his hands this way to recover from the "writing cramp"
which attacks him frequently.
(FRANCO GREMIGNANI-BLACK STAR)

SOMERSET MAUGHAM studying the chapters of a book in work.
(ILLUSTRATED-COULTER-BLACK STAR)

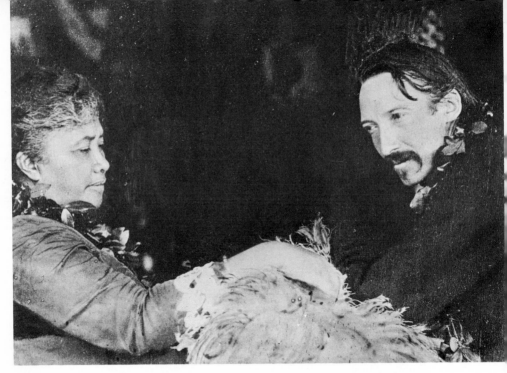

Robert Louis Stevenson and the last ruler of Hawaii,
Queen Liliuokalani, during a visit he made to Honolulu
in October, 1893.
(MENARD PHOTO)

Robert Louis Stevenson
and the last King of
Hawaii, King David
Kalakaua.
(MENARD PHOTO)

JOAN CRAWFORD as Sadie and Walter Huston as the
Rev. Davidson in the motion picture "RAIN".
(R. R. STUART COLLECTION)

GLORIA SWANSON as Sadie Thompson in a scene with
Lionel Barrymore.
(R. R. STUART COLLECTION)

JEANNE EAGELS as Sadie Thompson in the stage production of "RAIN"
(CULVER PICTURES INC.)

RITA HAYWORTH as MISS SADIE THOMPSON, in the
motion picture of the same name.
(R. R. STUART COLLECTION)

JEANNE EAGELS
as Sadie Thompson
and ROBERT
KELLY as the
Rev. Davidson in the
stage production
of "RAIN".
(CULVER PICTURES INC.)

GRETA GARBO and
HERBERT MARSHALL
in a scene from
"THE PAINTED VEIL".
(R. R. STUART COLLECTION)

CHARLES LAUGHTON
with ELSA LANCHESTER
in THE BEACHCOMBER
based on
VESSEL OF WRATH
(R. R. STUART COLLECTION)

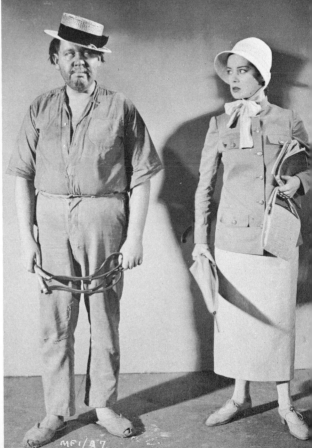

ALEXIS SMITH and PAUL HENREID in "OF HUMAN BONDAGE"
(R. R. STUART COLLECTION)

BETTE DAVIS in a scene from *THE LETTER*.
(R. R. STUART COLLECTION)

TYRONE POWER in "THE RAZOR'S EDGE"
(COURTESY OF 20TH CENTURY FOX)

GENE KELLY in a scene from "CHRISTMAS HOLIDAY"
(R. R. STUART COLLECTION)

12. Gauguin on Glass—a Mistress—and a Son

"I lived in Paris from about 1903 to 1905, after enjoying a mild success at playwriting in London, and it was there one day that a friend of mine, Gerald Kelly, who later became president of the Royal Academy[1] and was knighted, took me to a small restaurant where they had a room reserved for struggling artists to drink and eat reasonably with their friends, models and mistresses. In due course he introduced me to a surly, glowering Irishman by the name of Roderick O'Conor, who had a long time before painted with Gauguin in Britanny. I questioned him about Gauguin, as

---

[1] And who was later to paint one of the finest portraits of Maugham, with the Moorish insignia included in the upper right hand corner. Gerald Kelly was the real-life "Griffiths" of *Of Human Bondage*, and proof-read this novel and *The Moon and Sixpence* for authenticity in their art-painting sequences.

I was interested even then in doing a novel or play on the life of this controversial French artist. But O'Conor took an instant and active dislike to me. Most Irishmen resent Britishers, something to do with Home-Rule contention I suppose. I went to his place later, to try and get him to talk about Gauguin, but he had a filthy temper, and was about as communicative as an old turtle. But I did buy some of his paintings which I still have. Such lovely art from such a beastly man! Anyway, O'Conor didn't tell me much of a personal nature about Gauguin that was of any value, except that he was constantly rowing with him.

"That is the time that my interest in Gauguin seriously became a writing project for the future. I thought of the idea from time to time, and several times I was on the verge of packing and sailing for Tahiti where Gauguin certainly had spent the most absorbing period of his life. However, the years passed swiftly, and, of course, I had sufficient to keep me busy. Notwithstanding, all the time I had Gauguin neatly docketed in my mind."

But it was to be a considerable number of years later before Maugham was to voyage to Tahiti and commence the preliminary research there, so vital for the background of Paul Gauguin's life in French Oceania.

When he did eventually set out for Tahiti he had even then only a rudimentary idea just how he intended doing a novel on Gauguin's life. But he was hopeful that the visit to French Oceania would further advance the writing project and provide material to bolster many weak points in his brief story-outline.

His stay at the Tiare Hotel in Papeete was fuitful. Louvaina Chapman,[2] its proprietress, had known Gauguin very

---

[2] Her real name was Louisa Chapman, but she preferred to be called by the Tahitian equivalent of "Louvaina."

well and had many intimate anecdotes of him to relate. And it was Louvaina who introduced Maugham to a Tahitian chiefess living some distance down the coast from Papeete, who casually remarked one day that there were some paintings by Gauguin in a house not far from hers.

"Gerald Haxton was, of course, as you know, with me on the trip to Tahiti, and he and I drove down in a car to the native's home in the bush, reached by a swampy path. The house was rickety and weather-beaten from age, and the verandah was crowded with dirty children. The father, a flat-nosed Tahitian, came out and greeted us. I told him that I was interested in the Gauguin paintings, and he took me inside, and the first thing I saw was the Gauguin study, painted on the upper divided panes of a door. There were three doors in the living-room, all of the upper parts being of glass, and they, too, had at one time been painted by Gauguin. The Tahitian owner told me that Gauguin had been ill in his home, and he had taken care of him.[3]

"Now, many people think that I found the Gauguin painting in a hotel in Papeete, confusing me with someone else who had come along a few years earlier and found a similar glass-paned door painted by Gauguin. But it was in a native's house, as I say, far out of Papeete, on the western coast. I've always tried to correct this misunderstanding, and, of course, you yourself had been told that my Gauguin-on-glass had come out of a waterfront hotel of the port. Therefore, I feel

---

[3] Gauguin had made an attempt at suicide by taking an overdose of arsenic, because of a heavy depression caused by his destitute circumstances and unhappiness over being parted from his children, but the excess dose had caused him to regurgitate the arsenic. He had crawled to the home of a native, who took him in. During his convalescence, he used his last canvas to paint *The White Horse*, which now hangs in The Louvre, and, having no money to buy canvases, he turned his talents upon the glass panes of the doors.

I should later drop you a note concerning the true facts about it, so you will have verification in writing, in case you wanted to correct the error in a possible story you might write about me or Gauguin.

"So, to continue, the children of the house had scraped away the paintings on two of the doors, almost entirely, and there was no more than a trace that they had ever been painted. They had already started on the door that you see there, and were having great fun scraping the thin paint off with their nails. One of the damaged doors must have been a masterpiece, because I could still see the traces of a native woman's torso thrown backwards in an attitude of passionate grace. I knew that if I left the remaining door where it was, it would be ruined within several months.

"I told the native owner that I would like to buy the painting on the top part of the door, and he agreed, but he said he'd have to replace it with a new door. I asked him how much it would cost, and he said: 'A hundred francs.' I told him: 'I'll give you two hundred francs.'[4] He was surprised at my generosity in offering double his price, and he helped Gerald and me remove the door with the car's tools. We placed the door carefully in the car and drove back to the chiefess' home, where we sawed off the lower wooden part to make it more portable and secure for the remainder of the trip into Papeete.

"That evening the chambermaid of the Hotel Tiare announced to Gerald that a native man wanted to talk with me. She said he was a little drunk and unpleasant. The

---

[4] Then the equivalent of about $20. It was sold in the auction of Maugham's paintings and *objets d'art* at Sotheby's in London, in April of 1962, for $47,600, and was purchased by Philip Berman, an American banker of Allentown, Pennsylvania, who installed it in his home.

Tahitian told Gerald that he owned half the door, and was now demanding his share. I knew he was lying, but I didn't want any trouble that would delay my departure from Tahiti, so I give him two hundred francs and sent him on his way.

"Gerald and I took great care in transporting the Gauguin-on-glass to New York City, and then on to France. We didn't let it out of sight or personal handling for a second. We were both nervous wrecks, you can be sure, when we finally got it to a safe place. We had been so apprehensive that it would somehow be shattered on the trip."

He remained silent for a minute or two, his eyes fixed reverently on the Gauguin-on-glass in the window opening.

"I had a lot of sympathy for Gauguin long before I even started work on *The Moon and Sixpence*," he said, clearing his throat a little emotionally. "I made him a Britisher, Charles Strickland, in the novel, because I wanted to make him as credible as possible. Many critics claim that I modelled him after my own character, which was why I gave him British nationality instead of French. They further accuse me of expressing my own ruthless and cynical attitude toward women by having *Strickland* treat his women brutally and forever heaping verbal abuse upon them. Well, be that as it may, I have never understood why Gauguin was ever able to countenance and remain so long with that plump, sexless Danish sow, who, perhaps attempting to ape George Sand, sometimes wore men's clothes and smoked smelly black cigars. Gauguin's wife Mette was a mess! I imagine Gauguin was deliriously happy to get to a South Pacific island so well stocked with nubile Polynesian girls. I haven't forgotten his description of his favourite young mistress, Tahura: 'The amorous passion of a Tahitian courtesan is something quite different from the passivity of a Parisian cocotte—something very different!' "

Maugham continued staring at the Gauguin-on-glass, his expression rather wistful, as if reflecting again upon all the long-ago pleasant memories associated with his Tahitian interlude on the Gauguin research. Then he sighed, and turned toward me.

"I really don't know how much longer I will be able to enjoy my Gauguin and my other pictures, because according to my friends, the mayor here, and the insurance people, I am getting too many valuable masters under one roof."[5]

His eyes focused speculatively on the figure of the Tahitian girl of his Gauguin-on-glass.

"Tahura, Gauguin's child-mistress, was only thirteen when he found her that day far down on the isthmus of Tahiti. I never knew, until you told me, that she had posed for this painting." He folded his hands in his lap and settled back in his chair behind the writing-table. "I would like very much to hear of your long-ago meeting with Tahura. I never met her when I was in Tahiti, you know. I thought she had died, or disappeared to a faraway island of French Oceania."

So I told him my anecdote relating to the Gauguin-on-glass:

In the mid-Thirties, my father and I had arrived in Pa-

---

[5] Maugham finally decided in late 1959 to auction off most of his art collection because of the repeated art thefts along the French Riviera by a gang of organized thieves. He felt it would only be a matter of time before they would invade his villa. The irksome security measures now demanded by insurance companies to protect valuable art collections were becoming too stringent. So he had his paintings and art objects appraised by an agent from Sotheby's of London in 1960-61, and they were auctioned off in the spring of 1962. The proceeds from the entire sale totalled $1,500,000, and Maugham stipulated that the money was to be turned over to a philanthropy of his, Britain's Incorporated Society of Authors, Playwrights and Composers, to spare, as he prescribed, "needy authors from doing hack work."

peete, Tahiti aboard a passenger-freighter of the Union
Steamship Company, and a few days later we noticed a news-
item attached to the bulletin-board of the *bureau-de-poste,*
of Henri Matisse's account of a Gauguin painted on the
glass panes of a door that he had viewed in the villa of
Somerset Maugham on St. Jean Cap Ferrat, and his evaluation of its neo-impressionistic and monetary worth, declaring it to be an excellent Gauguin study.

A small group of Tahitian and white residents of the
island were clustered around the bulletin board, making
comments. Suddenly, one of them, a part-Tahitian man,
dressed in neat white drill, with a ludicrously small pandanus hat atop his huge head, broke away and rushed down
the steps of the post office. At the bottom he turned and
glared back at the announcement. It was then that my father
and I received a shock! *The man was Gauguin!* Not the old
Gauguin, of course, but a younger one, in his early thirties,
stalwart and brown-skinned. He had the same lean gaunt
face of the French painter, the protuberant eyes, the long,
slightly beaked nose, high cheek-bones, even to the suggestion of the familiar moustache.

The late James Norman Hall who had been conversing
with my father, remarked casually:

"That's Emile a Tai, Paul Gauguin's Tahitian son."

The next morning, my father and I, travelling by taxi
from Papeete, located, after many inquiries and wrong leads,
the a Tai home in Punaauia, on Tahiti's west coast, a sun-
and-rain ravaged wooden frame hut set back from the palm-
shaded lagoon-road.

Emile, with a *pareu*-sarong girdled about his bulging
loins, came down the path to meet us. Close, in the sunshine,
we had a chance to study him. Physically, he was a young
Gauguin, mentally a Tahitian. He shook hands politely,

murmuring a greeting in French, and then led us to the sagging, termite-riddled verandah with its overhanging roof of rusty corrugated sheet-iron. Seated, he seemed ill-at-ease, distracted.

Finally, he broke his brooding silence to inquire:

"Did you see the notice on the bulletin-board at the entrance of the *bureau-de-poste?*"

We nodded.

"It is the painting by my father that the *Peretane* (Britisher) stole from the Anani home in Mataiea. It really belonged to us. Now it is worth much money. Just a fraction of that money would keep me and my mother for a lifetime in all that we want, and plenty left over for all my children. I will go into Papeete tomorrow and talk about it with *avocat* Brault."

My father surmised what he had in mind. Gently, he said: "Court cases are long and costly, Emile—and in the end you would probably lose your claim. The painting was not in your possession at the time, a price was set by *Monsieur* Anani in Mataiea and agreed upon by *Monsieur* Maugham, so it was a legitimate transaction. And I don't think you have any rights to the Gauguin estate." And he added kindly: "Be content with what you earn with your fish and vegetable sales to the market in Papeete."

Emile sat with downcast eyes and slumped shoulders for a long time, then he stirred himself and spoke dully:

"Yes, I suppose you are right. After all, my father Paul Gauguin never recognized me as his legal son. He never cared enough for my mother to marry her."

"Could we meet your mother?" my father asked eagerly.

"She is far up the valley tending pigs for a *tinito* (Chinese). I will have to send for her." He sighed. "She will be very unhappy when I tell her about the Gauguin-on-glass in the home of the British writer in France. We have often spoken of the fine home we would build, and the radio and new electric phonograph, and all the expensive *popaa's* (white man's) things we would buy, if we could just lay claim somewhere to a painting of my father's."

A girl with a clubfoot limped onto the verandah with a portable phonograph and placed a thick disc on the turntable. A militant march-tune by John Philip Sousa blared out upon the hot, humid air of Punaauia. Then another younger girl brought us a green drinking-coconut. My father sat beside Emile and turned the pages of a handsome volume of Gauguin's reproductions which he had brought to Tahiti.

Emile glanced at them briefly with no appreciation. "I see no beauty in my father's paintings," he said flatly. "He makes the Tahitians look too gross, too *vilain*. If I owned one, I would sell it immediately, not hang it in my home, and let someone else enjoy its ugliness. But, then, who am I to pass judgment? They tell me that he is famous and his reputation, in painting, of the highest, and that fortunes are paid for just one of his simple sketches.

"I myself have no talent, otherwise I would be painting. But I can't even draw a straight line."

One of the Tahitian girls of the household, partly hidden by the half-length lace curtain in the doorway, stared at me brazenly, and, while I blushed, motioned with a crooked forefinger for me to join her, at the same time baring a golden globe of a breast.

So the time passed.

Then there was a low rustling sound at one end of the verandah, and when I glanced up warily, expecting to see the native girl moving toward me, I saw an old barefooted

Tahitian woman in a tattered Mother Hubbard-dress, smiling shyly and blinking her eyes.

Emile arose and said in a low voice: "This is my mother."

Tahura, Gauguin's pretty little *vahine,* of whom he had written such a glowing tribute in his book *Noa-Noa!*

Premature old age, as is the fate of most females in the islands below the equator, had degenerated her face and body. She was almost toothless, and in one leg she had symptoms of the grotesque *fefe,* or elephantiasis, the repellent malady that causes the limbs of its victims to sometimes swell seven times their normal size. Her crinkly hair was drawn tightly back from her wrinkled forehead and plaited in a thick grey braid over a thin shoulder. The parchment-like skin was stretched taut over her sunken, emaciated face. The voluptuous form which Gauguin had loved to paint, and had transferred to so many of his Tahitian canvases, had shrunken into a scrawny, feeble body.

It seemed inconceivable that this almost senile Tahitian *vahine* had once been the gay Tahura, Gauguin's thirteen-year-old mistress, of whom he had written: "Through her dress of almost transparent rose-colored muslin, one could see the golden skin of her shoulders and arms. Two swelling buds rose on the breasts; she was a large child, slender, strong, of wonderful proportions. . . . Happiness inhabited my home. Each morning it rose radiant with the sun; the golden hue of Tahura's face filled the house with joy and light . . . and she gave herself to me ever more loving and docile. I am embalmed with her! . . . These nymphs, I want to perpetuate them, with their golden skins, their searching animal odor, their tropical savors."

Emile had assisted his mother to a nearby chair, where she immediately dozed off, quite exhausted from the long walk down the Punaauia valley from the Chinese's pig-sty.

Emile shook her hard, and she opened her eyes. "The *popaa* and his son wish to hear stories of my father that only you can tell, *Maman*."

Tahura clapped a hand over her toothless gums and began to giggle. Yes, she was the *vahine* of Koké (Gauguin's Tahitian name), whom he had found that day on his horseback ride on the white horse down to Taravao on the isthmus of Tahiti. She had been frightened of him, because of his fierce eyes and his strange manner, and although her nursing-mother made her get up behind him on the horse and ride back to his *fare* in Punaauia, she had immediately run away. But he had come for her again, and he had some gifts for her, and was kinder and spoke softer, so she went back to him, and never ran away again.

She ran trembling, gnarled fingers over her face, as if to brush away the cobwebs of forgetfulness and restore memory, as my father plied her with questions of her painter-lover. No, she did not remember too many things about him now. He drank very much, that she recollected well, and sometimes when she was precocious he spanked her, or if she fidgeted with boredom when he painted her, he would pull her by the hair and slap her face. He had *fefe* in one leg, but which one she did not remember now. Yes, yes, he painted all the time, and the walls of their *fare* were always covered with unfinished paintings. And there were many carved wooden pillars and planks, also ugly *tikis* (idols).

What had happened to all the paintings and carvings on wood in Gauguin's studio-hut? Tahura shrugged her shoulders, as if they were of no importance. Oh, they disappeared long ago. Ask Oscar Nordmann, who once owned the Mariposa Bar in Papeete, as his father bought the property when it was lost by Koké because of many debts.

Emile interrupted her to tell the news about the Gauguin-on-glass owned by Maugham. Tahura's eyes brightened, and she nodded knowingly. Once, long ago, she had seen the paintings on the glass panes of the doors in the Anani home in Mataiea. The figures in all of them were of her, made from some sketches he had executed earlier.

"Yes, yes, it was I who posed as the girl holding the apple!" she exclaimed. "I remember it well, because I had a pet white rabbit, and there it was on the glass of the door, my dear sweet rabbit Timi, which Koké gave to me as a birthday gift. One day, when I was out swimming in the lagoon, some bad boys stole my Timi, killed him and ate him. I cried my heart out over that. Koké gave me another rabbit, but I did not like it as well as the first.

"And then there was the one of me lying *noho* (naked) on the couch at night." She stroked slowly the bony ridges of her body. "Of course at that time my body was young and ripe."

She was holding up the book that my father had handed to her, and it was opened to one of Gauguin's most famous studies.

This painting recalled, for Tahura, a low ebb in Gauguin's morale in Tahiti. He was destitute, sick and discouraged. He had exhausted sources of income from France, and the traders in Papeete were threatening to take him into the tribunal for non-payment of bills. Gauguin had walked into town to beg his last creditor to extend him expenses for canvas and oils. Refused, Gauguin had become roaring drunk and staggered through a tropical tempest back along the lagoon-road to Punaauia.

He lurched into his hut, and at this precise instant a flash of lightning revealed Tahura lying on the couch. Typical of all Tahitians, who have an uncontrollable fear of stormy nights, with evil *tupaupaus* (ghosts) riding the gales, she had wept and trembled for hours. Gauguin had struck a match to guide him into the room, and in its flare he saw Tahura. He stopped short, exclaiming. Never could he hope to get such an effect in a modelled pose! He struck another match so he could study her longer. When the flame burned out, he had the idea indelibly fixed in his mind. He hadn't a single *sou,* but he had the inspiration for one of his greatest works!

Gauguin's *Mano Tupaupau,* or Ghost of the Dead Watching,[6] painted in 1892, is of a nude Tahitian girl lying upon a low mat-couch, her face half-turned over her bare shoulder, the expression one of intense fear; in the background hovers the hooded phantom of the Tahitian Te Po, or Stygian regions.

"And then there was the other painting which sold for so much money in America!" cried Tahura. "The one in which Koké placed me in the center.[7] The notice on the bulletin-board at that time told how much the *musée* paid for it. Such a lot, that it was hard to believe so much money existed anywhere." Her lips moved soundlessly, and she touched lightly the tips of her fingers with the other, in her simple computing of trying to convert French francs into American dollars. "So much money! So much money!"

Emile stiffened and a growl started in his throat. "And there was not even a single franc for us from any of his paintings! Every time one sold it was announced on the bulletin-board at the *bureau-de-poste,* the same as today. There seems to be no end. The *Peretane* stole that painting. By rights it is ours!"

Tahura rose to her frail limbs. "I must go back up the valley. The pigs will get into the vegetable gardens, and then

---

[6] In the A Conger-Goodyear Collection in New York City.
[7] *From Where do We Come? Who are we? Where are we going?*

the *Tinito* will be angry with me, curse me, and strike me with a stick."

Emile assisted her to the end of the verandah and a short distance up the pathway toward the valley.

The brash Tahitian girl reappeared, cranked the phonograph, and placed another disc on the turn-table. A scratchy fox-trot, played by Isham Jones and his orchestra, drowned out the distant roar of the surf over Tahiti's barrier-reefs.

A few minutes later there was a loud clamor from the lagoon-front road. We stood up and craned our heads over the hibiscus bushes, and saw two men rolling over and over in the dust, slugging and cursing. A bicycle lay on its side in the ditch, the front wheel still spinning. One of them finally broke away, grabbed for his bicycle, righted it, and treadled desperately off. The other stood up, panting and yelling. *It was Emile.* He made a futile chase, gave up, and stood there in the middle of the sun-drenched roadway, shaking his fist and shouting: "Robber! Swindler! Cretin! Eater of dung!"

He stumbled up the path to the house, wiping with half of a banana-leaf the dust and perspiration from his body.

He sat down, breathing hard, eyes rolling furiously. At last he said, with an effort: "Please excuse me. I do not often lose my temper, but today, what with the combination of events, I have no control of myself. That was one of the Anani family of Mataiea, the son of the low-born thief who sold my father's painting on the glass door to the *Peretane.* He heard today about the news on the bulletin-board of the post office, so he wanted to go in and see for himself. The sight of his face drove me crazy, because he looks just like his father. Well, so you saw what happened. Disgraceful, of course. But, then, on that subject I become a little *maamaa* (crazy). There was nothing to do but pull him off his bicycle and give him the thrashing that he and his whole family deserve. His father had no right to sell that painting! It really belonged to us. I hold the entire Anani family to blame now. So whenever I see any of the men of that family, I will assault them, no matter where, even if I am arrested and sent to jail for disturbing the peace and attack."

We left Emile a Tai sitting morosely on his verandah, with the phonograph still sustaining its clamor, this time with a Paul Whiteman arrangement of *Dardanella*.

"If you ever see that *Peretane* in France, you tell him that you've talked to me, and that I've told you my intentions!" he hollered after us. "Say that someday I shall surely come to France and take that *sacré* painting on glass out of his villa and sell it, the gendarmes be damned!"

We located Oscar Nordmann, of Tahitian-Scandinavian extraction, supervising a gang of native prisoners repairing a stretch of roadway in Papeari, near Tahiti's isthmus. He himself was serving a sentence for barratry. He was fat, smiling and friendly. He seemed pleased and complimented that we would take the trouble to seek him out for a talk concerning Gauguin. "Not many stop to say *bon jour*, now that I am a *gibier de potence* (jail-bird.) "

He led us over to the shade of a breadfruit tree, after he had released the prisioners to have a swim in the lagoon, and related calmly how he had destroyed a huge quantity of Gauguin art, perhaps ten million dollars' worth on the market today.

"In the late summer of 1901 Gauguin decided to quit Tahiti and go to the Marquesas islands to the north, to the island of Hiva Oa where he died and is now buried in a tomb. He owed a lot of bills here in Tahiti. He had made a lot of enemies. Tahiti had ceased to be a pleasant island for him, so he wanted to escape to some lonely isle of French Oceania. At the auction my father bought his land and studio-home in Punaauia.

"One day my father instructed me to go down to Punaauia and clear up the littered property of palm fronds and coconuts, and remove and burn all the rubbish in the house, no matter what. But I did not relish that job, believe me, because I had heard that Gauguin was on speaking terms with bad ghosts. His property, so the rumor went, was under an evil *pifao* (curse). My teeth were chattering and my knees were knocking together when I walked onto the property, that you can be sure!

"I saw that the doors, window panels, house-posts and beams were all carved strangely, of Tahitian gods and symbols, and some quite naughty scenes for a young boy to look upon. I ripped them all down and chopped them up and burned them. The walls of the *fare* inside were covered with paintings, which I burned in a big bonfire. Many of Gauguin's statuettes and planks with half-finished carvings I broke up to make a fire for cooking my food and boiling my coffee. The ceilings were also of carved boards, and I gave these to a schoolteacher who happened to be passing by at the time. I think he sold them later to a tourist for a few francs. The huge carved posts and heavier objects of ironwood I carried to a canoe and took out to the reefs and pushed over the side into the ocean. I felt it was the only way to remove the *pifao* from the land.

"But when I had finished, I saw that my body had broken out in an ugly rash that itched horribly. I was sure it was the result of the *pifao* because I had handled Gauguin's paintings and carved things. I was sick for a very long time."

Oscar shrugged his shoulders. *"Eh bien,* at the time I performed what people now call a sacrilege, there was no value on Gauguin's art. Gauguin was thought to be a madman, and that anything belonging to him should be destroyed, lest evil ghosts inhabit the place where they were.

"Later, of course, I was pointed out to tourists for a long time as the idiot who destroyed a king's ransom of Gauguin's paintings and carvings. My family would sometimes look at me and burst into tears. I began to feel like a criminal.

"Perhaps *l'affaire Gauguin* was responsible for my foolish act of loading a schooner with stripped automobiles and sinking them off Tahiti for insurance. But I must now accept philosophically the judgment of the tribunal. The French judge was in no mood to listen to influences of Tahitian ghosts, even though the ghost was Gauguin's.

"And *Monsieur* Maugham, wasn't he the clever one! He got his Gauguin for so little, not more than $40. Well, once long ago I looked upon, lifted, carried, and destroyed millions of dollars worth of Gauguin's work. A French director from Paris, of a *galerie de tableaux*, visiting here, once estimated that I had done away with about ten million dollars' worth. Now and again I am tormented by that staggering thought, that all those things could have been mine had I been more of a Swede in mind and less of a Tahitian in soul.

"Once I owned the Mariposa Bar, under the old Hotel Tahiti, and over the bar I hung a sign, to assist tourists in making trips around the island and shopping in Papeete. It said: 'ASK OSCAR, HE KNOWS.' Ah, *oui*, in another instance, it could mean I certainly knew what a fool I had been about the Gauguin art I destroyed.

"I've read Maugham's *The Moon and Sixpence,* whose title implies an unlucky dreamer looking at the moon, while overlooking the sixpence at his feet. Yes, I was looking over my shoulder that day so long ago, expecting the ghosts to strangle me and lacerate with spears of coral my bowels and brain—so I didn't see the millions of dollars that were at my feet."

Maugham, when I had finished, gave a quick glance at the Gauguin-on-glass in the window opening. "That work is the last representative example of Gauguin's art in Tahiti."

Then, as if the full import of my story about the son of Gauguin assaulted his consciousness, he frowned and his lips drew down sourly.

He said coldly:

"Yes, there are many people who consider me a villain for acquiring that painting. I'm still accused of cheating that native out in Mataiea, or Gauguin's Tahitian mistress Tahura and her son by him, out of a fortune. But, you must remember, that if I had left the painting where it was it would long ago have been completely destroyed. The owner of the house was quite glad to sell the whole door to me and I gave him what he asked. It is true that I didn't pay a large sum for it, but on the other hand, thirty-some-years ago Gauguin hadn't the reputation he has since acquired."

It was apparent that the subject of the Gauguin-on-glass, as it related to his critics and the a Tai family, was a rather rancorous one to Maugham, and I decided it was best to drop the matter. Obviously, it was the first time that he had heard of the a Tai family's attitude on it.

A strained silence fell between us, as he smoked a cigarette and stared morosely out of the window.

I knew that my time was up. Maugham wanted to be alone.

13. A Memory of Rupert Brooke, Stevenson and Loti

I was particularly anxious to hear more of Maugham's experiences and observations on Tahiti, of which, in most instances, he had only given me concise but fleeting insights during our first and second meetings. He had mentioned just briefly his approval of Polynesian sexuality, and had made superficial references to his travels in Hawaii and Samoa, usually of transitory recollections. He would introduce a topic, touch upon an anecdote, recall a name or person; or his memory would suddenly be stimulated by something that I had mentioned of a mutually familiar place or character, and then he would add to his reminiscences, which, in view of his intimate association and talent for detail, would be, for my intense engrossment, too compressed a summary or too ephemeral a glimpse.

He had told me of his interest in Tahiti because of his

preoccupation with the life of Paul Gauguin and the *Moon and Sixpence* novel which was the result of his research there; and he had, of course, told me the details of how he had found the Gauguin-on-glass during his time there. But it was all too evanescent in the limited conversation of two meetings.

There had to be more exciting experiences, more keen observations, more anecdotes of compelling magnitude, more story potentials from a place such as Tahiti. There had to be more skeins of real-life dramas and circumstances for his story-loom which he had partly woven into the fabric of his fiction and essays. In his tremendous reserve of actual events and real-life personalities, wound up on the reels of his retentive brain, there had to be untapped resources, of which he had rarely spoken, and most certainly had never put down on paper. Two lifetimes could never be sufficient to make use of such an enormous supply of writer's-wool.

Therefore, I made it my mission, in the ensuing days and weeks, following our first and second meetings, to elicit from him true stories of Tahiti that had remained dormant in his mind, and which he had, to my knowledge, never made use of in a short story, novel, play or volume of essays.

These were not educed in one, two, three or four subsequent meetings, but in many more and in many different places.

"There were still wonderful characters living in Tahiti and the outlying islands of French Oceania at the time I was there," he had told me. "These were the significant years of World War One, and there was an embargo of sorts on extensive travel, so not too many of the truly interesting white and native characters of Tahiti could wander too far afield. These persons were confined to Tahiti for the most part, and, certainly, I couldn't have wanted for a more ideal stage for them.

"One or two interesting personalities had come and gone. Rupert Brooke—whom the Tahitians affectionately had named 'Pupure,' meaning 'The Blond One'—had come two or more years ahead of me. In fact, I stayed in a hotel on the waterfront where Brooke had lived for a short time."

The British poet had written of his delight with this lagoon-front hotel:

"The extraordinary life of the place flows around and through my room—for here no one, man or woman, scruples to come through one's room at any moment, if it happens to be a short-cut. By day nothing much happens in the yard —except when a horse tried to eat a hen the other afternoon. But by night, after ten, it's filled with flittering figures of girls, with wreaths of flowers, keeping assignations . . . Occasionally two rivals meet, and fill the darker corners with cursings and scratchings. Or, occasionally, a youth intercepts a faithless lady, and has a pretty operatic scene under my window."

Brooke did have the faculty of discovering beauty in everything he encountered. In ugliness he seemed to find the redeeming vestige of the pure origin of its loveliness before the accidental corruption; more pleasures and sensory delights of the universe were revealed to him, through his lively imagination and insistence that the world and all in it were an eternal rhapsody, than to most mortals. He ennobled mankind, and he excused and forgave almost every human foible and dereliction, if there was just the barest suggestion, the most tenuous possibility, the most microscopic shred of evidence, that a force of circumstance, too fateful to escape, had overwhelmed mankind. He apparently harbored no hate or rancour for anyone or anything. He seemed to be constantly intoxicated by discovering in nature and humanity, to support his credence in the perfectibility of human society, some new, radiant facet, tone and hue, as if he had just come, unspoiled and without disillusionment, from some distant star to this earth-satellite—and that nothing, to him, could be distorted, vicious or sordid.

Maugham had this to say about Brooke's vision of things around him:

"His ravishment over Papeete was an example of his unrelenting romanticism. He thought it a fascinating place, which called for remarkable forbearance, to say the least! That revolting dive-port of open sewers, filthy noxious odours, blue-bottle flies, mosquitoes, nasty cockroaches, mangy pariah dogs and cats, toothless, disease-ridden prostitutes, drunken seamen, the decaying hovels along the waterfront and backstreets! To say nothing of the accommodations in the mouldy hotels, vermin-infested mattresses, scummy latrines and gangrenous bathrooms, the abominable service and the stomach-turning, maggoty food."

Maugham still had a vivid memory of his one and only meeting with Rupert Brooke, in London.

"It seems to me that the year was 1908, when I had several plays running at the same time in London theatres, and I had read one of Brooke's poems in a journal, perhaps the *Cambridge Review* or the *Westminster Gazette,* that took my fancy. I recall it was titled *Jealousy,* and its bohemian tone rather reminded me of Ernest Dowson's unconventional verse. In fact, some critics caustically insinuated that Brooke could be the spiritual offspring of Dowson.

"I don't remember now who introduced us, but it could have been John Drinkwater, a poet-playwright friend of Brooke's, or perhaps an impecunious newspaper critic in the gathering, helping to celebrate the opening night of one of my plays, had brought him along. Anyway, I recall that he was a very exuberant young man, not more than twenty-one, rather carelessly attired, as if auditioning for the part of a Parisian artist in *La Bohème*. I was in my early thirties, but he seemed so young in comparison. I suppose it was his contagious *joie-de-vivre* that made him seem so much younger than he was, and yet there was a mature wisdom and fatalism about him. The total impression I had was that he had the most charming smile I had ever seen on a man. It made you feel that life and death were a very gamesome experience.

"He was, of course, exceptionally handsome, with wavy blond hair, and the most startlingly blue eyes, very large and friendly and eager. I would say that he was one of the handsomest Englishmen I had ever met. The *literati* had started calling him 'a golden young Apollo.' What made him so distinctive, apart from his physical attractiveness, was his passion for life and a wide-eyed wonderment of all that was beautiful about him. He radiated the healthy impetuosity of youth. He died at the age of twenty-eight or twenty-nine before he lost this enviable response to man and nature.

"Had he lived he would have become one of our greatest poets. He wrote his finest prose and verse during the period of his South Pacific travels," said Maugham.

Writing with inspiration, surrounded on all sides by the delirium of a tropical domain, of crystal-clear lagoon, of palm and coral strand, green valley and wooded hillside, and again surrounded by "the loveliest people in the world, moving and dancing like gods and goddesses," the young unsullied British poet had, on the wide verandah of a native's home in Mataiea, on the south coast of Tahiti, composed during his several months' stay here, his finest poems: *The Great Lover, Tiare Tahiti,* and *Retrospect.*

At sea he had written of his farewell to Tahiti:

"Last night, I looked for the Southern Cross as usual, and looked for it in vain—like the moon from Omar Khayyam —it had gone down below the horizon. It is still shining and wheeling for those good brown people in the island—and they're laughing and kissing and swimming and dancing beneath it—but for me it is set. And I don't know that I shall ever see it again. It's queer. I was sad at heart to leave Tahiti. But I resigned myself to the vessel, and watched the green shores and rocky peaks fade with hardly a pang. I had told so many of those that loved me, so often, 'Oh, yes, I'll come back—next year perhaps, or the year after.'—that I suppose I'd begun to believe it myself. It was only yesterday, I knew that the Southern Cross had left me, and I suddenly realized I had left behind those lovely places and lovely people, perhaps forever. I reflected that there was surely nothing else like them in this world, and probably nothing in the next, and that I was going far away from gentleness, and beauty and kindliness, and the smell of the lagoons, and the thrill of that dancing, and the scarlet of the flamboyants, and the white and gold of other flowers . . . so I wept a little, and very sensibly went to bed . . ."

Brooke arrived back in England in time to volunteer for training at Blandford Camp in Dorsetshire. He sailed in February of 1915 with the British Expeditionary Force for the Mediterranean. But he was not to reach the Dardanelles. In late April of that year, he met his untimely death from blood-poisoning aboard a French hospital ship at the Aegean island of Scyros, the mythical island of Achilles.

By torchlight, at midnight, a mile or so inland in an olive grove, the British poet was carefully lowered into a hastily dug grave, which, despite the abundance of white and pink marble of the Grecian isle, was marked only by a small wooden cross.[1]

Winston Churchill, a close friend of Brooke and one of his sincerest admirers—at the time of his death First Lord of the Admiralty—had written a eulogy:

"Rupert Brooke is dead. A telegram from the admiral at Lemnos tells us that his life has closed at the moment when it seemed to have reached its springtime. A voice had become audible, a note had been struck, more true, more thrilling . . . The voice has been swiftly stilled. Only the echoes and the memory remain; but they will linger . . . He expected to die . . . and he advanced toward the brink in perfect serenity . . . Joyous, fearless, versatile, deeply instructed, with classic symmetry of mind and body, ruled by high, undoubting purpose . . ."

Rupert Brooke's visit to Tahiti had not been forgotten by the islanders, white and brown, by the time Maugham arrived there. The Europeans admired the poet for his friendliness and good cheer, and the Tahitians for his love of play and swimming and fishing in the wide, reef-bound lagoons.

"Gerald and I drove down to Mataiea to the house where Brooke had lived for a time," said Maugham. "It was a wooden frame house, set attractively in a coconut grove and close to the lagoon, where Brooke swam almost constantly.

"And we met there the Chief of Mataiea, Tetuanui, and he and his wife burst into tears when we told them that we

---

[1] In 1914, as if with a presentiment of death far from England, he had written:

"If I should die, think only this of me:
That there's some corner of a foreign field
That is for ever England . . ."

had come to see where 'Pupure' had lived and written his three finest poems. They had come to think of him as their son, and, of course, they had heard of his death at Scyros. 'He was young and *beau* and happy!' sobbed the chief's wife Haamoura. 'We expected him to come back and live with us forever.'

"I met also some of the native girls whom Brooke had named in his poem *Tiare Tahiti*—Miri, Matua, Te Ura, and Teipo. They too wept uncontrollably at the mention of his native name. That is the only name they knew him by: *Pupure,* The Blond One, or The Fair One.

"They told us everything that Brooke did while in Mataiea, his trips to ancient heathen *maraes,* or temples; his hike to the lake high in the mountains, up the Valley of Vaihiria, with a laughing, flower-wreathed band, singing and shouting as they climbed, to watch dawn break in the east and then to keep their vigil beside the black waters of Lake Vaihiria, hoping to sight the legendary eels *with human ears,* who were supposed to be Tahitian demi-gods reincarnated. Miri told me how she had taken 'Pupure' to a wedding of a friend of hers, and how he had danced the Tahitian *upaupa* with the bride, and that the smitten Tahitian girl was all for leaving the new groom and going to live with Brooke."

Maugham and Haxton had swum in the lagoon off the Chief's small wharf, in the same spot, as Tetuanui said, where Pupure was forever diving and splashing.

"It was a delightful place to swim, about twenty-five or thirty feet deep, very clear in the sunshine which was reflected from the white floor of sand and coral. Tropical fishes swam rather boldly about us. They were of every shape and hue. I had never felt so relaxed and peaceful as floating on my back in the Mataiea lagoon, the sunshine warm on my face and limbs, and thinking of Rupert Brooke."

Miri had confirmed the poet's absorption with lagoon and sea and coral reef:

"Pupure not make too much scratch-scratch on paper wit' *plume,* mebbe one hour, two, then he run like hell to beach, in front of *chefferie,* an' he call us come join him, have fun, laugh, splash each ot'er, hold each ot'er, an' pull to bottom. He in water all time. I t'ink mebbe his family-god a fish, yes? At night he go to lagoon too, when moon vairee big an' make blentay light, and he swim long time, all time *noho* (naked) like little boy, an' Miri swim him wit'out *pareu.* Oh, we have blentay fun!"

"It was true that Brooke spent most of his time in the water, or on the reefs exploring," said Maugham.

For the poet there was in the eternal rhythm of the sea a clear message, a bond, a solace, and the affinity to him was enriching. When he was immersed in the sea time and destiny seemed to be mystically suspended. The contact with the lagoon and sea, above or below, established for him a world where he found an immediate solution in movement; below the surface civilization was washed smoothly from his body, with the attendant reflex of survival as in the aeons past when man was a mere struggling cell of the sea. Cleaving through the water was, for Brooke, like sliding obliquely through time, a ripple that flowed back imperceptibly on the surface: he was exploring a submarine world that had remained the same for incalculable centuries.

Maugham was visibly moved by his stay in Mataiea.

While close to the isthmus of Tahiti, Maugham decided to continue to Tautira, by a short route across the Isthme de Taravao, the narrow neck of land which connects the greater bulk of Tahiti to the peninsula. He had been told that in Tautira he could find a High Chief who had been a close friend of Robert Louis Stevenson.

"It was a very difficult trip for us, and had I known of the hazards, the heat, the mosquitoes and the gruelling trek, I'm afraid I never would have started," said Maugham. "The seashore was steep, and in some parts we had to pick our way over treacherous coral ledges. We had started out by horse and buggy, loaned to us by Chief Tetuanui, but shortly we had to abandon this vehicle for a sailing-canoe. Now we were at the mercy of the current and the wind that was extremely strong as we approached Tautira on the end of the peninsula; we almost foundered once in one of the passes. But finally we arrived in Tautira, wet, tired and miserable, hungry, too."

But the long arduous trip had proven fruitful.

"There I was to meet Oro-Oro,[2] Stevenson's friend. He was a very venerable Tahitian, six-foot-three or four, direct descendant of ancient chiefs, imposing and immaculate in his jacket of white starched drill, buttoned with silver buttons tight to his neck. His hair was grizzled and his magnificent moustache very white.

"He was a perfect host, in the approved Polynesian manner. He made us welcome, and sent servants off to prepare a meal. Then he talked to me of Robert Louis Stevenson, referring to him, because there is no *L* in the Tahitian alphabet, as 'Rui.' "

Ori-a-Ori had moved out of his European-style home, turning it over to Stevenson, his mother, wife, and stepson. He would never forget the banquets that Stevenson hosted on his lawn.

"Never had so rich a man come to Tahiti, and in such a god's ship," Ori had told Maugham. "Rui gave me many

---

[2] Ori-a-Ori.

presents, and one day he brought me fine dishes off the *Tatto*[3] and knives and forks and spoons. After Rui left Tahiti, my *fetii* Tati (Salmon) asked if he might have them. He entertained more than I, being closer to Papeete, and visitors of high standing sat at his table, so he would be proud to set such things before his guests. So now he has them, and I, as before, still eat with my fingers."

Here in Tautira, in the house of Ori-a-Ori, Stevenson's health, undermined by the rigors of the yacht trip (during which he had suffered hemorrhages) improved greatly. He sailed the *Casco* into the lagoon of Tautira for the Tahiti anchorage, and took over occupancy of Ori-a-Ori's home, completely satisfied that . . .

> . . . here I was at last;
> Here found all I had forecast:
> The long roll of the sapphire sea
> That keeps the land's virginity;
> The stalwart giants of the wood
> Laden with toys and flowers and food;
> The precious forest pouring out
> To compass the whole town about;
> The town itself with streets of lawn,
> Loved of the moon, blessed by the dawn,
> Where the brown children all the day
> Keep up a ceaseless noise of play, . . .
> And late at night in the woods of fruit,
> Hark! do you hear the passing flute? . . .

"There could be no doubting the fact that Stevenson until his dying day was a devout admirer of the Polynesians," said Maugham. "He liked their good manners and deference,

---

[3] Stevenson's yacht *Casco*, in which he had voyaged to Tahiti by way of the Marquesas and Tuamotu archipelagoes.

their warm-heartedness and carefree indifference to work and commercial congress. If he had had his wish he would have been born a Polynesian, I'm sure."

When Maugham talked with old Tahitians in Tautira of Stevenson, some remembered him. But they did not call him "Rui" because to them, the commoners, he was "The Rich Man." They would never forget the sumptuous feast he had spread for them on the lawn of the home of Ori-a-Ori.

"I'm inclined to think," remarked Maugham, "that Stevenson's reputation with the Polynesians he loved so well was based solely on his generosity with his demi-johns of wine and tables groaning with great platters of food."

One morning, after breakfast, on the verandah of the Hotel Tiare in Papeete, Maugham was diverted from his reading by the rustle of bare feet just behind his chair. His frown of annoyance changed to a smile of tolerance when he saw it was Louvaina, the proprietress.

"Oh, Mawg-ham, I happy see you read *Rarahu, ou le mariage de Loti!*" she exclaimed, still staring over his shoulder at the book he was holding. "My fat'er know Loti vairee well, an' Mama she know Rarahu of Bora Bora. But Loti not his right name. Real name Viaud. An' that not make-believe story, I tell you, like cinema. It really happen. Vairee sad story. I read it long time ago. 'Most break my heart. Too bad for Loti, too bad for Rarahu."

She lowered her three-hundred-pound body into a chair, carefully arranging her huge flowing Mother Hubbard over its back, then touched lightly, coquettishly, at the chaplet of flowers in her hair.

"Why you not go wit' friend up Fautaua Valley see *le bain de Loti*? It vairee pretty trip. I have Vava drive you up mos' way, then you walk. I fix nice food an' bottle of wine you make cold in mountain water. Have swim, then have picnic, mebbe sleep little, afterwards read book where Loti fin' Rarahu at pool. I think that bes' place read *Le Mariage de Loti*. What you say?"

Maugham had in his library the complete volumes of Pierre Loti's voyages to exotic lands, which he had visited as a midshipman under his real name of Louis Marie Julien Viaud[4] aboard a French naval frigate in the latter part of the 19th Century: Morocco, Egypt, India, Siam, Japan. Now, for the third time, in its proper setting, he was reading *The Marriage of Loti*, in French.

"The original edition, which I had brought all the way from London, had some striking illustrations by the author, which I admired very much. They were painstakingly drawn, with a fine attention to detail, and there was no trouble in identifying them as being executed by one who knew Tahiti intimately.

"I had always considered *Le Mariage de Loti* as Loti's most sensitive work. It was obvious that he had been captivated by Tahiti and the very young and pretty girl whom he called Rarahu."

The French frigate *La Flore*—the *Reindeer* of *Le Mariage*—had brought Loti, or Viaud, to Tahiti, and was to remain in Papeete for many months on a special mission. The midshipman had many leaves ashore, and it was inevitable that Loti was to meet his Rarahu. He had gone to a deep, cool valley beyond Papeete, and there he had seen her for the first time. He parted a growth of mimosa and saw her bathing nude in one of the pools of Fautaua Valley.

He described her in detail:

"Rarahu was small, beautiful in proportion and mould; her bosom was purely formed and polished; her skin was of

---

[4] Viaud was born in 1850, and died in 1923.

the same hue all over, from her forehead to the tips of her toes; a dusky-brown, like that of old Etruscan terra-cotta pottery . . . her eyes were tawny black, full of exotic languor and coaxing softness, like those of a kitten when it is stroked. Her nose was short and delicate, like the nose in some Arab faces; her mouth had deep corners deliciously dimpled . . . her hair, scented with sandalwood oil, was long, falling in heavy locks to her bare shoulder . . . over one ear she was placing a large hibiscus flower, whose vivid red contrasted with the paleness of her coppery cheek."

"Loti saw in his pretty little playmate Rarahu more than actually existed," said Maugham. "Surprising, too, that he, so widely travelled and experienced with so many types of loose women in almost every port of the world, would expect to find in his precocious Tahitian *vahine*, all the virtues of a maiden reared in a cloister. He wrote of his jealousy of Rarahu with the unreasoning fury of a Victorian, rather than dismissing it with an indifferent shrug of his shoulders as would a sophisticated Frenchman."

The French midshipman had come suddenly upon Rarahu at the pool, accepting a length of bright red ribbon as payment for permitting an ancient and skeletal Chinese to place his scurfy lips below her naked shoulder close to her bosom. And it was not perhaps the first time she had given such liberties to a Chinese. Rarahu liked pretty things, and she was poor, and before Loti had found her she had frequented the Chinese shops and restaurants of Papeete.

But for what Loti saw, the Chinese in Tahiti were to suffer for many decades following the publication in 1881 of his *The Marriage of Loti*.

In this volume he turned his wrath upon all Chinese:

"The Chinese merchants of Papeete were objects of disgust and horror to the natives. There was no greater shame

W. SOMERSET MAUGHAM
courtesy: Editta Sherman

Celina A Tai, daughter of Emile A Tai, made this drawing of her famous grandfather, Paul Gauguin, when she was twelve years old. She copied a reproduction of a self-portrait painted by Gauguin in 1889.

(MENARD PHOTO)

GAUGUIN'S famous group-canvas, WHO ARE WE? WHY ARE WE HERE? WHERE ARE WE GOING? The central figure was posed by his native mistress Tahura.

(MENARD PHOTO)

An example of the art work that Emile Gauguin was selling in Papeete, Tahiti a few years ago for one dollar each.

(MENARD PHOTO)

NAFEA FOA IPO IPO?
(When are you to be
married?) One of Gauguin's
famous paintings, executed
in Tahiti in 1892.
(MENARD PHOTO)

GAUGUIN'S *Te Matete* (The Market) painted in 1892.
(MENARD PHOTO)

THE ANANI HOME IN MATAIEA, where Maugham found the famous GAUGUIN-ON-GLASS.
(GEORGE LOGUE PHOTO)

A VIEW OF TAE O HAE, Nuku Hiva Island, Marquesas Islands, where Paul Gauguin wrote and painted.
(MENARD PHOTO)

A VIEW OF THE MARQUESAS ISLANDS where Paul Gauguin
spent his final years.
(GEORGE LOGUE PHOTO)

The Grave of
Paul Gauguin
(GEORGE LOGUE PHOTO)

EMILE a TAI GAUGUIN, with his
mother, Tahura a Tai.
(MENARD PHOTO)

EMILE a TAI GAUGUIN, in 1934.
(MENARD PHOTO)

EMILE a TAI
GAUGUIN, holding a
reproduction of self-
portrait painted by his
father, Paul Gauguin.
(MENARD PHOTO)

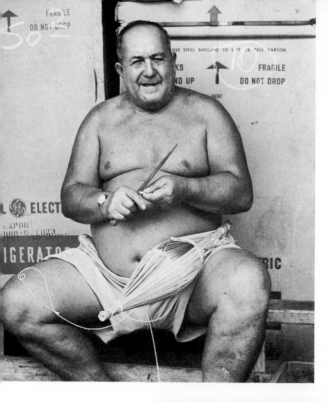

EMILE a TAI
GAUGUIN seated in
front of the Oceanic
Garage in Papeete,
in 1962.
(MENARD PHOTO)

mile a Tai Gauguin as he
is today in Chicago.
(CHICAGO TRIBUNE PHOTO)

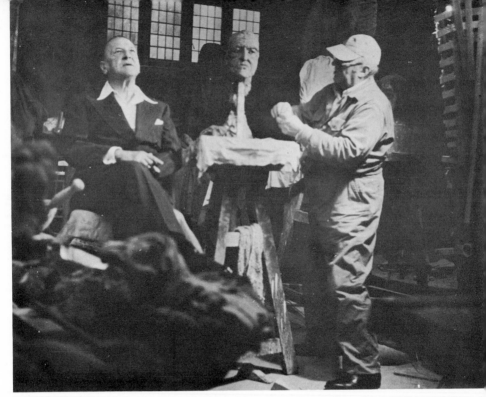

SOMERSET MAUGHAM in the studio of Sir Jacob Epstein, who is modelling a bust of him.
(IDA KAY-BLACK STAR)

SOMERSET MAUGHAM in the pose made famous by Graham Sutherland's masterly portrait of him. Mr. Maugham is seen with Alan Searle, his secretary-companion for many years.
(CAMERA PRESS-PIX)

SOMERSET MAUGHAM shown with Malayan dignitaries at the coronation of
Sultan Sir Ismail of Jahore.
(KHOO-PIX)

Pier 7, Honolulu, where Maugham boarded the steamer *Sonoma* for Pago Pago.
(MENARD PHOTO)

The *S. S. Sonoma*, aboard which Somerset Maugham and the heroine of *Miss Thompson* (*Rain*) sailed from Honolulu to Pago Pago. (MATSON LINE PHOTO)

A VIEW OF PAGO PAGO, which Maugham used as the setting for his short story, *Miss Thompson*, later titled "Rain". (MENARD PHOTO)

BEN KNEUBUHL, shipping
agent and trader of Pago Pago
who knew the real-life
Sadie Thompson.
(MENARD PHOTO)

IOSEFO SUAFO'A, Samoan
High Chief of American Samoa,
who was the real-life Sadie
Thompson's lover. He is shown
at the entrance of the Court
House in Pago Pago, where he
stood trial for
cohabitation with her.
(MENARD PHOTO)

IOSEFO SUAFO'A seen
today with some of his
children by his marriage to a
young Samoan woman.
(MENARD PHOTO)

Additional Marine

VESSELS TO HAWAII
To Honolulu unless otherwise specified

Foreign Ports

	Days Out
erie str., Chile	23
a. Olsen. schr.. Antofagasta	11
gara. str.. Sydney	16
na. str.. Yokohama	10
sia Maru. str.. Yokohama	9
o Maru, str.. Yokohama	9

Domestic Ports

to, str.. New York	
Bede, str.. New York	33
aar Coburu, sp.. Port Townsend	27
a. str.. New York	20
nent. schr.. Willapa Harbor	14
bert Lewers. schr.. Port Gamble	13
nbridge. schr.. Eagle Harbor	16
mington. schr.. Eureka	13
g of Clyde. sp.. San Francisco	9
sap. schr.. Port Blakeley	7
tsonia. str.. San Francisco	8
ades. str.. San Francisco	5
den State. m. s.. Seattle	5
bert Meyer, schr.. Port Ludlow	4
ank H. Buck. str.. San Francisco	4
nie Larsen, schr.. Sound	1

PORT OF HONOLULU

ARRIVED
December 4, 1916

Str. Great Northern from San Francisco, n Pedro and Hilo, 9 a. m.
Str. Sonoma from San Francisco
Mtr. Bt. Kuaihelani, from lagoon, p.

DEPARTED

Str. Sonoma for Sydney, 7 p. m.
Str. Maui for Kauai, 5:10 p. m.
Str. Claudine for Maui, 5:15 p. m.
Str. Hamakua for Hawaii, 4:50.
Str. J. A. Cummins for Kahaluu, a. m.
Mtr. Bt. Kuaihelani for Kahaluu, a. m.

DUE TODAY

Str. China, from Yokohama, noon.
Str. Matsonia, from San Francisco.
Str. Kilauea from Hilo.

SAIL TODAY

Str. Mikahala for Molokai, 5 p. m.
Str. Kinau for Kauai, 5 p. m.
Str. Manoa for San Francisco, noon.
Str. Gozan Maru, for Vladivostok, (bond ermitting).

DUE TOMORROW

Str. Maui from Kauai, a. m.

SAIL TOMORROW

Str. Kilauea for Hilo, 10 a. m.

DUE THURSDAY

Str. Claudine from Maui, a. m.
Str. Thomas, from Manila.
Str. Persia Maru, from Yokohama.

SAIL THURSDAY

land, Oregon; Kee, Sam. Honolulu; Kerr. L. B. San Francisco; Lyon, Geo. A. Boston; Mrs. Geo. A. Boston; Levi, I. E. San Francisco; Lilienstein. Mrs. K. A. Santa Barbara; Lewis. Miss M. Los Angeles; Lawry. Mrs. J. Pasadena; La Chau. C. F. Seattle, Wash.; MacDonald, Mrs. F. K. Honolulu; Mallory, C. C. Portland, Oregon; McLaren. Miss Annie. Santa Cruz; Mouts. Miss Georgia, Minneapolis; Morgan. E.. Portland, Oregon; Metzger, Mrs. D. E. Colorado; Murray, Mrs. W. J. Denver, Colorado; Malloy, Miss Minnie; Walla Walla; Malloy. Miss Angelena; Walla Walla; Malloy, W. S. Walla Walla; Movins, Mrs. E. A. Minneapolis; Mable, W. B. Pasadena; Mihron, Miss Claudea, Los Angeles; Mihron. M. B. Los Angeles; Mihron. Mrs. M. B. Los Angeles; McDonald, Jno. Sioux City; McDonald, Mrs. Jno. Sioux City; Montenegro. R. A. San Francisco; McCree. A. A. Portland, Oregon; McCree, Mrs. A. A. Portland, Oregon; Newton. Miss New York; Norman, G. Newport, R. I.; Osterhouse. Mr. Kansas City; Osterhouse, Mrs. Kansas City; Oberndorf, Jas. Chicago; Olson, Beni. Tacoma; Olson, Mrs. Beni. Tacoma; Oliver, Mrs. R. N. Honolulu; O'Rea, G. A. El Paso, Texas; Rigby, Jno. Chicago; Rockwell. Mr. San Francisco; Rockwell, Mrs. San Francisco; Ravenhall. Miss Rose, Brooklyn, New York; Ravenhall. Miss Edith, Brooklyn, New York; Ravenhall. R. Brooklyn, New York; Rosenberg. Sam'l. Seattle; Rosenberg, Mrs. Sam'l. Seattle; Reed, J. A. San Francisco; Ranft, Mrs. Agnes, Portland, Oregon; Reiser, Miss May. Honolulu; Riley, Miss Jessie. Salt Lake City; Smith, Clifford M. San Mateo; Thompson, Wm. B. San Francisco; Thompson, Mrs. Wm. B. San Francisco;

PASSENGERS DEPARTED

By str. Sonoma for Sydney, Dec. 4—Somerset Maugham, Mr. Haxton, W. H. Collins, Miss Thompson, Mr. and Mrs. J. J. Mulqueen.

By str. Maui for Kauai, Dec. 4—

Victoria Cruz, Jose Cordeira. Mrs. L. K. Nihoa, L. Y. Aiona, Mrs. Aiona and infant. Miss Aiona, Master Aiona, K. F. Yap, William Barkow, M. S. Depont, U. Taira, Victor Forslund, Eris Carlson, M. O. Olsen.

PASSENGERS BOOKED

By str. Manoa for San Francisco, ten o'clock this morning—G. Belloni, E. Gauffel, Philip Hottinger, A. Robbius, C. Raymond, Mrs. R. J. Pratt, C. H. Wells. Mr. and Mrs. George Sykes, Miss E. T. Wells, Miss Maybelle Broz, Miss Rosie Lerman, J. B. Cunliffe, W. L. Kersten, A. B. Arleigh, Mrs. H. B. Coonley, Mrs. M. Southard, Mr. and Mrs. R. W. Thompson, C. S. Goodrich, Mrs. Goodrich, Mr. and Mrs. A. Smith, Mrs. Clifford M. San Mateo; Spitz, Joel, Chicago; Schneider, Miss Margaret, Portland, Oregon; Scaront, Miss Corinna, Santa Cruz; Smoot, P. M. San Francisco; Stigen, B. A. Seattle; Stanley, C. Astoria, Oregon; Stone, Burt, Astoria, Oregon; Sachreiter, J. E. Grimes, California; Sachreiter, Mrs. J. E. Grimes, California; Sato, Miss M. Honolulu; Stitson, A. L. Los Angeles; Stitson, Mrs. A. L. Los Angeles; Stege, L. G. Louisville, Kentucky; Schnee, G. San Francisco; Schwartz, H. A. New York; Tassie, B. M. San Francisco; Town-

land, Oregon; Kee, Sam. L. B. San Francisco; Ly-ton; Mrs. Geo. A. Boston Francisco; Lilienstein. Barbara; Lewis, Miss Lawry, Mrs. J. Pasadena Seattle, Wash.; MacDon Honolulu; Mallory, C. gon; McLaren. Miss An Mouts. Miss Georgia, Min

E. Portland, Oregon; Me Portland, Oregon; Murray Colorado; Murray, Mrs. la; Malloy, Miss Angelen Malloy, W. S. Walla Wa E. A. Minneapolis; Mat dena; Mihron. Miss Cleo Mihron. M. B. Los Ange M. B. Los Angeles; McD City; McDonald, Mrs. Montenegro. R. A. San A. A. Portland, Oregon; A. Portland, Oregon; N York; Norman, G. Newp house, Mr. Kansas City; Kansas City; Oberndor Olson, Beni. Tacoma; Tacoma; Oliver, Mrs. O'Rea, G. A. El Paso, T Chicago; Rockwell. Mr. Rockwell, Mrs. San Fra Miss Rose, Brooklyn, Ne Miss Edith, Brooklyn, hall. R. Brooklyn, New Sam'l. Seattle; Rosenber attle; Reed, J. A. San Mrs. Agnes, Portland, Or May. Honolulu; Riley, Lake City; Smith, Cliffo Smith, Mrs. Clifford M. Joel, Chicago; Schneide Portland, Oregon; Scaro Santa Cruz; Smoot, P. Stigen. B. A. Seattle; S Oregon; Stone. Burt, A chreiter, J. E. Grimes, er, Mrs. J. E. Grimes M. Honolulu; Sti ngeles; Stitson, Mrs. Stege, L. G. Louisville, York; Tassie, B. M. Sa cond. B. R. St. Paul; T Clair, New Jersey; To Mont Clair, New Jersey Victoria; Urbahn. Albe Washburn. G. H. Bosto Lancaster. California; Chicago; Winkley. H. ren, J. T. Honolulu; land, Oregon; Zeliff. M Oregon; Ambrose. S. F bey, Wm. Oakland; Oakland; Abbey. Mrs. W bach, G. A. San Antc Jas. F. Honolulu; Be Honolulu; Baptist, A. Banning, Claude C. O F. San Jose; Cozier, M City. Utah; Coop, Mrs Crittenden. Edw. San Mrs. A. Los Angeles; ter, California; Debney Dashby. Mr. Cincinna Mrs. M. San Francisco la, Los Angeles; Fuller California; Fuller, Mrs. fornia; Girdler, Ralph Gardner, Mrs. M. San S. Long Beach; Herr Beach; Herron, C. H. ey, A. H. Rodeo, Cal S. Rodeo; Jones, Jas. rence. Seattle; Jones Johnson, W. H. Hart Los Angeles; Jones, J vada; Jones, Mrs. J. M Legg, R. F. San Fran

Passenger list of the steamer Sonoma.

Grand Hotel de l'Europe
Badgastein

8th June, 1960.

Dear Mr. Menard,

I was pleased and interested to get a letter from you from Pago Pago. I am afraid I cannot remember what month I was there in 1919 - after all that is a hell of a long time ago. I forget how long I stayed, I only stayed long enough to take the inter-island boat. I spent some months in Tahiti and the neighbouring islands.

I am sure that Sadie Thompson was not the real name of my heroine. I would never have been so foolish as to risk such a thing. She might easily have started an action against me and claimed half a million dollars in damages. I have no idea what happened to my own Sadie Thompson.

I see in the newspapers that you have just had great waves of water flowing over you, I hope they have not done too much damage.

Yours sincerely,

W.S. Maugham

P.T.O.

I have just read your letter again. You ask about your dates. On thinking it over I am more the impression that I was in Pago Pago in 1917.

WSM

This letter was written to the author while he was in Pago Pago doing research on Maugham's visit there.

13th September, 1950.

Dear Mr. Lenard,

As you see I am away from home and that is
why I have taken so long to answer your letter.
So far as I am concerned, the information you have
received about my Gauguin painting is erroneous.
I found it in a cottage in the bush in Tahiti, inhabited by a large family of natives. There were
three doors in the living-room, the upper parts
which was of glass. They told me that Gauguin had
been seriously ill in that house and during his
convalescence had painted the glass portions of
the three doors. The children of the house had
scraped away the paintin of the doors almost
entirely, and there was no more than a trace that
they had ever been painted. They had already
started on the third door, and were having great
fun scraping the thin paint off with their nails.
If I had left the painting where it was it would
long ago have been completely destroyed. The
owner of the house was quite glad to sell the whole
door to me and I gave him what he asked. It is
true that I didn't pay a large sum for it, but on
the other hand, thirty five years ago Gauguin hadn't
the reputation he has since acquired. It may
interest you to know that the subject is Eve in the
Garden of Eden, holding the fatal apple in her hand.

Yours sincerely,

W. S. Maugham

This letter was sent to the author while he was living
in Nice, France.

LAURENCE HARVEY with Somerset Maugham at St. Jean Cap Ferrat, during the filming of "OF HUMAN BONDAGE"
(UPI PHOTO)

SOMERSET MAUGHAM shown on his 91st birthday at his villa on January 25, 1965.
(UPI PHOTO)

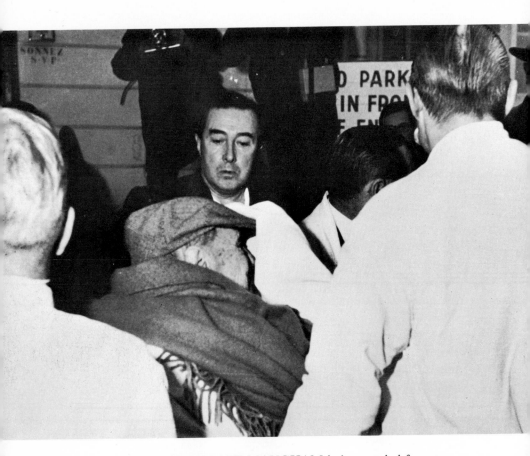

An ailing SOMERSET MAUGHAM being carried from an
ambulance into the Anglo-American Hospital in Nice
on March 5, 1965.
Alan Searle is seen in the background.
(UPI CABLEPHOTO)

than for a young woman to be convicted of listening to the gallantries of one of them. But the Chinese were wicked and rich, and it was notorious that several of them, by means of presents and money, had obtained clandestine favors which made amends to them for public scorn."

"It was vicious, damaging propaganda that affected the Chinese in Tahiti for almost fifty years," said Maugham. "When I was there I don't think that there were more than two thousand Chinese in French Oceania. They had originally come from Kwangtung Province in the 1860s to plant cotton, because of the Civil War in America and the shortage of cotton in the northern states, but when this experiment failed, they were released from indentured labour to shift as best they could.

"A Chinese is a very industrious, versatile and self-sufficient person, so by hard work, long hours and deprivations, he became a farmer, or opened up a small shop or eating place in Papeete. And he prospered, as he so deserved."

The French officials in Tahiti accorded them few privileges, other than that they pay their license fees and other tariffs and cause no trouble, sternly hinting that for any infractions there was always Devil's Island. The white bureaucrats and traders, because of the orientals' shrewd commercial enterprise, intrigued and conspired against them. And the Tahitians hated the former coolies from Canton, calling them "tinitos,"[5] because they could not run up debts at their shops and restaurants, which, in line with the Polynesians' reputation as the poorest credit risk on earth, they, of course, had no intention—and never the cash—to discharge in any case. Tahitian mothers did bring their teen-age daughters at night to the back doors of the Chinese places of business,

---

[5] The Tahitian's phonetical pronunciation of the American word *Chink.*

in exchange for Spanish shawls, combs, scent-water and sundry gew-gaws, and they were always the most vociferous in the natives' maligning of the Chinese.

"And whenever anyone was in doubt about the 'sinister Chinese' of Tahiti, there was always the warning in Loti's book.

"But they were allowed to remain in Tahiti. The Frenchman likes his food, and if it had not been for the Chinese agriculturists, no *legumes* would have been cultivated in Tahiti, no *poulet* raised, no fresh eggs laid for his *omelette*; no fine silks for his *madame's* gowns and other varied luxuries."

Anyway, Pierre Loti had contributed much to the original condemnation of the Chinese in Tahiti. For the lecherous peck that one of their countrymen took at the bare brown shoulder of Loti's little Tahitian girl-friend, the French writer was to wreak revenge upon them collectively for almost a century.

"Notwithstanding, make no mistake about it, Loti's *Rarahu* is most engaging reading, giving an accurate and colorful picture of life in Tahiti at this period, one of ingenuous delight."

Loti became completely captivated by Tahiti, with its spell of tropical languor, always smiling and poetical, a realm of flowers and beautiful women; the tors of basalt, the dark forests clinging to the mountains' flanks; the slender coconut palms and the thatched huts of pandanus strewn along the very edge of the coral reefs and the immense sunlit ocean; the groups of Tahitians lounging beneath the shade of great trees, idle, happy, singing and dancing; the endless murmur of the breakers on the barrier-reefs, the coral gardens of the lagoon swarming with fantastic, brightly-tinted fish, like figures in an oriental tapestry; the plaintive sound of the *vivo*, the reed flute, from the depths of the wood, and the distant note of conch-shell trumpets—all this safe in the midst of the vast, immeasurable southern ocean.

But Rarahu had her intuition, as with all island women, that Loti would not remain with her forever. The early navigators, the whalermen, the sailors of the French men-of-war, had come to Tahiti, taken the *vahines* casually and then had sailed away, most times never to return.

She dared not imagine that Loti deeply cherished her—a half-wild nymphet of fifteen—but that she was to him just as all island girls considered themselves: nubile companions for the sleeping-mat.

"This *Le Mariage* was more autobiographical than fictional, although I'm sure Viaud, or Loti as he called himself, didn't intend for readers to consider it as such. And you can't read too far into the volume without understanding that he had fallen deeply, madly in love with Rarahu." After Loti received his orders to board *La Flore* and return to France, Rarahu knew she would never see him again.

One day, in November of 1875—she may have been about eighteen—she had set out with her infirm old cat for her native island of Bora Bora, where she had gone to die, and where, as it would seem, she lived only a few days.

Rarahu's last letter to Loti was written just before her death:

"O my dear Loti, o my fragrant flower of the evening! My heart is very sick since I will see you no more. O my star of the morning, my eyes melt into tears because you did not return! I greet you by the true God, in the Christian faith.
                                                      Rarahu."

Loti, seized with unrelenting remorse, had written in his anguish:

"But at night, when I am alone again in silence and darkness, a gloomy dream weighed on my soul, a vision born neither of sleep nor wakefulness—one of those phantoms which fold their bats' wings to settle on a sick man's pillow, or to squat on the panting heart of a criminal."

Maugham was still charmed with *Le Mariage de Loti*.

"It was an added pleasure to read it in the true setting particularly so that Gerald and I did make the excursion, as Louvaina had suggested, to the Valley of Fautaua to see *le bain de Loti*."

Louvaina's deaf-mute servant, Vava, had driven them as far into the valley as possible, and then they had gone the rest of the way on foot.

The narrow trail along the Fautaua River was overarched with large *mape* trees, the native chestnut of the tropics, acacias, breadfruit, guava and *purau* (hibiscus) bushes, forming a tunnel of greenery. Dominating the end of this valley was Maiauo, the high mural-crown of peaks, which, because of its silhouette, the French called *La Diadème*.

At last Maugham and Gerald reached the famous pool.

"It was rather an unforgettable sight to look up at the natural *couronne* of the mountain and to see a slender waterfall leaping out from its side and, like a torrent of fluid crystal glass, plunging hundreds of feet to the valley below."

The Falls of Fautaua fill the stream and the series of pools, and the cascade drops from such a lofty height that much of it never reaches the pool as water, but, blown by the gentle breeze, the spindrift falls like gentle rain in a wide radius upon magnificent tree-ferns, elephant-ear *ape* plants, delicate maiden-hair and golden-green mosses, all sparkling in the sun with the shower of iridescent drops from the waterfall.

"We rested, then swam in the cool water of the pool, and afterwards we had the very satisfactory lunch that Louvaina had prepared for us. I then read some of the passages from *Le Mariage* which concerned the Pool."

One of Loti's descriptions of *le bain*:

"The pool had numerous visitors every day; beautiful young women of Papeete spent the warm tropical days here, chatting, singing and sleeping, or even diving and swimming like agile gold fish. They went here clad in their muslin tunics, and wore them moist upon their bodies while they slept, looking like the naiads of the past."

Maugham and Gerald, when they returned to Papeete, found Louvaina waiting for them at Hotel Tiare.

"I think you happee you go to *le bain de Loti!*" she exclaimed. "That vairee prettee place. I wish I go, too, but I too fat. Mebbe walk ten minute, fifteen, then I haf sit down, rest, catch breaf. If I walk too far up vallee, then they mus' carry me back down, an' I no think that vairee easy. Mebbe three, four man mus' carry me all way back Papeete!"

And, then, seemingly as a casual afterthought she added:

"Oh, I forget tell you, Mawg-ham, but you know Loti he have babee by Tahitian *vahine*. She live in Moorea, mebbe you like go see, talk. I think Loti write to her, an' she show you letters. You let me know an' I write letter you comin'."

"I never got to Moorea to visit with the daughter of Loti,[6] which I always regretted," said Maugham. "At the time of my stay she must have been a mature woman in her early forties. It would have been interesting to have learned her attitude concerning her famous father. But time was against me. There was still much work to be done on Gauguin."

---

[6] The Tahitian granddaughter of Loti's, with the appropriate name of Ta-Rarahu, is still living in Moorea.

14. London, Levy and Gauguin

Maugham, in his research on Gauguin's life in Tahiti for *The Moon and Sixpence*, was to have, apart from Louvaina's valuable assistance, some interesting encounters with European and Tahitian residents who had known the controversial French artist.

"Gerald fraternised with a number of the characters of Papeete," said Maugham, "and because of the ease with which he socialized, he was able to add immeasurably to my material on Gauguin."

Maugham, at Haxton's insistence, paid a visit to a part-Tahitian man with the first name of Dominique, whose brother Fortuné had known Gauguin intimately.

"Dominique had a ramshackle building across Pont de l'Ouest, not far from the Hotel Tiare, where he bottled sweetish, synthetic lemonade for local consumption. He was a tall, agreeable fellow, more French than Tahitian, chronically drowsy, with a ridiculously small pandanus hat set back on his head, and he had a native cloth draped around his enormous stomach. He brushed a keg-top clean for me with the end of his skirt, and then squatted down on the earthen floor, native-style."

And he told Maugham about his irrational brother Fortuné.

"I did not know Koké (Gauguin's native name) well, because he was not very friendly. If you said *bon jour* to him, it was as if he were deaf. He would never nod or return a greeting. So I said to myself: '*Je m'en fou!* I will not take off my pandanus hat to such an angry wolf.' And from then on I passed him indifferently in the streets as if he were a coconut husk or horse-droppings, nothing more."

He handed Maugham a small bottle of his *limonade*. It was warm, with an obscure citric acid flavor.

"*Eh bien*, as I have said," continued Dominique, "Gauguin was hated there, especially in Papeete among the *fonctionnaire*. I do not know how my brother Fortuné met him and got along with him, but he was always speaking of him with extravagant words. 'Dominique,' he would say to me, 'that man Gauguin who has come from Paris is a genius, and one day the world will honor him.' I did not take Fortuné's words too seriously, because Fortuné always made too much out of nothing.

"Every time I saw Gauguin he was either angry or drunk, never pleasant or smiling, just a vicious animal. He had a very ugly temper, I can tell you. I do not know how Fortuné managed their friendship. They would drink and argue, argue and drink, pounding the table, cursing one another, sometimes shaking a fist under the other's nose. I think once they had a terrible *combat* with their feet, as Frenchmen do with their *sabots*. I don't know who was the *champion*, but for weeks Fortuné hobbled around like an old man, rubbing his *derrière* and groaning. Then they were friends again, for a while. Fortuné told me that Gauguin was at his worst when he was drinking absinthe, which must have been all the time. Drinking, painting and sleeping with the *vahines* were the devils that possessed that *sacre* Koké.

"The last time I saw him was the morning before he left for Hiva Oa in the Marquesas Islands. He came here to the house to borrow some money from Fortuné to settle some of his debts in Papeete. Fortuné gave him part of the money, I don't remember now how much it was, and Gauguin gave him a large parcel, wrapped in pandanus matting.

"So this Koké went off on the schooner to Atuana, and my brother Fortuné waited and waited for a letter from him, but none came. Gauguin had promised to repay the loan within two months or so. After six months, Fortuné began talking to himself, having violent conversations as if he were arguing with Gauguin.

"Now, hark to this, *Monsieur*! One night, a year after Koké had been in the Marquesas, Fortuné came home, staggering under the influence of too much Atimono rum. He took a knife, cut away the matting of the bundle that Gauguin had given him, and out fell many paintings, I don't know how many. My brother stamped upon them like a wild bull. 'Worthless! Worthless!' he shouted. 'Not worth ten *centimes*! I've been tricked!' And he yelled at me: 'Where's the *petrol*, I'm going to burn all this rubbish!' I tried to reason with him, saying that we would use them to cover the holes in the walls, or maybe a *tinito* would buy them to hang up in his shop. But he pushed me aside, carried them all out into the coconut grove, emptied a can of *petrol* on the pile, and had his private bonfire. It made quite

223

a conflagration, I can tell you. And Fortuné cursed obscenely while the paintings burned to ashes."

Dominique gripped his head in his hands, as if it were about to burst, rocking forward and backward on his haunches, moaning.

"Fortuné never lived to understand what he had burned up. And it is only now that I realize it. Gauguin has become a famous painter in Europe, and that bundle of canvases which he left with Fortuné would have meant a pretty penny. For the drunken stupidity of my brother—peace to his soul—I will have to continue bottling *limonade* to wash the gullets of *les Canaques!*

"It was only six months ago that a Frenchman called upon me. He handed me his card, which said he was an agent for important art galleries in Paris, London, The Hague and Hamburg. Someone had told him that my deceased brother had known Gauguin. He wanted to know if there were any Gauguin canvases in our home. I told him how Fortuné had disposed of the bundle of paintings, and he closed his eyes and drew in his breath weakly, as if he were about to faint. He sat down, and I saw that his face was quite pale, so I got him a bottle of *limonade.*

"Then he told me. Two shocks, he whimpered, were too much in one day! He had been to see the Nordmann family. And they had told him what little Oscar had done out in Punaauia with all of Koké's things. He sat there shaking his head, and he kept saying miserably: 'I don't understand! ... I don't understand . . . even the canvases without any paint on them would have been worth something! What a destruction! *Quelle desastre!'*

"Finally, he calmed down, and became rather businesslike. He said to me in a scolding tone, as if I were the guilty one: 'For just one of those paintings burned out there, and just one carving that the Nordmann boy let go up in smoke out there in the country, someday they would have kept in luxury both of you, your families, and all the children you might have conceived, for the rest of your lives.' He put on his hat and took up his walking-stick. 'I hope you can live with that monstrous idea!' he growled at me. And he went off down the road in the sunshine, wobbling a bit, stabbing the earth with his stick as if it were a personal enemy.

"So now how is it possible, *Monsieur*, for me to live with such a thought? How does a human manage to be philosophical about such a catastrophe? Consider now my labor for life, filling bottles with stomach-burning tonic-acids—when I might have enjoyed a life of leisure, drinking fine champagne."

Maugham left Dominique collapsed in grief on the floor of his lemonade bottling works, lamenting the madness of a brother, whose first name had the ironical spelling of *fortune,* but who had disposed of a potential treasure trove.

"There were many others in Tahiti who had thrown away Gauguin art," said Maugham. "As early as 1910 collectors had started picking up his drawings and canvases. It was only by a stroke of luck that I found the Gauguin out in that native's house in the bush. It was just that the collectors had not heard about it, and neither would I, if the good Chiefess hadn't casually mentioned it."

And Maugham was to have meetings with other residents of Tahiti who had their private recriminations concerning Gauguin.

He and Haxton often went to a coffee shop near the market-place for coffee and *croissants*. It was Drollet's Coffee Shop, long a famous gathering-place for early morning risers who had marketing to do, or for those who were coming back into Papeete from all-night *areareas* (happy times) in an outlying country district. Inside and outside you were certain to see or meet someone you knew, who had something pleasant or interesting to say, some choice gossip, and the latest report on the sexual infidelities of native and white residents.

"One of the Drollet family, Alexandre, a rather distinguished middle-aged man with a slight strain of Tahitian blood, came into the shop and looked around as if he were looking for someone," said Maugham. "He saw me and came over and introduced himself. I invited him to sit down with Gerald and me.

"He was good company. His father had been a Breton sea captain,[1] and his mother Tahitian-American. I was particularly interested in his experiences as an official controlling pearl diving on a low coral atoll of the Tuamotu Archipelago, northwest of Tahiti.

"He asked me if I had met Jack London or read any of his stories of the South Seas. I informed him that I had read almost everything that Mr. London had written."

"I became a good friend of his when he came here in the *Snark*," he told Maugham. "He arrived here at the end of 1906, and the American Consul at that time, Mr. Dyer, knowing that my mother was part-American, asked if we could possibly let *Monsieur* London, his wife Charmian and the Japanese boy Nakata, occupy our guest-cottage during their stay in Papeete, as he had much writing to do. I agreed, and they moved in, and so in consequence we became close friends."

Maugham interrupted him to remark that he was surprised to read in the account of London's voyages in the

---

[1] He could have been the "Captain Brunot" of *The Moon and Sixpence*.

South Pacific, *The Cruise of the Snark,* a very bitter paragraph on Tahiti.

London had written:

"Tahiti is one of the most beautiful spots in the world, inhabited by thieves and robbers and liars, also by several honest and truthful men and women. Wherefore, because of the blight cast upon Tahiti's wonderful beauty by the spidery human vermin that infest it, I am minded to write, not of Tahiti, but of the Nature Man."

"It was unfortunate that he had trouble with the yacht while here in Papeete," explained Alexandre Drollet. "Thieves stole many things from it, and he did not get along with some of the officials here."

"And who was the 'Nature Man'?" inquired Maugham.

"His name was Ernest Darling, and he was what we call here in Tahiti a *natura,*" replied Drollet. "He wore a long beard, and let his hair grow down to his shoulders, and he lived in a valley, and ate only fruits and vegetables. But he gave no one trouble. *Monsieur* London when he was here had visited him, and had boxed with him for exercise. He told me that the *natura* was a strong man, and that the administration should not bother him. But Darling was finally sent away from Tahiti, and I think he died in Samoa.[2]

"I forgot to mention also that *Monsieur* London had trouble with Emile Levy, the pearl buyer here, because he used his real name in a story he published."

Maugham's interest quickened. He smiled wryly. "I thought I was the only writer with the habit of innocently using real names for my characters."

"But for *Monsieur* London it was *tres grave,* because Levy sued him and received judgment—which is perhaps why

---

[2] Ernest Darling died in Fiji, at the age of 52, during the devastating 1918 influenza epidemic.

Monsieur London wrote the thing he did about Tahiti,"
said Drollet. "My wife and I had hoped that he would return to Tahiti, so that he would change his mind. We wept
when news was received here in December that he had died.
I considered him a very good friend."

"I do seem to remember that there was a story in which
an avaricious pearl buyer came into possession of a large
pearl," murmured Maugham.

"Yes, it was in a short story with the title of *The House of
Mapuhi*. In fact, while *Monsieur* London was my guest, one
night I told him the true story. During my time as director
of pearl fisheries in the Tuamotu archipelago at Hikueru, I
met an old native woman who had had a fantastic experience in the hurricane of 1903, which drowned almost 500
natives in the Tuamotus. She was swept to sea, but she survived by hanging onto some floating things, and she finally
was washed up on an atoll called Tekokoto, seventeen miles
from Hikueru. She lived there for almost three weeks, eating
only raw sea-life and a coconut or two that drifted onto the
reefs.

"Finally, she made a crude raft for herself and was able
to return to her atoll. When she knocked on her son's door,
at night, he refused to let her in. He thought it was the *tupaupau* (ghost) of his mother. But finally she convinced him
she was alive. That was the whole story. But *Monsieur*
London, of course, made much more out of it, so that it
became a dramatic and highly colored fiction story.

"He had the son of this old woman find a most wonderful
pearl, one which had never before been found in any lagoon
of the Tuamotus. It was at the important atoll of Hikueru.
A strong young diver by the name of Mapuhi had brought
it up, and he wanted only that it would buy him a house
for his wife and daughter and old mother. It must be like

a white man's house and be filled with the things of a white man.

"The first trader who saw the pearl, and wanted it badly, made a total of how much such a house would cost, and it was at least four thousand dollars, so he went away to think it over—but he still wanted the pearl. But before the first trader could return to accept the conditions, another trader was told about the pearl, and he came to Mapuhi, looked at it, and took it to settle Mapuhi's long-standing debt for trade-goods. And that is when Levy arrives . . ."

Now, Maugham recalled the story clearly.

"Yes, I remember it all," Maugham interrupted him. "The pearl buyer from Papeete buys it from the second trader for a low price, but before he can get back to Tahiti where he plans to sell it for five times more than he paid for it, the hurricane sweeps across the atoll, the old mother of the diver is washed far out to sea, lands on another atoll, and while there finds the dead body of the red-haired pearl buyer washed up on the beach—and, of course, the pearl. She makes a miraculous return to Hikueru through seas swarming with sharks, knocks on the door of her son's hut at night, is able to prove to him that she is not a ghost, and gives him the pearl. And at the end it is understood by the reader that Mapuhi will get the home he has dreamed about."

"If *Monsieur* London had not written so badly about Emile Levy there would not have been any trouble over the publication of the story," said Drollet. "But Levy had friends in San Francisco."

Jack London had not only used the pearl buyer's actual name, but had accurately described him:

"Huru-Huru, watching from the beach, saw a third schooner that he knew heave to outside the entrance and drop a boat. It was the *Hira*, well named, for she was owned

by Levy . . . a fat man with massive asymmetrical features
. . . the greatest pearl-buyer of them all, and, as was well
known, *Hira*[3] was the Tahitian god of fishermen and
thieves."

And when Mapuhi's mother, Nauri, finds Levy's body on
the beach where she has also been cast by the hurricane,
there is another description, quite gruesome, of Levy, which
most residents in French Oceania and traders thought London had gone far beyond the bounds of common decency
in writing:

"Coming out of a stupor, she became slowly aware that
she was gazing at a patch of sandy-red hair on the head of
the corpse. The sea flung the body toward her, then drew
it back. It turned over, and she saw that it had no face. Yet
there was something familiar about that patch of sandy-red
hair . . .

"But at the end of the hour she sat up slowly and stared
at the corpse. An unusually large wave had thrown it beyond the reach of the lesser waves. Yes, she was right; that
patch of red hair could belong to but one man in the Paumotus.[4] It was Levy, . . . the man who had bought the pearl
and carried it away on the *Hira*. Well, one thing was evident: the *Hira* had been lost. The pearl buyer's god of fishermen and thieves had gone back on him . . ."

Drollet shook his head ruefully:

---

[3] *Hiro* is the correct spelling.

[4] The Lower Archipelago of French Oceania, northeast of Tahiti,
which numbers more than eighty coral atolls, is called both the
Tuamotus and the *Paumotus*. This broad belt of coral isles, possessions of France, stretch in irregular lines in a northwest and southeast
direction. There is no collective name among its inhabitants, but the
Tahitians in the south call this group the *Tuamotus* or *Paumotus*,
whch means "The Cloud of Islands." The French-Tahitian and Chinese
skippers call the group *Les Iles Dangereuses*.

"*Monsieur* London, you will have to admit, went a little too far with Emile Levy. When the story was published, friends of Levy's in San Francisco sent him at least six copies of the magazine, and there were those who thought that Levy had met his death exactly as in the story.

"Here in Tahiti we laughed about it, and whenever we saw Levy we would pretend he was a *tupaupau*, like the mother of Mapuhi, and walk across the roadway to get out of his way, just to be amusing, nothing more, certainly not to torment or insult him. We thought he had a sense of humor, and would accept it all as a huge joke.

"But he didn't. He stopped me one day and threatened me. 'If you do not stop making me an object of ridicule, I shall certainly sue you and all your friends!' he shouted at me. He was sure that, because I was a friend of the *Monsieur* London, I had been responsible in a way for the whole thing. Later, he came to my house and apologized to me, saying that his nerves were bad, and that even his family were affected by the story. His wife was part-Tahitian, and she thought that because *Monsieur* London had drowned her husband in the story and had his face eaten away by sharks or slashed off by coral reefs, that this would be the way that her husband would meet his death. That is how Tahitians are, they let their imaginations run away with them, especially about such things. She refused for a while to permit him to sail into the Tuamotus and do anymore business there. 'So you see my business is being ruined, too!' Levy told me. And I saw the look on his face, and I knew he was to make trouble for *Monsieur* London.

"And so he did. He started it here in the Tribunal. *Monsieur* Dyer, the American Consul here in Papeete, communicated with *Monsieur* London. The case dragged on for a long time. And in the end Emile Levy won a big judgment against him for defamation of character. And *Monsieur* London was compelled to pay much money to Levy.

"Now, I wondered why *Monsieur* London had used Levy so badly in the story, but I didn't find out for a long time. Levy and he had had a quarrel while he was here, over some supplies for the *Snark*. And *Monsieur* London, when he sailed through the Tuamotus, from the Marquesas to Tahiti, had talked with the natives there. They told him that Levy traded cases of cheap cat-salmon for the pearl shell and pearls of the divers, so the atmosphere, you must understand, was suitable for a storm between them. *Monsieur* London accused Levy of cheating the Tuamotu natives, and building his fortune on the collapsed lungs of the pearl divers. Levy ordered him out of his office. And that is how it all started.

"*Monsieur* London is not the only important man with whom Emile Levy has had trouble. There was Gauguin, too . . ."

Maugham bent toward him eagerly.

"And what sort of trouble did Levy have with Gauguin?" he asked.

"Gauguin when he published here his journal, *Le Sourire*, wrote an article that took up the whole front page. He did not name Levy, but it was certainly he. The subject was about white men exploiting the Tahitians. As Gauguin was a poor man while living here, he, of course, hated the business men, the traders and the bureaucrats."

"And so what happened?"

Drollet smiled and shrugged his shoulders. "A typical Gauguin *geste*. He personally delivered a copy of *Le Sourire* to Levy's office, put it down in front of him, and said: '*Tien!* Now, read about yourself!' Levy threatened to call the police, and Gauguin invited him out on the waterfront to fight. Levy slammed his door shut, and finally Gauguin went away.

But someone said that Gauguin and Levy met one night near the Cercle Bougainville Club, and that they came to blows, but of that I am not certain."

"And did *you* know Gauguin?" asked Maugham.

Drollet frowned slightly. "Ah, *oui, oui,* I knew him, we all knew him. I talked to him many times. I was interested in art, and he had all the latest news from Paris. But there was never any friendship between us, we never had a drink together, not once did he visit my home. Gauguin was not a very likeable man, you must understand."

"What was your personal opinion of Gauguin?"

"A drunkard, a dope addict, a very rude savage man," Drollet replied immediately. "He was a *bête noire,* a shocking disgrace to the decent European residents of Tahiti, that is all I can say."

"But what of his art?"

"*Eh bien,* that is something quite different. I do not think that Tahitian *vahines* are the grotesque creatures he painted on his canvases, but, still, there is something he caught, a spirit, a mood, an expression. You know that they are Tahitians, not Samoans, or Cook Islanders."

Maugham wondered if Emile Levy would talk with him about Gauguin.

"That is difficult to say. If he is in the right mood, and if his stomach is not bothering him, he could be very cordial to you, and hold a pleasant conversation. If not, he could be very short and unfriendly. You would just have to accept the disposition he is in. He is always sitting on the verandah of the Club every afternoon, having a drink. That is the best place to see him, where he is relaxed. In his office he is too concerned with making money, and he would keep looking at the clock, calculating how much money, in time, you were wasting.

233

"I must say, in all fairness, that Levy is not a bad man. No one likes a very rich man, particularly here in Tahiti, where there is not too much money in circulation. So much of the dislike of him is envy. And, let us face it, he can never escape the bad publicity that *Monsieur* London spread, no matter if he did win in the Tribunal. The story will always remain in black-and-white for anyone to read, forever. But I have known Levy to do some very kind, generous things, and he does support a large family."

Gerald Haxton was able to supply Maugham with the information that, every afternoon, at 4 p.m., Emile Levy closed and locked the door of his office and walked a short distance to the Club, where he climbed the rickety stairway to the second-floor open verandah. There he sat down at his favorite table at the railing, which commanded a fine view of the lagoon-harbor of Papeete and Moorea Island on the horizon, and ordered a lime squash. Then he opened his journal and read.

So Maugham appeared there one afternoon and requested that the manager of the Club introduce him to Levy.

"As we crossed the wide verandah to his table, I couldn't help but remember, almost word for word, his gruesome end in the London story," said Maugham.

The manager had to speak to Levy twice before he jerked his head up from his reading. He stared at Maugham coldly during the introduction. He squirmed irritably. He made no motion to take Maugham's extended hand.

"This is the only time of the day that I can call my own, when I can take a few minutes . . ." he started to say impatiently. He spoke French with a strong accent that was either Algerian or Moroccan, but very cultured.

Then he put aside his journal, and nodded toward the

opposite chair. "Well, as long as you're here, sit down, if you like, but I will be leaving soon. I have an appointment."

Maugham quickly explained that his interest in Gauguin had brought him to Tahiti, and that he was seeking any interesting and personal anecdotes concerning the French painter.

"Well, what do you expect *me* to tell you about that wild artist?" demanded Levy. His face tightened. "So *what* am I supposed to say that you might think is interesting? I am not an agent whose business it is to supply material to every writer who passes through Papeete! I had an experience with *one* writer; you might have heard about that. And I'm sure he had a lesson that he didn't forget in a hurry."

Maugham held his temper in check; he was not one to accept such a tirade lightly. But the irascible man seated across from him had known Gauguin, and the possibility of an unusual reminiscence would mitigate the offense that he felt.

"And as for that Gauguin. What a *bruit* they are now making over him! And, the poor miserable one, there he lies far off up there in *les Marquises*. Not a *sou* did he leave for a decent head-stone, nor is there anyone there to place flowers on his grave. How his bones must be moulding in the damp, black earth of that Catholic cemetery!

"Now what am I supposed to tell you about him? Tell you what a great painter he is? Admire him, excuse him, rave about him? *I think not!* I am no idolater. Gauguin is no idol of mine. I never understood his school of painting, and I don't now, and, *Monsieur,* I *don't* like it. I prefer to see the human form as God made it, not the sick interpretation from the inflamed brain of a madman. How far afield from truth or nature is an artist permitted to go to express his mania for imagery? His confusion was obvious, drink, dope, women, and attempts at suicide. So for the originality in his art, he became a wretched wanderer, a bitter man, a violent man. *Eh bien, tant-pis,* so he got in the soup! And the price of pearl shell doesn't go up or down one *centime, n'est-ce-pas, Monsieur?*"

Levy spread his fingers, and touched the tip of each one with a forefinger as he continued in a vitriolic tone:

"He was a disagreeable man! . . . he was dirty and untidy! . . . he insulted almost everybody! . . . he drank until he fell over on his side like a glutted pig! . . . he tried to seduce every *vahine* that he met! . . . he ran up bills everywhere he could and never paid them! . . . he wrote dirty things in his journal about innocent people here! . . . he ridiculed people who were honorable and hard-working! . . . he didn't believe in God or immortality! . . . he spoke of love only in terms of lust! . . . and, worst of all, he had little or no respect for himself! Does a man who punctures his stomach with vials of morphine sound like a human of any self-esteem? . . ."

"He was a very sick man towards the end," Maugham said quickly. "I understand he had elephantiasis in his right leg. This can be very painful in the tropics—that and many other serious organic ailments. The morphine served to ease his pain, at least medical science so recommends it."

Levy gave an angry grunt.

"His most serious pain was in his head!"

He folded his paper, consulted his watch.

"Now, so it is said, romance and adventure have been associated with Gauguin. Friends and disciples in Paris are publishing his letters, writing his biography. They speak of him as if he is some sort of Messiah in the world of art, a great exponent of a new school of painters."

"He has pioneered in a new technique," Maugham reminded him.

"His technique? Well, I have studied his canvases. I am not entirely ignorant of art. I have lived in Paris. I have an appreciation, and I have read much. Gauguin's art is organized around his reds, which some critics interpret as fire and blood. Some of his toadying followers, the stupid poseurs and pretentious intellectuals, swoon over his style, and argue that his paintings are like an autobiography, recording in color and design the life of a mad sensualist, egotist, cynic and beachcomber. Some fools even say that his Tahitian and Marquesan scenes and figures are true to Polynesia: that one can almost feel the heavy tropical verdure, smell the fragrance of island flowers, and sense the mystic blue reverie of Tahitian jungles. Many say that his colors are all in turmoil. Well, his grandmother was a social agitator, a suffragette, and certainly he was anti-social. His disposition was like a volcano.

"I know that some of the females of Polynesia have coarse features, often rather masculine, and I think that Gauguin instinctively, through a strange compulsion deep within himself, gave them a hermaphroditic appearance."

Maugham interrupted to say:

"I'm afraid that too many people are under the delusion that the distortions in his canvases of the anatomy of Polynesian women are just a deliberate artistic perversion, simply because they themselves have formed their own conception of South Seas femininity through the agency of travel postcards and the exaggerated stories of seamen and writers."

"The writer August Strindberg had some very pointed things to say about his art, when Gauguin asked him to write a foreword for an auction-catalogue for the sale of his paintings in the Hotel Drouout, in Paris," said Levy.

He looked around, snapped his fingers at the Chinese waiter dozing in the inside bar, and, when he had his attention, shouted:

"Quick now! Bring me the large book of mine there on the shelf! Yes, yes, that's it, the one with the clippings sticking out of it! *The Gauguin book!*"

When the book was being brought to him, he said to Maugham: "Now, I'll read you something, something very appropriate, that will support well what I am saying."

He put on his glasses, turned the pages hurriedly, and found a place.

"Ah, now, yes, here we are! This is what the great dramatist and novelist Strindberg said when he saw some canvases of Tahitian women on the walls of Gauguin's studio:

" 'I cannot grasp your art, and I cannot like it . . . and in your South Seas paradise dwells an Eve who does not conform to my ideal—for truly I also have an ideal of women, or two!' "

Maugham replied: "I'm afraid that the eminent playwright, Mr. Strindberg, had a number of private neuroses, one of them being that he was an anti-feminist. No matter what the anatomical proportions of Gauguin's *vahines* had been he would never have approved of them.

"And I think Gauguin replied very neatly in a letter to Strindberg, so well that I have committed it to memory. I'm sure you will remember it, too: 'The Eve of your civilized conception makes you and makes us all misogynists. The Eve of old, she who terrifies you in my studio, might perhaps smile on you less bitterly some day. . . . The Eve I have painted (and she alone), logically, may remain nude in our presence! Yours, in that condition, could not step forth save immodestly, and too fair (it may be) evoke pain and sorrow.' "

"Ah, yes, yes," said Levy impatiently. "We can sit here all week arguing about Gauguin, but there is one thing I can say that is self-evident. I wonder if he would have become so important if he had gone to Siberia to paint instead of Tahiti. Hardly! The islands of the South Pacific did much for him, believe me. Now let me read to you from a clipping I have here in the book. His friend, Charles de Monfried, knew a thing or two about this when Gauguin wrote him that he wanted to leave the Marquesas and return to Paris. He advised him in a letter to stay where he was. And this is what he wrote: 'It is to be feared that your return would only derange the growing and slowly conceived ideas with which public opinion has surrounded you. Now you are that legendary artist, who from the depths of Polynesia, sends forth his disconcerting and inimitable work—the definitive work of a man who has disappeared from the world. Your enemies—and you have many, as have all who trouble the mediocre—are now silent, do not dare to combat you, do not even think of it: for you are so far away. You must not return. You are as the great dead. You have passed into the history of art.'

"*Eh bien*, so now you have it." Levy reached for his hat and journal. "Certainly, one has to admit that Tahiti had much to do with whatever success his paintings are having." He stood up and moved toward the stairway. "But I do not want to be quoted on anything, you understand. I once had trouble with a reckless, drunken American writer. Therefore, I know how to settle such matters." He gripped the railing as he started to descend gingerly. "Anyway, I'm afraid you've wasted your time talking to me about Paul Gauguin."

Maugham didn't think so.

15. The Agony of Paul Gauguin

Gerald Haxton, during the Tahitian sojourn, spent many hours along the waterfront of Papeete. It held a special fascination for him. Ships and the sea had always been part of his life. Conrad and Melville and Jack London were three of his favourite authors. Later, in the mid 1930s, in the harbor of Villefranche, adjoining Villa Mauresque on Cap Ferrat, Maugham's yacht was registered in his name, and he was always at the helm when cruises were made into the Mediterranean.

Tahiti's sailing crafts and their brown-skinned seafarers in scarlet loin-cloths were exactly as adventure writers had described them. The copra schooners and pearling luggers, sterns against the esplanade of Papeete and lines snubbed ashore to the butt-ends of half-buried ancient cannons, once used in the French-Tahitian wars, gave strong credence to the phrase "the South Seas," the certitude of faraway coral atolls scattered like green garlands across the shimmering expanse of the Pacific, and the promise that they could transport one to them if one were of a mind.

Gerald wanted desperately to book passage on such a boat to the Tuamotu Archipelago, or far north to the Marquesas, where Melville, as a young man, had once deserted a whaleship at the island of Nuku Hiva and escaped into a paradise valley. But important work was pending in Tahiti on the Gauguin novel and it was with a sense of great good fortune that one day, Gerald and Maugham met Captain "Winny" Brander.

He was a short, solidly built, trading-schooner skipper, in his forties, with a strong jaw and a large blondish moustache, and his keen blue eyes were in startling contrast to the deeply tanned face. His schooner was the *Kaeo,* and he sailed from Papeete into the Tuamotus, and beyond sometimes to the Marquesas, with an occasional call at the isolated Gambier island of Manga Reva.

"When he walked onto the verandah of the Hotel Tiare with Gerald, I knew instantly, before being introduced, that he was a sailing-ship mariner," said Maugham. "He had a rolling gait that could only come from a long, steadied, balanced footing on the plunging deck of a schooner. And the hand that gripped mine was hard and calloused. He wore an open-necked white shirt, khaki pants and strap-leather sandals. In uniform it would not be inappropriate to imagine him coming down the gangway of a windjammer in Sydney or Liverpool.

"He was a soft-spoken, polite and modest man, with a command of cultured English. It was obvious that he read a lot, or that he had been reared in a family of substance. Finally, I learned that his father John Brander had come from Bamfshire in Scotland, and that he himself was of one-eighth Tahitian blood.

"His father had amassed one of the greatest fortunes in the islands, and had built the first sugar-mills in Tahiti," said Maugham. "He had, also, owned at one time the Island of the Stone Gods, Easter Island,[1] the 'Riddle of the Pacific,' which was eventually sold to Chile."

It was only after a considerable consumption of gin and rum, that Maugham learned something else about the Brander family of Tahiti: old John Brander had married a chiefess of royal blood, one of extraordinary beauty in keeping with her lengthy name, Tetau-nui-reia-i-te-ra'i-atea[2] Salmon, and that if France had not seized Tahiti and the outlying islands in the mid-Eighties, Captain Winny would have now been called Prince Teri'i-tino-rua Marama—a name which meant "Prince Dual-Body-Moon." And that, furthermore, the Clan Branders of Scotland had been Scottish chiefs, with a notable mention in Richard Blackmore's *Lorna Doone*. Also, he had two brothers, Arthur Te-ra-tane (The Man Sun) and Norman Teri'i-tua (The Ocean Sovereign).

Maugham told him of his intention to write a novel on the life of Paul Gauguin.

Captain Winny put down his glass of rum, and his eyes widened in surprise.

"Oh, now are you going to write something about Koké? That's what we called him here. Name doesn't mean anything in Tahitian, just how the name sounded to the natives." He nodded his head slowly. "Yes, he was a queer one, that's for sure. A lot could be told about him. Fancy that, you're going to write a book on him! Arthur will be inter-

---

[1] A modern account of Easter Island exploration is Thor Heyerdahl's *Aku Aku*.

[2] English translation: Great-Princess-Roaming-in-the-Spacious-Palaces.

ested when I tell him. Gauguin's all right in his book. He always said he was a great painter, and Arthur should know. He went to Oxford, and afterwards travelled around Europe, touring through museums and studying the old masters."

"Did Gauguin travel to any of the other islands of French Oceania?" inquired Maugham. "I can't find a single record of any trips, until he left for the Marquesas."

"No, I don't think he did," replied Captain Winny. "And for a very good reason. He was so stony-broke he couldn't even pay for a one-way passage to Moorea. He owed everybody in Papeete, especially the *tinitos*, and they ran most of the copra and pearling schooners to the Tuamotus and Marquesas. So he was stuck here on Tahiti. I think he would have left Tahiti, if he could, and gone to another island, because he was fed up with this place. He'd had too much bad luck and hell here.

"However, it will interest you to know that when he finally did make the last trip that he was to ever go on, it was aboard a schooner I sailed on."

"He sailed with you to the Marquesas?"

This was more than Maugham had anticipated from Captain Winny!

"Yes, one morning, in August of 1901, when I came down to the dock, the supercargo told me that we were taking a sick Frenchman to Hiva Oa in the Marquesas. I asked him who it was and he said, 'The painter from Punaauia.' I said, 'Oh, hell-damn! What does he want to go to the Atuana for?' The super said that he was going there to live, judging from all the bundles of things he was taking with him. And I said to myself: Hiva Oa is the last place for anyone to go to who's sick. What was all this bushwah?

"I went below in the sleeping-cabin to see Gauguin. He was lying on his side, his head on his arm, and his eyes were closed. He reeked of absinthe, so I figured he had been up all night with some of his cronies having all his goodbyes from Tahiti. There was a native woman with a two-year-old boy squatting on the floor beside him, and she was holding his hand that dangled over the edge of the bunk. When she lifted her head, I saw it was his *vahine* Tahura, and she was bawling, so I knew right away that he wasn't taking her or the kid with him.

"I went over to the bunk and looked at him. He was in bad shape, all right. I shook him and asked him if he felt up to making the trip. 'Dr. Cassiou[3] just left,' he grunted at me, 'and he told your *capitain* that I was fit to travel. After all, I'm not dying—*yet*! I asked him if there was anything I could do for him, and he rolled over on his side away from me, and muttered: 'Yes, please leave me alone! And, for the love of God, get this stupid snivelling woman out of here! I want to sleep.'

"I took Tahura and her little boy Emile up on deck. I asked her if Koké would be coming back from Atuana some day, and she shook her head, and walked off down the plank and away. I felt sorry for her. It was clear he didn't give a damn for her or the kid."

The next morning Captain Winny found Gauguin slightly improved from his sleep, but still not able to come on deck. There was a bottle of lotion in the chest made from the laurel-shaped leaves of the *ati* plant, and he washed out his festered eyes. Cataracts had started to form, and the irritation was intense. For his stomach cramps he administered a double dose of laudanum. That evening Captain Winny went below for another talk with Gauguin.

---

[3] Dr. Cassiou was the "Dr. Coutras" of Maugham's *The Moon and Sixpence*. Dr. Cassiou was beloved by whites and Tahitians and administered medically to them for many years.

He found him moving about slowly, rearranging his pile of baggage.

Captain Winny asked him:

"Are you sure it's a sensible idea, this move of yours to the Marquesas?"

Gauguin shrugged his shoulders. "How does one know what is sensible until you have tried it? My time was up in Tahiti, so I move on, that's all. I don't think I have any other choice."

"You won't get mail for months and months."

"I don't receive many letters of importance. Besides, if one doesn't receive messages from the outside world, one's peace of mind is more assured."

"And there is no doctor in Hiva Oa or Nuku Hiva," said Captain Winny. "Just a few native *tahuas.*"

"The *tahuas* can perhaps do more for me than the European doctors in Papeete," muttered Gauguin. "At least they have no tricks to get high fees. And they do know the healing barks, leaves and roots that grow wild in the valleys."

"I'm surprised you didn't take your *vahine* and boy with you. She could take care of you until you are better."

"She bored and annoyed me," said Gauguin. "And it's better for the boy to stay here in Tahiti with his people. The Marquesans don't like the Tahitians." He handed Captain Winny a large can of linseed oil. "This is leaking, could you please try to fix it? I will need this for my painting in the Marquesas, so it's precious to me." He didn't want to converse longer with Captain Winny.

The schooner made short scheduled stops at Fakarava Atoll and Takaroa, one of the northernmost isles of the Tuamotus, and then slanted away for Hiva Oa in the Marquesas.

"The night before we arrived in Atuana, Gauguin came

on deck," Captain Winny told Maugham and Haxton. "He had taken a bucket-bath and shaved and looked much improved. He had been able to eat some bland foods on the trip, so his stomach condition, caused by the previous suicide try with arsenic while living in Punaauia, was not as serious. His disposition had improved, too."

Gauguin had moved about the deck for a while for exercise, and then had come to the stern to talk to Captain Winny at the wheel.

"I've read much on the Marquesas," he told Captain Winny, "and they sound as if a man could live well there for little money. I need badly such a place now. I am practically destitute. Had I remained in Tahiti I would have been in jail for debts, sooner or later. Now I can start over again."

There was a note of wistful hope in his voice that surprised Captain Winny.

"I told him all I knew about the Marquesas, and he listened with interest. When I had finished, he nodded and said: 'Well, I'll just have to make the best of it, that's all. There are foods growing wild in the valleys, so I shall get along.' I wasn't so sure. The climate of the Marquesas is not healthful, it rains a lot, and the *nono*-flies are terrible. For a young, strong man they are all right, but not for a middle-aged sick man."

Gauguin started to go below, then he came back and put out his hand to Captain Winny. "I wish to thank you for being so kind. If I have been rude, and seemed not to appreciate what you have done for me, it is just that my body is always filled with agony. I have my supply of morphine for that, thank God. Would that I had a narcotic for my mental torture."

Then he asked a favor. "The boy I left back there, Emile,

he is named after my son in Copenhagen,[4] and when he grows up he will need to find something to do, to earn a living. I would appreciate it if you'd try to interest him in the sea. It's a clean life and he'll be much better for it."

Captain Winny promised that he would do what he could to encourage the boy, when he was of sufficient years, to sign on his schooner.

"Gauguin then said goodnight, and goodbye, and that he perhaps wouldn't see me in the morning, as he'd go ashore right away," Captain Winny told them. "I was ashore early on business in Atuana, and when I came back to the schooner Gauguin had left. The super said the last he saw of Gauguin was him talking with a Marquesan on the beach and bargaining over the price of a mustang to carry his things into the valley behind Atuana.

"In 1902, in the summer, I met Gauguin on the sea road of Atuana, and he was very agitated. He asked if he could come out to the schooner and talk with me. I told him that I had to remain ashore for a while. But he didn't seem to want to talk ashore, and kept looking over his shoulder, as if he thought someone was listening to him.

"Finally, he followed me down to the copra shed, came inside and said: 'I'm having trouble with the dirty missionaries here! They don't like the way I live. Because I took one of their converts away, a young, pretty girl, they have it in for me. I think they have written back to Papeete. And the *sacre* French gendarme here is supporting their complaints about me. He, particularly, is a scoundrel, and has been cheating the natives, and he molests the women here more than I do.'

"I asked him if he wanted me to speak to an *avocat* in

<hr />

[4] Gauguin's legitimate son Emile Gauguin, an engineer, who became an American citizen, died in retirement, in his 80s in Florida in the 1950s.

Papeete about his problems, and he said he would appreciate it if I would, just in case. I said I would have a talk with Brault, and he made a face and said: 'Isn't there any other?' I told him that Brault had influence with the administration, so he said: '*Eh bien,* then Brault it is, but he may not like the idea of helping me. I think I offended him once.'

"That was the last time I was to see Gauguin alive. I did talk to Brault, but he was not too eager to help him. 'He insulted me and did not apologize, ever!' But later he reconsidered. 'Oh, well, the man is a good artist, and most artists are lunatics, inspired idiots and must be protected after a fashion. If necessary I shall represent him.'

"When I came back to Atuana later that same year, a Swiss by the name of Vernier said that he thought Gauguin was now completely deranged. 'He is doing strange things!' 'Such as what now?' I asked him. 'Well, he has been carving on slabs of wood showing the priests of Hiva Oa chasing naked women.' And he told me that the missionaries were preaching sermons against Gauguin in their mission stations. I told him that I didn't think that Gauguin was acting strangely, as it was the sort of thing he was capable of, sober, drunk or out of his mind."

Secretly, Captain Winny was amused over Gauguin's attacks upon the missionaries. He had little use for them himself. He had always questioned their role in Polynesia. The islanders were worse off than before the self-appointed savants had come, and were now riddled with just about every-known disease of the white man and addicted to all of his vices, lazy, shiftless, conniving, promiscuous, and as far removed as ever from being succored from the missionary-threatened punishment of a fiery purgatory.

"There isn't one native in a dozen here today who can give you the faintest idea of the spiritual value of Christianity, and how it's going to give him a better life than what he had before the *mitinares* came here. A relative of mine, Marau Taaroa, the last Queen of Tahiti, spoke well when she said: 'The natives looked at the missionaries as a kind of children, or idiots, incapable of understanding the simplest facts of island politics or society.' "

Maugham, an avowed atheist, agreed.

"Later, I heard that Gauguin was in real trouble," said Captain Winny. "The case had been prepared against him, and he was tried and sentenced to three months' imprisonment and a fine of one thousand *francs* for defaming the *gendarme* of Atuana, and inciting, so the complaint read, the natives to 'rebellion.' I think that the Marquesans of the village had made a demonstration in Gauguin's behalf outside the *gendarme's* house. Gauguin appealed in a personal letter to the colonial tribunal in Papeete, but such things move slowly, and of course, they were not *sympathique* to him. But Brault prepared his review.

"Gauguin at this time was in better shape financially. His paintings were catching on in Paris and Amsterdam, and some payments were reaching him, which, if he had lived longer, would have given him a good guarantee of not worrying about money for life. In fact, when I talked to a trader of Hiva, a chap by the name of Keane, he told me that Gauguin had told him he might leave Hiva Oa and return to Paris. He said: 'He's homesick, and I think he's had a belly-full of the islands, and maybe he's afraid he might die, and he doesn't want to be buried so far away from his own country. He's not painting anymore island stuff, but things such as snow scenes in Brittany.' "

Captain Winny was in Taahuku, the next bay to Atuana on May 8, 1903, loading a cargo of copra, when in the afternoon a whale-boat manned by eight Marquesans swept around the low cliff point and bore down upon the schooner.

"Some of them were yelling and waving their arms to attract my attention. And when they came closer, I heard the name '*Koké*!' I knew instantly that Gauguin was dead. Otherwise they would not be so excited. When they came alongside, I found out that I was right. Gauguin had died in his hut in the Atuana Valley just before noon. And they told me that the Catholic priests had refused to have anything to do with his body.

"I found Vernier in Atuana the next morning and we went up to Gauguin's place. The *gendarme* was there and a lot of natives, who were carrying on, wailing, and looking in the door. I asked the *gendarme* if I could go in to see the body, and after much haggling he said it would be all right. Inside I found a Marquesan, who said his name was Tioka. He was bawling his head off. He told me that Gauguin had taken a strong injection of morphine to rest easier, and had laid down. When Tioka came back an hour later, he found Gauguin with an arm thrown across his face. He thought he was sleeping. He touched him to be sure, and then felt no heat on his skin. He ran out of the hut. But he came back a few minutes later, and, using an ancient Marquesan custom that is supposed to awaken the dead, he bit Gauguin on the head. But Gauguin did not move. He was fifty-five years old when he died; he had finally found in death the peace that he couldn't find in life."

Captain Winny had come closer to examine Gauguin's body. The stench of tropical putrefaction had already set in, that and the suppurating pustules that covered his body, and the seepage of eczema. The leg swollen with elephantiasis had many open lesions and the discharge had soaked into the mattress; vermin had already found the human dissolution. One eye was open, the other half-closed, filmed and oozing pus. The sphincter muscle had lost its tension in death, and faeces contributed to the incredible physical corruption. It was as if some cleansing spiritual force within the body was now completely rejecting and throwing off the accumulated organic filth of a lifetime.

"He wasn't very pretty, I can tell you. The natives were afraid to touch him, and the *gendarme* was too squeamish and of no mind to remove the body to a cleaner place. Vernier and I finally got some help in Atuana and came back and prepared the body. Then we tidied up the place a bit. But native looting had already taken place, and many of his things had disappeared."

Formally, the government official at Atuana had written to the administration in Papeete:

"I have the honor of informing you that the painter Gauguin, Eugene, Henri Paul, died at Atuana on the Eighth day of May, 1903, at 11 a.m. in the morning. I have notified his creditors . . ."

And a seven-page inventory of Paul Gauguin's belongings accompanied the death notice to Tahiti. There were more than a hundred tins of food, many bottles of beer, two litres of absinthe, a half-dozen demi-johns of wine. There were also listed a sewing machine, a guitar, a mandolin, a stove, crockery, cooking utensils, miscellaneous books, mildewed and worm-eaten, weapons for hunting, ammunition, a horse and a carriage, on and on and on, item for item, in precise columns. Far down at the end of the list, as if of negligible value, was a brief statement of drawings and canvases, hundreds, that had been gathered up in the littered house.

And at the end of his report, the French official in Atuana had affixed his summation of the dead man's effects:

"Already I am convinced that the debts will far surpass the assets, since the works of the deceased, because he was a decadent painter, have little chance of finding a buyer."

16. Maugham
on a Private Island

During his Tahiti visit Maugham was to meet Dr. Walter Johnstone Williams, the Canadian-born dentist and once acting-consul for the United States, who later became the British Consul in Papeete, from 1916 to 1935.

"He was a very distinguished, perhaps the most distinguished man in Tahiti, and he enjoyed a unique privilege; he was the only dentist within three or four thousand miles, and he had an exclusive monopoly, approved by the French Tribunal, of dentistry in French Polynesia. He was, of course, very rich, in consequence, because in the tropics teeth go bad very quickly. He enjoyed his position, and the Tahitians always referred to him as 'Eez-Onor-Weelee.' He was well-liked by everyone. He had been a close friend of King Pomarè the Fifth,[1] whom he described to me as a heavy

---

[1] His tomb in Tahiti is topped with a large replica of an absinthe bottle, of which he was inordinately fond—a thirst which his friends and family appropriately commemorated.

drinker and playboy, but a good-hearted and happy man, who had spent most of his days in travelling around the island, giving parties with a huge entourage of dancers and musicians and friends.

"Willie was over seventy, plumpish and cherubic, but he had never had a sick day in his life, and he said to me: 'It's this wonderful climate below the equator that keeps the pores open, empties the body of poisons, keeps the skin lubricated. In the forty years or more that I've been here I only wear clothes at work, and then damn few, and, of course, when I have to attend official functions and *soirées* at the Governor's palace. The rest of the time I'm in a *pareu*. Of course, I'm not overlookin' the worry-free life here where a man doesn't have his conscience botherin' him all the time if he's sinnin'. And, Lord!, the *vahines* have contributed a lot to my health!—don't sell *them* short. I have to give credit where it's due.'

"But the most outstanding privilege Willie enjoyed was that he owned an island, his own private, paid-in-full, Land Office-approved coral island—and not too far from Tahiti.

"I secretly envied Willie his own South Seas island. I had always imagined it would be the most wonderful thing to possess a picturesque island, with blue sunlit water all about, and the coral reefs holding back the surf, and just the sea-birds and gaily tinted marine life as companions for inviolable solitude. It would have to be a tropical island, below the equator, because most uninhabited temperate-climate islands are just too barren and windswept. And not a large one that would take too much effort and time to walk around, one you could easily stroll around in an hour or so.

"I have from time to time received in the mail offers of islands for my own private use and ownership, but always they were so far away, in some inaccessible ocean, that would require an expensive steamer or plane ticket to reach. Not suitable for permanent living most of them, and if just for a vacation-island the arrangement wouldn't be practical. If I left it unattended, I'd always be worrying if beachcombers had somehow heard about it and taken possession *en masse,* or if someone had come in the night, affixed a hook, and towed it off to God knows where.

"I asked Willie how he had ever come by the island, and he casually told me: 'In payment of a dental bill.' I told him that it must have been an enormous bill for the island to be tended as payment. And he said: 'That's correct. The Royal Pomarè Family of Tahiti came to me for all their dental work, and, of course, you don't send bills to kings and queens. It went on this way for years. Most of their dental work consisted of pullin' out perfectly good teeth and re-placin' them with gold teeth for the 'golden smile' that was popular at that time. The Tahitian royalty saw gold in the teeth of the French officials and their wives here, so they wanted to be in fashion. So one day they casually gave me Tetiaroa.'

" 'And just where is this Tetiaroa?' I wanted to know.

"I expected him to say it was hundreds of miles away.

" 'It's about twenty-five miles north of here,' he replied offhandedly.

"That interested me. I knew that he'd have no objection if I visited it, perhaps lived there for a time, to see just how *I* would enjoy owning a private island.

"But, then, Willie told me a rather startling thing about the island. He announced that it was dangerously over-run with . . . cats! Yes, that's what he said, *CATS!*

"I didn't think I had heard correctly. 'Did you say *cats?*' I exclaimed.

" 'Yes, that's right, a whole bloody gang of cats. And wild as the devil, too.'

" 'How in the hell did *cats* ever take over your island, Willie?'

"If he had said crabs, snails or sea-birds, I would have understood. But *cats*, and way off down here in the South Seas, too!

"And he told me how it happened."

When Dr. Williams had made his first ownership-inspection of Tetiaroa, he found it plentifully covered with mature, bearing coconut palms. He, also, found ruins of old *maraes* (temples) and stone-covered graves. The coral atoll had been a possession of the Pomarè royalty for centuries, and had been used as a combination pleasure resort and sacred meeting-place for *tahuas* (priests) of the *Arioi* Society, a sex cult that had dominated the islands, finally usurping the power of even the highest chiefs. A phallic god, Oro, previously worshipped as a war god, had become their *ti'i* (Idol) of sexuality and fertility, and was transported in a double-canoe—that was also a nautical temple and exclusive brothel of royalty—from island to island of what is now French Polynesia, attended by singers, musicians, dancers and beautiful women. The voyages were intended as regular excursions to recruit more islanders to licentious idolatry. The erotic rituals were witnessed by Captain James Cook, and he was mortified when he first saw them. The influence of the *Arioi* Society spread over the entire archipelagoes and became the tradition, in name, for every variety of venery; the sect dominated eastern Polynesian culture up until France seized the islands in 1848. Shortly thereafter, the missionaries, appalled at the power of the *Arioi* that was circumventing their Christianizing of the natives, appealed to the French Naval Fleet to disband the pagan cult, and this was finally accomplished.

Tetiaroa was also the atoll where the women of the Pomarè Family went to indulge in the art of *ha'apori* (fattening), generous avoirdupois being the criteria of sexual charm of high-born native *vahines*. And in the dark, cool groves of enormous and heavy-foliaged *tou*[2] trees on Rima-tou—islet of Tetiaroa—the former site of the Pomarè royal residence, they languished in regal splendor, attended by servants, so that their skins would bleach with the native emollients used, thus establishing the necessary complexion-contrast between fisher-woman and noble *vahine*.

Dr. Williams noted that the series of about a dozen islets that comprised Tetiaroa were enclosed by wide protective coral reefs, with a shallow entrance in the northwest for canoes and small craft. There were a few natives living temporarily on the atoll, descendants of the former retainers of the Pomarè Family who had originally occupied Tetiaroa at the behest of Pomarè the First or Second—dark, squatty people of the Tuamotus, who delivered to the Royal Family fish and sea-life from the "Cloud-of-Islands," as the Tuamotus was known in the pagan era, but they complained to Dr. Williams that it was no longer possible to gather coconuts because the thousands of rats on the isle were damaging the palms.

"I made a survey and found that they were right," Dr. Williams told Maugham. "Criminy! They were dashin' about, climbin' up the palms, duckin' into holes, fightin' over spoiled fish, even tacklin' each other, no matter where you looked. I knew I'd have to do somethin' about them, if I wanted to make any money off the copra.

"I told the natives to start clearin' up the littered groves, lop off the dead fronds, and to plaster mud from the swampy part of the atoll high up on the trunks of the palms to stop

---

[2] *Cordia-supcartata.*

at least the giant coconut-crabs from climbin' up them and snippin' off the young coconuts. Crabs are stupid things, even when they're climbin' for food. Once their claws touch earth, they'll let go their hold, and so, with the sun-baked, hard collar of mud they'd drop about thirty or forty feet and knock their brains out on the hard coral.

"I made a survey, too, about takin' out the old, diseased palms and replantin' with young shoots I could bring from Tahiti, for a rotatin' crop.

"I wondered, also, if there was any treasure buried on the island, because Pomarè the Fifth had told me that at one time, durin' tribal wars, his ancestors had taken their valu-ables there for safekeepin'. However, I haven't found any to date, and don't think I didn't look a lot from the time I took over. If Pomarè the First or Second did leave any behind, someone had got to them long ago."

When Dr. Williams made another trip back to Tetiaroa, with a cutter's deck filled with young coconut plants, he found the natives apprehensive and discouraged. They had, as the new owner had ordered, tried to start exterminating with rocks and clubs, but sometimes the rats turned on them, and they didn't dare chance antagonizing the giant, vicious rodents to the extent that they might organize forces against the humans and gobble them up alive. The next morning, when Dr. Williams returned to the coral strand where he had left the cans of coconut shoots, he found every one de-stroyed. The rats had eaten the tender hearts out of the in-fant palms. And it was clear that the rats were also gnawing off coconuts from the thick clusters in the mature palms. Rats in the islands, especially on low coral atolls, are ca-pable of making a hole with their sharp teeth through the fibrous husk and eventually reaching the water and the meat.

Dr. Williams was alarmed.

"I knew I couldn't afford to band every palm on Tetiaroa with strips of anti-rat and anti-crab metal to stop those rats from gettin' to the coconuts. I began to wonder if the gift of Tetiaroa was a bargain after all. I went back to Tahiti depressed and discouraged. I tried to think of a solution."

And as he was cogitating, his large maltese cat leapt onto his lap and snuggled down, purring and kneading with its paws, and he stroked the tom absently trying to solve the scourge of rats on Tetiaroa.

One of the cat's claws lightly scratched his knee. His eyes widened, and he looked closer at the tom. Then, with a happy exclamation, he seized the pet by the scruff of his neck and held up the startled feline in front of him, eyeing him with inspiration. The cat returned his stare with increasing annoyance.

"The perfect solution to those damned rats! Turn a whole slew of cats, the natural enemies of rats, loose on Tetiaroa!"

"Incredible that you would have thought of it," remarked Maugham, with a faint smirk. "Commendable perception, indeed, Willie."

"Well, so I got busy and took a walk around Papeete. Funny, but before I hadn't paid much attention to the feline population of this island. But, criminy! There were cats everywhere, fightin', scroungin' food at the back doors of the *tinito* restaurants, makin' love, chasin' dry hibiscus flowers, sunnin' themselves, asleep. Lord! There were enough just in Papeete alone to raise bloody hell on Tetiaroa. I tried to pick up a few, but they just wouldn't let me get too close. So I knew I'd have to pay for them."

The Dentist-Consul posted a sign on the front of his waterfront office:

CATS WANTED!
Two Francs each. Payment promptly upon delivery

Within an hour of the announcement a steady stream of Tahitians descended on his place of business, and a Tahitian assistant directed them to the rear garden, where a Chinese carpenter was building slatted cages. The bags and nets of yowling, spitting cats were unceremoniously emptied into them.

And when Dr. Williams had 200 cats, which just about depleted Papeete of its midnight serenaders, he called a halt.

"Lord! What bedlam in the yard! I didn't plan to feed them, so they'd go ashore at Tetiaroa with growling bellies, and it got so I didn't dare to even put a hand near a cage out there. They'd have chewed the fingers down to the palm.

"I made a deal with one of Levy's cutters to haul them over."

It must have been a scene of panic when the rats of Tetiaroa first smelled, or heard, the cats approaching the coral strands of Tetiaroa. The savage chorusings of the felines must have carried for miles.

"I'd have given anything to have been there with Willie when he gave the order to release all those enraged, starved cats," chuckled Maugham. "They had to pile the cages in a dinghy and row them in to the beach of white sand. And two of the boys knocked off the slats with hammers."

Standing on the deck-house of the cutter, jumping up and down with glee, Dr. Williams shouted:

"Go get 'em! Eat 'em up! Give 'em hell!" Then: "Lord! Look at that, will you! Just look at that!"

The beach had suddenly come alive with cats, charging in every direction. They scrambled wildly, but with purpose, over the fringing reefs, leapt from coral shoal to coral hillock, swept in a furry tide into the groves, in frenzied pursuit of the terrified rats.

Dr. Williams had made a rough estimate that there were between two to three thousand rats on Tetiaroa.

"And those two hundred-or-so cats over a time must have made short work of them. It must have been an incredible orgy of rodent slaughter," remarked Maugham.

Those that had not been caught and eaten within the first week must have crawled far down into crab holes or hidden in the tops of palms. But when starvation and thirst did force them out of their hiding-places, there was always a skulking cat ready to pounce upon them.

Gorged at last on the rats, the cats now merely killed them and left them for the scavenger-crabs.

Dr. Williams, grinning triumphantly, sailed back to Papeete, leaving the toms to guard his island's coconut crop.

"But he didn't consider one simple law of survival," said Maugham, with amusement. "The delicate, but inexorable, balance of nature. He didn't take into consideration that the feline birth-rate would soar."

Over a short period of time the original two hundred cats multiplied three times over!

"So now that the rats had almost become extinct, the toms were faced with eventual starvation."

"Lord! You wouldn't think that animals could propagate so fast!" Dr. Williams had told Maugham. "I told the workers over there to kill off the litters of kittens, but they couldn't find them all. And they didn't feel so easy facin' all those wild tomcats. They were wild, fierce as bob-cats."

Then the inevitable took place. First, the toms and tabbies raided nests of new-born kittens; then they waylaid the older and weaker cats. Gangs formed against each other, with stronger bands overpowering the lesser rivals.

"It was fantastic, but cat cannibalism raged on Willie's private paradise," said Maugham.

Dwindling numbers forced gangs to break up, with smaller units attacking each other. The smarter and stronger cats soon vanquished and ate the weaker ones in this bizarre feline survival of the fittest. And it undoubtedly would continue, unabated, until at last only two cats remained to face each other in final combat.

Dr. Williams then told Maugham the most astounding reversal of the warring toms on Tetiaroa:

"I don't know when or how it started. But, all of a sudden, the cats weren't killin' each other. Perhaps cat-sense came to the hundred or so cats left on the island."

"It's plausible that they must have held some sort of a conference, or meow-meow, with all agreeing finally to cease the insane war of extinction," remarked Maugham.

And, incredible as it may seem, they reverted to an almost forgotten feline instinct: *fishing!*

The lagoons of Tetiaroa swarmed with the most succulent and tame fish in the South Pacific. Lying on their shrunken, bony stomachs across the coral strands they hooked with their sharp claws at the schools of fish that passed in the shallows close to the beach, or were trapped by the eddying tide in the many coral pools.

"The cats up there now," Dr. Williams told Maugham, "are ruled by a king and queen, and they're wild as ocelots, can't get near them. But they don't hurt anyone, and they keep the rats to a minimum. Fishermen toss fish up on the beach when they have more than they can use. The cats leave us alone, and we leave them alone. And, thank the Lord, the coconuts are doin' fine on Tetiaroa."

"It was really most interesting," said Maugham. "And Willie hadn't exaggerated the account. The cats had actually worked out a satisfactory system of how to survive—and, importantly, let each other live."

Maugham had thought about Tetiaroa many times in the ensuing few days, and the idea of assaying a trial in isolation on such an almost uninhabited isle became most attractive.

"I asked Gerald if he'd care to make the visit with me to Tetiaroa, and he was very enthusiastic. He was quite an athlete, and a true adventurer at heart, and he was sure there would be good swimming and fishing there.

"So I asked Willie if we could use his private paradise for a week or so, and make all arrangements for us. I was having a gin with him at the time, and he said casually: 'Why, of course, no trouble at all. I think you'll enjoy it there, be a change from the noise and distractions of Papeete. And there are not too bad accommodations for you up there.' He made me the offer as if he were handing me a copy of *Punch* or *Illustrated London News*. I liked the casualness of it, his handing temporarily over to me and Gerald the entire island, with no obligation or proviso. Anyway, it was an opportunity to find out how *I* would enjoy the proprietorship of a private island."

The next morning, after coffee at Drollet's Coffee Shop, Maugham made his customary stroll along the waterfront to the small Parc Bougainville. The small oasis of greenery that bordered the *quai* contained a bust of the intrepid French navigator and discoverer, Monsieur Louis Antoine de Bougainville. There were comfortable benches here, and he enjoyed coming to sit and look out upon the lagoon-harbor of Papeete, in whose center the tiny island of Motu Uta, the Quarantine Station of the port, floated like a faery isle—and across the barrier-reef, sparkling-white with a ruff of surf, to the majestic blue silhouette of Moorea Island. At the same time he could see all who passed along the shaded waterfront road.

"Levy's establishment was between the park and the roofed cement pool where the Papeetean washerwomen and the seamen off the schooners came to soak and pound their clothes with wooden clubs, and while I was sitting on the bench, smoking, Levy came outside his place and waved to me. I nodded, and in a minute or two he came over.

"He advised me that Willie had sent a message to him asking if he could take me and Gerald on his cutter to Tetiaroa. He told me he would be only too happy to arrange passage on his craft, and added: 'It will be a pleasure to take you and your friend there without charge.' Before I could remonstrate, he added: 'I would like to see Tetiaroa again. It is a pretty little island.' He suggested that we avail ourselves of netting and oil of citronella, inasmuch as the mosquitoes were bad there, breeding in the brackish water of a section that was somewhat swampy. He promised to see that a supply of food was put aboard his cutter for us, a bag of rice, a good selection of tinned goods, gin, whiskey, and a number of cases of Perrier water, as there was no fit drinking-water on the island; also a first-aid kit as an insurance against cuts and coral scratches which are particularly dangerous in the tropics. There were other items, such as lanterns, petrol, fishing-gear—and a portable gramophone which he felt would be worthwhile. 'Music will fill in the lonely hours on such a place as Tetiaroa,' he said in explanation of this afterthought article of luxury."

When Maugham returned to Dr. Williams' office with the news of Levy's gracious offer, he found a scrawny Chinese awaiting him on the verandah.

"Willie, before I could tell him that the trip to Tetiaroa had already been arranged, said: 'Yes, yes, now everythin's all set, and the *tinito* out there can cook for you. I've never sat down to one of his meals, but at least he can boil an egg or two, and wash the dishes.' The cook turned out to be a most inefficient and unimaginative chef, but his disposition was so infectiously and delightfully happy that he proved to be a never-ending source of amusement for Gerald and myself. Without him I doubt if we would have had so many laughs, so he well deserved his wages, and he was helpful in so many other ways." Levy's cutter left the esplanade of Papeete at about one o'clock in the morning for the imperative daybreak arrival at Tetiaroa, when the seas would be calm and a safer passage over the near-surface reefs accomplished.

"Willie was down to see us off and, as we pulled away from the sea-wall, he called across the widening stretch of dark water: 'Enjoy yourselves at Tetiaroa! Don't worry about anythin'!' I couldn't know then, but later I was to have reason to reflect ironically on his instructions to have no *worry* concerning Tetiaroa.

"It was not possible to sleep, what with the back-firing of the marine engine, and my excitement was such that any thought of closing my eyes was out of the question. It was a particularly lovely night, the sea very quiet and the stars bright. There was a gentle breeze blowing, and it was heavy with the fragrance of tropical flowers and vegetation. We arranged a rug on deck and settled down.

"While at sea Levy came up on deck and talked. I had now formed a very favorable opinion of the pearl buyer. He was, fundamentally, a decent sort, and it was evident that he had been greatly disturbed and injured by the London story. And he wanted us to understand his side of the defamation-of-character action against the now deceased American writer.

"*Monsieur* Londre was not what one would call a very diplomatic person," he told Maugham. "If he was drunk, which was often, and someone annoyed him, he would curse that person. He was, besides, not a very impartial man, and had some very stubborn opinions on racialism. He was just one of the millions of rather deluded gentiles who blamed the Jews for all the ills and catastrophes of the world. Just because I was a South Seas trader, and made a profit from pearl shell, pearls and copra, he, knowing that I was a Jew, automatically assumed that I was cheating the Polynesians out of their rightful products, and should be banished—as the money-changers who were flogged from the temples by Christ—from the islands. He cursed and threatened me over a very minor affair. When I composed myself, I forgot the incident. But he did not. He had the unfair advantage of harming me by the process of machine-printed words on paper. The harm could never be undone when the story was published, even though a retraction and apology might be made. In consequence I felt he should be reminded that a human being has a right to his privacy and peace-of-mind and not to be insulted, even though he is a Jewish pearl buyer.

"I do not disparage *Monsieur* Londre as a writer. I have read his stories, his novels, and have found much true value in them. He was a talented writer, that I do not deny.

"So now that I have said these words relative to the unpleasant matter, I shall speak about it no more."

Levy was to tell them his many fascinating experiences as a pearl buyer in the Tuamotus; and of the faraway Manga Reva Island[4] in the Gambier Group, far to the southeast of Tahiti, where Honoré Laval, a mad despotic priest, had tried to enslave the native population and build for himself a South Pacific kingdom; and how his wife, Madame Levy, was a more capable pearl buyer than he was, sailing every year into the Tuamotus aboard the schooner *Hinano,* carrying bags of silver dollars, so that when a good pearl was bargained for, she had the advantage of hard cash rather than the questionable value of trading goods, and, therefore, customarily sailed back to Tahiti with the best pearls. "She always

---

[4] The Levy family in Tahiti today own an island in the Manga Reva lagoon.

gives them a decent price, contrary to what you might have heard, and she's very popular with the pearl divers. I am very proud of her, as a wife, a mother and a business woman."

So while the cutter sailed toward Tetiaroa, pearl-buyer Levy made them forget the loss of sleep with his observations, adventures and character studies in French Oceania.

He had more interesting information to impart on Tetiaroa.

He mentioned the *tou* groves on Rima-tou, which covered about three acres of the islet, the "beauty parlor" for the royal Pomarè females. He told how Queen Pomarè the Fourth, a sovereign of Tahiti from 1827 to 1877, had gone there, before her marriage, to fatten up and lighten her complexion.

"It is true what Dr. Williams has told you about the sexual orgies on Tetiaroa. Pomarè the Second, father of Pomarè the Fourth, took his entire court and priests and many beautiful *vahines* there, when the missionaries started to Christianize Tahiti, so he would not be spied upon by the *popaa* meddlers.

"Not many of the early explorers visited Tetiaroa. The only one who went there was Captain Bligh of the *Bounty*. He sailed there to look for three deserters who had stolen a cutter in Matavai Bay, Tahiti, this in the first month of 1789. He found and arrested them."

And he cautioned Maugham and Gerald Haxton:

"You will see the ruins of some ancient *maraes* on Rima-tou and some burial places. I would suggest that you do not touch them. I have been in the islands long enough to respect Polynesian *tapus* and *pifaos* (death-curses). The natives say that Pomarè the First's *tupaupau* (ghost) lives there."

He had an interesting anecdote to tell them how the Royal Family acquired the name *Pomarè*.

"Tu, the first king of Tahiti, came from *Les Iles Danger-*

euses. He was a fierce, bushy haired man and liked to battle the many *teva*-clans of Tahiti. Once, while on an expedition of war, he caught a very bad cold, from which he finally died. Until he breathed his last, he coughed and coughed and coughed. The subjects of Tu asked the Queen why he coughed so loudly. She told them: 'He has a *night-cough*.' Tu coughed night and day, until at last he died, and his last sound was a cough. Tahitians usually named their new-born infants on the word that a father might say upon viewing the child, or, if he travelled away or died before the child was born, on any circumstance relating to his absence. So when a son was later born to the queen, she said: 'His name shall be *Pomarè*. It was his father's choice.' The Tahitian word *Po* means *night* and *marè* is *cough*."

Maugham had thoroughly enjoyed Levy's company on the voyage to Tetiaroa. "He sat on deck with us, quietly telling story after story, which we never could have heard from any other person. His knowledge of French Oceania was quite astounding for a man who must have had to devote so much time to his commercial enterprises."

With the approach of dawn the cutter was still at sea, and there was now a long swell running. Then, suddenly, a Tahitian seaman stood up in the bow, peered ahead, and shouted: "*O* Tetiaroa! There is Tetiaroa!"

Maugham and Gerald went forward to watch Tetiaroa rise out of the early morning sea. Levy took his binoculars to study the approach to the reefs.

"First the plumes of the palms appeared, then the palisades of their long smooth trunks, and at last the white froth of small broken waves on the series of reef-islets that chalk-marked her permanent position in the South Pacific."

Islands had always suggested to Maugham a sanctuary beyond life, of time arrested in flight, of absolute escape.

The aspect of Tetiaroa from the sea was inspiring: a long elliptical formation of palm-covered reef-islets, enclosing and protecting a lagoon with no more than six feet of land above the surface. White seabirds were circling lazily, like flashing silvery reflections, above the palms. It was an isle more picturesque than he had imagined.

The cutter came up close to the reef and a boat was lowered. Levy gestured and shouted, and the anchor was dropped onto the reef, the line tightened, but the anchor held in the coral crevice.

Maugham looked vainly for the reef passage giving access to the isle.

Levy told him:

"There is no real opening, just a shallow declivity in the reef itself, which is why we had to reach Tetiaroa at flood tide.[5] I would suggest you start ashore as soon as possible."

The boat was loaded with their supplies, and Maugham and Gerald dropped down after the cargo stowage, making themselves as comfortable as possible on the precarious mounds. The Tahitian seamen pulled hard on the oars and they headed in toward the reef.

"Then we seemed to be sucked into a channel, and on each side were nasty-looking coral outcroppings, and then, quite suddenly, we were through and the seamen had vaulted over the side and were holding to the sides of the boat, walking slowly, vigilantly, up to their armpits, pulling us through a labyrinth of treacherous coral obstructions toward the beach of white coral rubble."

As they moved in to the strand of Rima-tou, Maugham glanced over the side into the blue translucence, where the

---

[5] A jetty has now been built out over the reef from Rima-tou, facilitating an easier landing, and a safer loading of copra and unloading of supplies.

primeval oceanic gardens, teeming with strange and colorful marine life, spread in canyoned mysteries.

"At last the keel of the boat scraped onto the apron of coral and we got out, stretched, and looked around. Safely ashore we could now appreciate fully the beauty of this atoll. There came in from the outer protective reefs of Rima-tou the ceaseless strong murmur of the ebbing and flowing of the southern ocean over the ramparts. And I remembered what Bougainville, the Pacific explorer, had written of the atolls of French Oceania."

Seeing his first atoll and natives in 1769, the French navigator had exclaimed:

"I admire their courage if they live without uneasiness on these strips of sand which a tempest can bury under water in the winking of an eye!"

The beach was blindingly white, with a layer of coarse white sand, pulverized coral and shells of dead crabs and the bleached skeletons of terns, boobies and other sea-birds. And walking through the colonnades of the palms beyond the beach, they reached a grove of gigantic ancient *tou* trees, beneath which the Pomarè *vahines* had once beautified themselves, but whose extensive leafy branches now shaded the six or more palm-thatched huts of the island settlement. There were two simple structures for the storage of copra, and, apart, was the headman's dwelling and another for the copra workers, and then, beyond, two well-made larger *fares*, for the use of Dr. Williams when he visited the island, and which Maugham and Gerald were to occupy.

"The Tahitian seamen and the copra-workers carried up our supplies, bedding and gramophone. Gerald and I hung one of the mosquito-nettings on the verandah of the living-hut, and placed a table and two chairs under it. At least, we could eat in peace, protected from mosquitoes and flies and other flying pests. While we were so engaged, Levy came to say goodbye and wish us well, promising to return for us in two weeks' time.

"The Chinese cook was in the small shed alongside the hut, and he was singing a nasal Cantonese song as he arranged his stores and prepared a fire to boil some water for tea.

"At tea-time we found that at least two dozen mosquitoes had somehow got under the netting, and we spent so much time searching and exterminating them that the tea became cold. We had to fight these devilish, pitiless mosquitoes the moment that the sun went down. If it hadn't been for the oil of citronella we would have been in a sorry state when we finally left the island.

"Gerald and I made a survey of our immediate surroundings before sunset, and found that most of the interior was rather barren, with swampy areas, the breeding ground for the infernal mosquitoes. We saw a number of rats, and at a distance cats, who watched us with baleful glares.

"Anyway, we decided that we would make the best of it, and were sure once we had a routine functioning we'd find life on Tetiaroa comfortable and interesting."

And so the days and nights passed uneventfully, yet each different in its subtle effect. The simplest occurrence now became an event of absorbing interest, as, for example, when a frigate bird landed on Rima-tou and the headman walked down to where it was standing, almost at attention, on the beach, and removed a note from its wing, which informed him that his grandmother on a far distant atoll needed a new charcoal iron from Papeete.

"So I learned that the frigate bird was the flying postman among the atolls of the Tuamotus where the mail service is unreliable and sporadic."

271

Frequently, Maugham would awaken in the middle of the night, unable to believe that he was actually living on such an island as Tetiaroa. He would turn his head and look through the raised latticed side of the sleeping-room, through which the moonlight filtered, making a pattern of grill-work that extended through the netting and across the bed. Beyond, through the motionless spaces of the lofty palms with their scroll-work of fronds, he could see the curving sweep of stars. Always there was profound silence.

"I was reminded of something Gauguin had written," said Maugham.

Gauguin had described a similar scene:

"Silence! I am learning to know the silence of . . . night.

"In this silence I hear nothing except the beating of my heart.

"But the rays of the moon play through the bamboo reeds, standing equi-distant from each other, and reach even to my bed. And these regular intervals of light suggest a musical instrument to me—the reed—pipe of the ancients, which was familiar to the Maori, and is called *vivo* by them. The moon and the bamboo reeds made it assume an exaggerated form—an instrument that remained silent throughout the day, but that at night, by grace of the moon, calls forth in memory of the dreamer well-loved memories. Under this music I fell asleep."

Or Maugham might walk in the late hour of night to the edge of the lagoon and stand there listening to the feathery sounds of the tiny wavelets lapping the irradiantly silvery beach, like secretive whisperings, beneath the over-arching coconut palms, and then, suddenly, a short distance out from the strand there would be the startling tail-lash of a night-foraging fish.

The adjustment to their atoll living was not as simple as it might sound. There were hot, enervating days, when one only became conscious of the dazzling glare of the lagoon and the mocking film of mist floating over the encircling reefs; the sky was brazen, every cloud dissipated by the glaring sun.

"It was well that from Rima-tou there was, when the horizon was not obscured by a haze, the reassuring outline of Tahiti and of Moorea, otherwise we might have felt that we could be marooned on this speck of coral forever."

Maugham never had to consult his pocket barometer for warning of a tropical storm. Flies, the voracious species, came in swarms into the hut and formed pulsating patterns on the thatched walls; on humid oppressive nights mosquitoes "collectively lifted the sides of our netting and swarmed over us."

"But most of the time the steady trades blew across the isle and carried away the worst of the flying pests. The headman took our Chinese out to fish, and showed him how to prepare some delicious native sea-food dishes, so our cuisine improved.

"Under daily contact with the coral strand and reefs the soles of our feet had become toughened and calloused. Wearing only brief shorts, my body no longer suffered from the rays of the strong tropical sun. I had always been a light sleeper, but on Rima-tou I was sleeping nine and ten hours. And in Europe I had always been in the habit of arising late in the morning, but here on the atoll I was loath to shorten the day by getting up late, but began to consider the mornings as the quintessence of life, almost sacred, so I was up an hour after dawn, to take my walk along the long coral strand."

Maugham would sit for hours, his back resting against a palm bole, with only reflections, light and shapeless as summer clouds, drifting through his mind. He would watch, entranced, the rippling course of a small coral snake, the sedate riding majesty of a brace of sea-horses, or the almost imperceptible movement of a *nohu*, the stone-fish, clinging with bony grapnels to the fringe of the coral ledge, its venomous quills stiffly erected for a careless stroller. A sea-bird might soar without wing-beats in the blue sky, a barely moving shadow. The lagoon's surface, lightly rippled, now aqua, now indigo, was like an expanse of rich brocade; as if ceasing its incessant activity the small ripples broke on the coral beach so softly, so limpidly, that in contrast the pleasant diapason of the sea upon the barrier-reefs was amplified and seemed very close.

And he and Gerald often paddled out upon the lagoon in an outrigger-canoe to be held fascinated for hours by the fabulous underwater domain. Far below, the occasional deserts of white coral sand refracted the sun's rays, and, seen through the natural filter, the amazingly tinted lagoon gardens and fish appeared to be magnified and were not unlike the fantastic designs in an oriental tapestry. In the deeper parts of the lagoon there were the shadowy suggestions of forests of coral trees, ferns and fans, and yawning shells of the giant furbelowed clam. Battlemented coral castles were struck from behind by rays of sunlight and irradiated a diffused glow through ornate windows. Snappers, groupers, trigger-fish, butterfly fish and cow-fish idled here and there; now, ominously, there was the swift eerie gliding of small rays, the shuddering spasms of eels and the convulsive crawling of small octopuses.

"But one had to be very careful in such an unfamiliar latitude, to strengthen caution, as for example the time when Gerald was swimming back to the beach from a reef-ledge with a string of edible fishes, which he had speared underwater, tied to his waist, and a small lagoon-shark slid up stealthily and tore every fish away, missing his stomach by a fraction of an inch.

"Gerald spent much time in the water, swimming and spear-fishing under the tutelage of the headman. He enjoyed spearing octopuses underwater, although I considered it a decidedly loathsome business. I shall never forget the time he came upon a small one ensconced in a coral crevice at the bottom of a submerged ledge and imprudently launched his spear. He made a perfect strike, but this particular mollusk proved to be a vicious one. I was watching through a glass-paned box, and I was seized with acute revulsion when this gorgon of marine life began crawling in jerking spasms down the spear-point and along the shaft, enlarging the hole that pierced it, and plastered sucking tentacles around Gerald's arms, neck and chest. He surfaced, blinded and nauseated by the sepia it was discharging. I reached down and eventually peeled the damnable creature from Gerald and flung it back into the lagoon. But for many days thereafter Gerald carried the red kisses of the little brute's tentacles around his chest and neck. Later, whenever I wanted to tease Gerald, in company, I would say casually: 'Gerald, why don't you tell us about the time at Rima-tou, near Tahiti, when you wrestled a hundred foot octopus into submission.' "

Whenever they tired of the sameness of the leeward side of Rima-tou they would walk across in a short time to the more active windward side. Here, as if with constant warning of its potential force, the combers smashed determinedly against the barrier coral reef, flooded over it deeply, frothing and sucking at the crenated inner mole. At regular intervals a heavier one would pound itself to destruction, growing louder and louder as it breached the open spaces between the reef-islets, throwing the spume high and arousing the screeching birds which swooped down for any small sea-life marooned in the crevices of the reef's flooded expanse.

Maugham had the headman prepare on the coral strand near their dwelling a roof of palm-leaves for shade, with open sides, and hung a mosquito netting inside, under which sand was spread and then a pandanus mat. Here, where he could be assured of the cooling trades, he enjoyed coming for his siesta. He could consider the slow and stately procession of the large masses of clouds as they passed over the atoll. The shadows they made when darkening the sun were imposed upon the sea and reefs, making the palm-margined coral strand blazing white, now laying briefly on the distant side of the lagoon's green surface and deeper-hued outer sea, "as if a celestial Gauguin were carefully experimenting with color tones, endlessly and effortlessly repeated."

"But there was a strange situation that presented itself at Rima-tou. I thought Gerald and I had covered every inch of this southernmost islet of Tetiaroa. One evening, at the extreme end of the island, I sighted a very small *fare*, and so we approached to see if it was occupied. We were about a hundred feet away, when a native man emerged from the low doorway and shook his fist at us to go back. He had a most ferocious expression on his face, and, as we imagined he might be demented, we withdrew.

"I asked the headman who he was, and he just shrugged his shoulders and said it was an unfriendly native of the Tuamotus, who preferred to live alone and have no congress with anyone. So we left it at that. But the idea of a man living all by himself, bereft of human company, a *vahine*, or a pet, bothered me. I saw him once again before leaving Tetiaroa, far out on a reef searching for shell-fish, and I waved to him, but he didn't return my greeting. I wondered about him now and again, and felt sorry for what must be his crushing, angry loneliness."

The time came for them to leave Tetiaroa and they reluctantly packed and had their belongings carried down to the beach.

Levy's cutter anchored off the reef, the boat was lowered to bring them aboard, and an hour later they were on their way back to Tahiti.

"Both Gerald and I felt a sadness over leaving the coral island. Although it had been our home for only a short two weeks, we had become deeply attached to it and the workers there. We were to speak often of our adventures on Rima-tou for many years afterward, and there was always the same nostalgic yearning to return there."

A few days after their return to Papeete, Maugham was sitting on Dr. Williams' verandah, chatting with him over a drink. Suddenly, he remembered the hostile native on Rima-tou.

"There was a man of the Tuamotus living all by himself on the island," he said. "He never came down to the settlement, he ate alone, he never seemed to talk to anyone, and he didn't want anyone coming near his hut which was located far away from the workers' *fares*. What is wrong with him, and why is he living there?"

Dr. Williams smiled benignly.

"Oh, dear me! I forgot to mention about him," he replied. "That's my leper that I've allowed to live there." He noticed the shocked expression on Maugham's face. "Knowin' you, I thought the situation would amuse you."

Maugham put down his glass, gave the dentist a cold stare. "Willie . . . I don't think I'll buy your island of Tetiaroa, even if you were willing to sell it to me for a few dollars. I'm sure if I came back to take possession, I'd find it turned into a nudist colony, or some other sort of bizarre refuge."

Dr. Williams chuckled, then shook his head.

"No danger of Tetiaroa ever bein' put on the market," he said, with finality. "That is my private island, and I intend to keep it always. I am now makin' plans, when I retire, to build a very comfortable European home on Rima-tou, and go there to live for the years left to me."[6]

"With your leper?" inquired Maugham with a wry smile.

"Even with the leper," assented Dr. Williams.

---

[6] Dr. Williams did not live to fulfill his plans for retirement. He died at Tetiaroa in June of 1937.

17. Farewell to Tahiti—and Louvaina's Death

Maugham's Tahitian interlude, as given, in part, in the preceding pages, is only a miniscule glimpse of the many, many experiences, adventures, observations, and reflections that Maugham had obtained from his visit there while researching for *The Moon and Sixpence*.

One writer had commented:

"I have often wondered why Maugham wrote much about Samoa but little about French Oceania. I believe it is because for the most part there is no fiction on Tahiti. There is no guile. In rigid, prudish Samoa, like rigid prudish most every place else, desires smoulder beneath the surface and often explode. There are no explosions of this sort on Tahiti, for no steam builds up. The escape valve is candour— Tahitians tell you everything at once. There is no suspense, so no story. Take Maugham's *The Letter*—here (in Tahiti) there would be no murder—all three, the wife, her husband and the lover, would get together over a bottle of red wine and talk about it and laugh and then someone would start beating a drum and the dancing would go on until dawn."

Maugham was partly in agreement:

"Yes, it is true that in a place where there are sexual licenses, excesses, the condoning attitude on infidelity, a tolerance of promiscuity, and an absence of sexual possessiveness, there does not exist the emotional tension that precipitates human drama, the personality conflicts, the violence of jealousies, the intrigue and self-inflicted agonies that are precipitated by the wanton conduct of an unfaithful wife or husband, who because of the ever-present code of public or community morality, is compelled to resort to clandestine assignations.

"The really significant fiction of the world today involves a husband-and-wife relationship, the problems that lovers encounter and overcome, a cuckolded man, a jilted woman, an unrequited or pretended love for the other. From sexual conflicts we have our revenge and homicidal motives.

"*The Letter* could perhaps not have had a setting of Tahiti, simply because, I must assume, it's doubtful, with so many predatory, loose Polynesian girls available, that the slain man would, in the first place, have had the inclination to even consider the heroine for an illicit affair.

"In a circumspect British colony in the tropics, sexual congress is furtive, and out of furtiveness there can be the sudden exposures and detections that can cause a man or woman, suffering the tortures of betrayal of faith and devotion and loyalty, to employ a pistol or a knife, or a vial of poison, to placate or assuage his or her outraged ego.

"Then, you must remember that Tahiti is a French possession, and the French with their *laissez-faire* and *ménage-à-trois* tolerance of sexual philanderings and indulgences don't really provide believable fictional protagonists for any human-triangle story or play, unless you want to make a comedy or farce out of a situation. You'll find interesting, complex and violent human drama in a circumspect community or way-station where the emotional safety-valve is jammed. With sufficient pressure, tempers erupt, equilibrium is lost, values are discarded, and someone ofttimes gets betrayed, maimed or killed.

"Tahiti is, or was when I was there, a very attractive setting, but not for drama. Strickland, of my *The Moon and Sixpence,* brought his pre-destined purgatory to that island with him, and the languor of this island, the Polynesian playfulness, the castrative sexuality that abounded there, could not save him from his ultimate and wretched fate. That, of course, was Gauguin's predetermined course of tragedy."

The day came, all too soon, for Maugham to go to the steamship office in Papeete and arrange for his passage back to London. He had finished his research on Paul Gauguin, and his notes were ample for the writing project. And he had made his commitment to the British War Office to go to Russia on the special intelligence mission.

"Gerald and I carefully placed the Gauguin-on-glass, that had been heavily wrapped with insulation material to guard against breakage and then crated, in the back of the car and drove down to the *quai,* where the steamer was ready to cast off. En route I stopped briefly to say goodbye to Emile Levy, slowed down past the Parc Bougainville where I had spent so many morning hours on one of its benches, waved *adieu* to Alex the manager of the Club who was calling his goodbyes from the second-story verandah, and Johnny Parè caught up with us on his bicycle to assure us he would see us off at the *quai*."

On the *quai,* where the entire population of Papeete customarily crowded to welcome or bid *au revoir* to every passenger vessel, Maugham found all of his friends and acquaintances there to wish him *bon voyage*. There was Tetuanui of Mataiea and his weeping wife, the girl Miri, whom Rupert Brooke had immortalized in his *Tiare Tahiti* poem, Ori-a-Ori and his wife, Louvaina and her deaf-mute driver Vava, all the chambermaids of the Hotel Tiare, Drollet, Willie Williams honking emotionally into a huge handkerchief, Captain Winny Brander and his brother Arthur, and many, many more friends and acquaintances.

"Gerald and I were deeply moved by those who had come down to see us off, bringing gifts of mats, baskets of fruit, shell necklaces, beautifully carved pearl shells, fine-woven hats of pandanus and rare Manihiki fibre, coconut baskets filled with unusual species of coral growths, and other examples of native handicraft.

"The women planted wet, smacking kisses on our cheeks, embraced us and wept copious tears. Louvaina was prostrated with grief at our imminent departure, and when the steamer's warning whistle blew for all passengers to be aboard, she hung on to both of us. 'No go, Mawg-ham! No go, Jaree! You stay Hotel Tiare always! Louvaina take good care of you! Nevaire min' you have money! Not necessary pay!' I had never been tended before such a wonderful farewell by people of any other land. You can be sure, I was emotionally choked up. I knew that they were genuinely sorry to see us leave.

"From the promenade deck, I looked down at all my friends, waving and calling *bon voyages* up to us, massive

Louvaina dominating the scene, tears streaming down her face, still crying: 'You come back, you hear, Mawg-ham! Jaree! You no forget Tahiti and fat Louvaina!', and trying ineffectually to capture some of the flower wreaths that we were tossing down.

"Even when the vessel was far down the lagoon-harbor, we could see our group of friends at the end of the *quai*, still waving, the distance now too great to hear their cries, and Louvaina had a *pareu* and was flapping it high above her head. Then, I saw the dummy Vava take her arm and lead her to the horse-drawn carriage.

"I couldn't know then that I would never see any of them again, even if I had returned to Tahiti. So many of them died in the 1918 influenza epidemic that swept the world, and which had not spared Tahiti. Louvaina, so Johnny wrote me in a letter, had been one of the first to die—and that news distressed me greatly. I never heard all the details of just how she was stricken."

Through a coincidence it was possible for me to tell Maugham some of the facts of Louvaina's death.

Frederick O'Brien, the author of *White Shadows in the South Seas, Mystic Isles of the South Seas* and *Atolls of the Sun*, three of the best travel books on French Oceania that exist today, even though now dated, had been a very close friend of Louvaina's during his long visit in Tahiti in 1913-14, and I had met him at his home in Sausalito, California while a young university student. O'Brien, an old man at that time, was indulgent over my secret plans to abandon a university confinement and run off to Tahiti and become a beachcomber. He subtly dissuaded me, but he did speak to me at length on Tahiti and the other romantic islands of French Oceania. And he told me of Louvaina, showing me a letter he had received telling of her death.

The letter was from a lovely Tahitian girl, Fragrance-of-the-Jasmine, and read:

"Ia ora na oe, Maru (O'Brien's Tahitian name)

"Great sorrow has come to Tahiti. The people die by thousands from a devil sickness, the *grippe*, or influenza. It came from your country as we were rejoicing for the peace in France. The *Navua* brought it, and for weeks we have died. Tati is dead. Tetuanui is dead. They cannot lay the corpses in the graves, they fall so fast. There are no people to help. The dogs and pigs have eaten them as they slept their last sleep in their gardens. Now the corpses are burning in great trenches, and drunken white sailors with scared faces burn them, and drive the dead wagons crosswise in the streets. The burning of our loved ones is affrighting, and the old people who are not dead are in terrible fear of the flames. It is like the savages of the Marquesas in olden times.

"Your dear friend Louvaina was the first to die of the *hotahota*, as some call this sickness. Louvaina had a bad cough. The man who looks after the engines of the *Navua* went to see her, and she kissed him on the cheek. Then the good doctor of Papeete who visits the ships was called to see her. Maru, could that doctor have brought the *hotahota* to Louvaina? She was dead in a little while.

"Louvaina had good fortune all her life, for, being the first one to die, she was buried as we have always buried our people. All of Tahiti that was not ill walked with her coffin. Oh, Maru, I wept for Louvaina. Vava, whom you whites call the Dummy, is dead, too. When Louvaina was taken to the cemetery, Vava drove her old chaise with her children in it; and then, Maru, he was seen again only by a Tahitian who had gone to bathe in the lagoon because the fever was burning in him. You know how Vava always took the old horse of Louvaina at sunset to swim in front of the Annexe (hotel). This man who was ill said that he saw Vava ride the horse into the sea, and straight out toward the reef. Vava signed farewell to the man with the fever. The man stayed in the lagoon to cool his body until the sun was below Moorea, and your friend, the Dummy, did not return. Maru, we loved dear Louvaina, but to Vava she was mother and God.

"It is strange, Maru, the way of things in the world. The lepers who are confined towards Arue were forgotten, and as nobody went near them, the *hotahota* passed them by.

"I cannot write more. O Maru, come back to aid us. It is a long time since those happy days when we walked in the Valley of Fautaua.

"Ia ora na i te Atua!

"NOANOA TIARE."

And there was a postscript:

"E tupu te fau, et toro te farero, e mou te taata!

"The hibiscus shall grow, the coral spread, and man shall cease!"

VI

THE SEARCH

18. Reunion in Europe

Maugham's path and mine were to cross a number of times in Europe, where I was to live for some years between our first meeting and 1962. Sometimes I visited at his villa at Cap Ferrat, other times, usually in early or late summer, at the cure-spas of Vichy, France and Bad Gastein in Austria, where he went for periodic rests and treatment. Maugham was never a well man, and encroaching old age aggravated a number of early complaints. There was a rumor that he was being injected with "youth shots" of testicular concentrates from unborn lambs. A friend of his verified that he was taking rejuvenation injections from Dr. Paul Niehans of Switzerland,[1] coupled with conventional vitamin shots from his physician, Dr. Georges Rosanoff, of Nice, France.

---

[1] Bernard Baruch convinced Maugham that he should take the Niehans Cellular Therapy, after undergoing the rejuvenation treatments himself, with remarkable results. The technique consists of ob-

Our conversations, when we did meet, were of short duration, because he was busy or not feeling too well. Some correspondence passed between us at intervals. Usually, the subject matter was of the South Pacific islands or the Far East, which, although he had written abundantly in glowing terms of these places and had travelled extensively there, appeared to hold a permanent fascination for him.

I recall that one of our most interesting meetings was in late April of 1958. I was staying at the Europa Hotel on the Piazza San Marco in Venice, and late one morning I walked to the San Marco landing to take a *vaporetto*, or small steamer, across the canal to the Chisa di San Giorgio and the Teatro Verde. Ahead of me I saw a familiar figure, walking slowly toward the Gritti Palace Hotel. The distinctive Tyrolean-type hat I would recognize anywhere. I caught up with him when he stopped to readjust his large velvet lavalière tie, and he seemed pleased to see me again. He was thinner, and seemed depressed.

"I've not been too well," he said, as if to explain his presence in Venice. "And when I feel low in metabolism and spirits this beautiful city of canals is a wonderful tonic. I've just come from the Gallerie dell'Accademia, where they have the best of the Venetian painters from the Fourteenth to the Eighteenth Century. I never tire of seeing the superb Bellinis, Carpaccios and Giorgiones.

"This morning I spent considerable time studying Veronese's *The Feast of the House of Levi,* a huge painting that covers a wall at the end of a long galleria."

---

taining *Frisch Zellen*, or fresh living cells, from unborn animals, preferably lambs or calves. The tissues obtained are made soluble in a saline solution for the "miracle serum." The efficaciousness of the treatment is to have the cells only fifteen-or-so minutes old from the time they are ground up from the unborn animal and injected into the patient.

I knew this masterpiece, a powerful work, showing Jesus presiding in the center of a long table, with St. Peter on his right, and John the Baptist on his left, and the other disciples and the host Levi and friends in their respective places.

"Well, I sat down about fifty feet away and stared at this painting for a long time. Then a curious phenomenon took place: Jesus, who was in profile, listening to what his disciple John was telling him so eagerly, seemed to slowly turn his head and look at me full face! It was a startling experience, believe me. I looked away, thinking that my strained eyesight was playing tricks with me, but when I looked back again I had the same impression. First Jesus was in profile, then, imperceptibly, in full-face. I removed the spectacles I use for distant vision, and rubbed my eyes. No change. Then I got up from the chair and moved closer. Jesus now remained in profile listening to John. I went back and sat down again, but the mysterious effect was not repeated. I cannot believe that it was an optical illusion."

He was visibly disturbed by this manifestation, and, after telling me of the incident in the Accademia, lapsed into a brooding silence as we walked along the *piazza*. I felt that it was odd that Maugham, an avowed atheist, would have been so profoundly affected.

Before leaving Venice, Maugham and I were to have a long conversation over tea concerning a visit I had made, during my European sojourn, to Hong Kong, Malaya and Java, and which concerned some of his short stories and novels.

He was especially amused over my meeting in Hong Kong with an ancient, hennaed hag, a venomous British dowager, formerly of Peking and Shanghai, who, after a number of triple martinis, began berating Maugham.

"I understand he's planning a trip out here again!" she screeched, making reptilian hissing sounds through her loose false teeth. "He thinks we're all dead and buried, we who remember! Well, I'm not, and I'm just waiting for him to show his face here in Hong Kong!

"Such humiliations he's caused so many nice people out here in the Far East and the Orient! I've been waiting for almost a half century to box his ears! Friendships and confidences were given to him so freely. He practically ruined the lives of Poor P—— and T—— C——, by calling them Walter and Kitty Fane in his *The Painted Veil*. P——, it's true, did some foolish and impetuous things out here, and perhaps was not always true to T——. But *who* was a paragon of virtue out here? The damned climate, the boredom, the drinking. It became the moral climate, I suppose. I'm broadminded, and I don't believe in hypocrisy, never have! I think a person has the human right to go to bed with someone they like without being insulted and held up for censure to society by such hack-writers as that dreary, atrocious Willie Maugham!

"So when you see that Maugham person again, you tell him that I'm waiting for him, waiting to tell him to his face just what I think about him!"

Maugham chuckled for a long time.

"Yes, I remember her, now that you tell me her name. A horrible person really, the prime gossip of the Orient. She must be quite a dreadful harridan now. She was fat, common and sheep-faced when I met her. I felt sorry for her husband, who was a decent chap. She shoved him into an early grave, so I understand. I used her in one of my stories, but I don't recall which one now."

In Singapore I had met a planter, whose father had entertained Maugham in Malaya, in one of the Federated States.

"I'm afraid he'll get a very chilly reception if he comes out here again," he informed me. "There are still a lot of old residents and planters alive out here who have never for-gotten or forgiven Maugham. A relative of my father's fig-ured in his *The Letter*. It was an unfortunate tragedy. But she was not the deadly bitch of Maugham's story and play. He treated her brutally, giving her no opportunity to defend herself.

"If Maugham had not written and published that story, the whole thing would have been forgotten. It almost had out here, when the damned story appeared in print. My father's cousin, the 'Leslie Crosbie' of the story, had only just recovered from the horrible ordeal, when news of the publication of *The Letter* in England was received out here. It was too much for her; she couldn't take anymore. She went to live in Italy, in Florence, I believe, and she died of alcoholism in a sanitarium in her early forties.

"Maugham exaggerated the facts, stretched them all out of proportion. He portrayed her as a cold-blooded, conniving strumpet, a pathological adulteress. In reality she was a high-ly sensitive and, except for one mistake, very circumspect woman. She was in her early thirties, married to a dour, un-sentimental man, much older than herself, and isolated on a large rubber plantation. There was little or no diversion for her, except a dance now and then at someone's bungalow. In England she had been very popular. Malaya was a shat-tering letdown for her.

"Her husband, a selfish, self-centered bastard, made no effort to help her adjust herself to the life out here. He was a fat, lethargic bore, who drank too much, laughed too bois-terously, talked too much nonsense, and usually staggered off to bed right after dinner to snore his fool head off. I don't see why she ever married him, nor could my father under-stand it. He had tried to prevent the marriage. It's difficult to explain some husband-wife situations, really.

"It's understandable that she was fed up to the teeth by the time this chap came out to Malaya, a young civil servant in the administration. He was a ladies man, and knew how to compliment and make a woman feel that romance was not entirely dead and buried in this hot dreary corner of the world. They were thrown together a lot. They had some common interests, literature, art, music. He was a good dancer, and he had a fine singing voice, and he was called upon to perform at many parties. She admired him, and after a while I'm sure she became infatuated with him. Anyway, they became lovers.

"I don't know how it would have ended, if she hadn't found out that he was bedding down on the side with a young Chinese girl, daughter of a Cantonese trader. There had been rumors, her friends had gossiped over his infatuation for the oriental girl, but she just couldn't believe it.

"One night, when her husband was in Singapore, he came out to the house drunk. She asked him to tell her the truth about the Chinese mistress. He hedged, became angry, told her it was none of her business, that she shouldn't pay any attention to gossip. She kept at him, tearfully, I suppose. He finally lost his temper and admitted that he was having relations with the Chinese girl. She quietly told him that if that was the case, they had best not see each other again. But he wouldn't leave it at that. He was very drunk and in a nasty mood. He called her some names, and I think she called him some names in retaliation. He inferred that she was lower in his estimation than the Chinese girl. And he said he enjoyed sex with the oriental more than he did with her. How the revolver came into play, is not clear. Anyway, it did go off, and he was fatally wounded. There was a trial, of course, and Maugham was here while it was on. She was cleared. Self defense.

"As I say, the whole thing would have died down, nothing would have come of it, if Maugham hadn't turned it into a distorted story of vengeance and murder. How true it is, quoting from my Sixth Form Latin: *Hinc quam sic calamus soevior ense patet*—'The Pen is worse than the sword'."

Maugham, who had listened indulgently, gave a sarcastic smirk.

"I'll admit that I've used a lot of real people in my stories, but, then, as I've always maintained, people are a writer's business. However, you mustn't overlook the fact that a lot of people will write themselves into a story, if they happen to be of the locale and have experienced an emotion similar to a character in the story. And it's difficult to convince them that they aren't the living, breathing human you've so 'cruelly exposed' in your short story, novel or play.

"I've been threatened many times with suits of libel and slander by persons who happened to have the same names as the characters in my stories. Every well-known writer must expect this.

"Finally, the only thing I could do was to state very clearly in prefaces to my volumes that all my characters' names were taken from the obituary sections of daily newspapers, implying, of course, that I would be ridiculous to libel a complete stranger."

But it is obvious that Maugham took bold liberties with the names of the characters in his stories. In his *Cakes and Ale* he named the strumpet-heroine Rosie Gann, and in Whitstable, where he lived as a boy in his uncle's vicarage, there was a respectable family by the name of Gann. A scoundrel in the same novel was called Lord George Kemp, and there was a prominent family in Whitstable by this name. Originally, in *The Painted Veil*, the bacteriologist and his wife were named Walter and Kitty Lane, but he was

295

threatened with a libel suit, when it was learned that there was an actual couple in China by this name. Maugham compromised by renaming them Walter and Kitty *Fane.* These are only a few instances of Maugham's penchant for using real names of people in his stories.

But, if he utilized actual persons in his stories, he also was very free about injecting himself. He was, of course, the Phillip Carey of *Of Human Bondage,* and instead of afflicting him with a stammer, he gave him a club-foot. In *Cakes and Ale,* he was the narrator; in *The Narrow Corner,* Maugham becomes the self-sufficient, and intolerant Dr. Saunders, who "took an interest in his fellows that was not quite scientific and not quite human . . . He regarded them dispassionately and it gave him just the same amusement to unravel the intricacies of the individual as a mathematician might find in the solution of a problem . . . It was with a little thrill that he sought to pierce into a man's consciousness . . . but the thrill was merely one of curiosity. His sensibility was unaffected. He felt neither sorrow nor pity . . ."; he became the narrator of *The Moon and Sixpence,* and was also not too unlike the strange artist Charles Strickland, whose philosophies, about women in particular, could have been spoken by Maugham himself: "A woman can forgive a man for the harm he does her, but she can never forgive him for the sacrifices he makes on her account. . . . Because women can do nothing except love, they've given it a ridiculous importance . . . When a woman loves you she's not satisfied until she possesses your soul. Because she's weak, she has a rage for domination, and nothing less will satisfy her. She has a small mind, and she resents the abstract which she is unable to grasp . . . The soul of man wanders through the uttermost regions of the universe, and she seeks to imprison it in the circle of her account-book

. . ."; Larry Darrell, of *The Razor's Edge,* could easily have been Maugham in his early twenties, forming his beliefs and curiosities about life, religion, spirituality, philosophy, the Universe, and man and morality, which parallel Maugham's jottings in his fifty years of reflections in *The Writer's Note-book;* and he was the hero-in-espionage in his collection of short-stories of World War One intelligence activities, *Ashenden.*

When I bade goodbye to Maugham in Venice in the Spring of 1958, I was forming plans to visit Samoa and Tahiti, by way of Bangkok, Singapore and Australia, em-barking in Genoa, Italy on a Norwegian passenger-freighter. I did not reach Samoa, however, until late in 1959. And here I found several cards and letters from Maugham with postmarks of Japan and Hong Kong. He had suddenly de-cided in 1959 to visit the Orient again for, as he put it, "the last time." At the time neither of us could anticipate the great adventure in literary discovery that awaited me.

19. Miss Sadie Thompson—and Her Lover

I found the steamy tropical waterfront of Pago Pago little changed since the time Maugham, Miss Thompson, and the missionaries were thrown together in the dilapidated rooming house on the edge of Tutuila's only port. America's island-poorhouse had fallen into sad decadence when the U.S. Naval Administration relinquished its control to the Department of Interior. The former spic-and-span atmosphere of Navy efficiency, neatness and cleanliness had vanished long ago; the coconut plantations had degenerated under invasions of rhinoceros-beetles and the disinclination of the indolent Samoans to remedy the situation; the once tidy native villages were now merely wretched settlements of mouldering, dry-rot thatch and sugar-cane leaf roofs; white office workers, school teachers, technicians, and the medical staff at the hospital were discontented, demoralized, indulging in malicious gossip, petty intrigues, sexual derelictions, and drinking heavily. American Samoa had a low priority for appropriations from the Department of Interior.[1]

But if the island generally had run to seed, the old hotel had somehow benefited. A successful German trader had bought the hotel, remodelled the second-floor for his living-quarters, converting the ground-floor to a modern general store. New lumber and paint had accomplished miracles. There was little vestige left of the run-down place where Maugham and his secretary-companion, Gerald Haxton, had been marooned next to the chamber of the ex-harlot of Honolulu, Miss Thompson, while "outside, the pitiless rain fell, fell steadily, with a fierce malignity that was all too human."

I walked down from the Rainmaker Hotel in Utulei to the former Saddie Thompson Hotel, and stood outside staring up to the second floor, where the present German owner, Max Halleck, then lived with his Samoan wife. It was difficult to conceive now, with the refurbishing, that this was the hotel where Maugham and Sadie had been quartered, and where she had stormed up to the missionary, Reverend Davidson, to yell: "You low-down skunk, what have you been saying about me to the Governor? . . . You poor low-life bastard!" I tried to guess which room she had occupied on the front, where "with her sins she had put aside all personal vanity, and . . . slopped about her room, unkempt and dishevelled, in her tawdry dressing-gown." And I wondered where she had delivered her last violent outburst: "You men! You filthy, dirty pigs! You're all the same, all of you. Pigs! Pigs!"

I heard the rustle of bare feet in the roadway, and when I turned I saw a slender, handsome Samoan man, of regal

---

[1] Congress voted funds to rehabilitate American Samoa a few years ago, because of adverse publicity on conditions there, and Samoa is now destined to become the model island-paradise of the Pacific.

bearing, approaching. He was briefly attired in a *lava-lava* sarong and a sport shirt. He smiled and extended his hand, and gave me the Samoan greeting of "Talofa'lii!" Then he glanced up at the second-floor of the structure.

"You come down see where Sadie live, yes?" he asked.

I nodded.

He pointed to the center section of the upper living-quarters. "Dat is where I raise hell wit' Sadie, drink, sing, play ukulele, play gram'phone. But one mornin' it all finish. Chief ob Police Jack an' Mike Laulu come get me an' t'row me in jail."

I fell back a step. "You knew the *real* Sadie Thompson?" I exclaimed.

He grinned widely. "Sure t'ing. I her number-one boy-friend." And he introduced himself: "I Iosefo Suafo'a, High Chief ob Amanave Village. I vairee old now, but when Sadie here I very young an' strong feller. She vairee crazee 'bout me."

"And you remember the British writer, Somerset Maugham and his friend who were here at the same time as Sadie Thompson?"

"I no savvy his name, but I know he make blentay trouble for Sadie. We keep him 'wake all night, an' he swear like hell an' pound on wall wit' fist. Oh, he vairee damn sore man! But me an' Sadie jes' laugh an' keep on make lub. Sadie an' me, we sure hav lots fun!"

Here was a find, indeed!

"Why don't we go to a bar and have a beer or two?" I suggested, taking him by the arm.

"No can do now," he said gently. "Mus' catch bus back to Amanave. But you come out my village anyday, an' I tell you ebryt'ing 'bout Sadie an' me."

Which gave me time to do some checking on the veracity of Iosefo's statements.

I called upon Benjamin Franklin Kneubuhl,[2] 73, the oldest American merchant and shipping agent for the Oceanic and Matson Lines, who lived with his Samoan wife above his prosperous store. He was white-haired, but still rugged and healthy. He had come to American Samoa as a Chief Petty Officer in the Navy, and remained, after mustering out, to make a fortune in trading and shipping. I liked him instantly. He was a no-nonsense individual, and what he had to say you could take as the gospel truth.

"Iosefo, or Joseph, isn't giving you a line," he said brusquely. "He *was* Sadie's lover. Not many know that. He doesn't talk about it, simply because he's afraid that some clerk over in the Court House might dig up the fact that he never paid the fine imposed upon him for being brought to trial for fornication and cohabitation with Sadie. That he saw you outside the old Saddie Thompson Hotel, and had a few beers under his *lava-lava,* might account for his speaking to you."

"Do you recall the woman whom Maugham wrote about in *Rain?*" I asked hopefully.

"Hell, yes, I ought to. I was shipping agent for the old Oceanic Line. I don't remember the year now, because all the records have been destroyed, but I do know that Sadie Thompson and Maugham came down on the old *Sonoma* from Honolulu, together with the missionaries, just like he told it in the story."

"You call her 'Sadie Thompson.' Don't you remember her real name?"

Ben gave me a sharp look, scratched his chin thoughtfully. "As far as I can recollect that *was* her name."

"Maugham would never have dared to use her real name," I said. "Particularly because of the unflattering manner in which he presented her."

---

[2] He died in December of 1964.

Ben pondered hard, stared out the window upon the green *malae,* or grassy common, of Pago Pago.

"No . . . No, I suppose not. Still, I'd almost swear that was her name. However, maybe it's because I've read the story. It's so long ago, and, besides, as I say, the passenger manifests of the *Sonoma* were burned years ago."

Ben's still pretty Samoan wife, Lena, spoke up quietly from a corner of the verandah living-room. "It seems to me, also, that she called herself Miss Thompson." And she added: "The missionaries, I remember, were Mormons, from America."

"And the hell they gave poor Sadie!" chuckled Ben. He winked at me. "With some justification, of course."

"And you remember Maugham being here at the same time?"

"Oh, yes, I met him. A rather uppity Britisher, who was annoyed at being detained because of the storm and a small-pox scare. He was on his way to Apia, Western Samoa. The fellow with him, a sort of travelling companion, did a lot of drinking while they were holed up in Bella Bartley's boarding house in Fagatoga."

"How did Maugham's description of Sadie compare with the original?" I asked.

"I'd say, very true to life," replied Ben. "Sadie—I'll call her that because I don't know any other name to call her by —was a flashy-looking blonde of about 25 or 26. She told me, when she came into the office, that she was a laundress from Honolulu, down here for a little vacation. I'd say she was about five foot six, with a fashionable hair-do coming down to her shoulders, blue eyes, with shapely hips and big bosoms. When she took a walk around the Station in her big white picture hat, she wriggled her backside and gave the glad-eye to just about every husky, goodlooking Samoan she passed. I knew it would only be a matter of time before the

Naval Administration would lower the boom on her. She was causing too much commotion and talk. And the missionaries were after her scalp.

"About her drinking, I got to admit that she could sure hold her booze. And, believe me, she sure did raise the Old Nick night and day. She was one helluva disturber of the peace! From the few words I had with her, I got the idea that she was sick and tired of white folk, and now just wanted to live with the Samoans. There was never any positive proof just how she had earned her money to come down to Pago Pago, and I do know that Governor Jack Poyer, the Navy Commander running the island, wired up to Honolulu to find out if she had a police record of prostitution—but there was nothing.

"She liked music all the time. You could hear her gramophone blasting out any time you walked past Bella's place. She could play the ukulele and sing a few Hawaiian songs. The young Samoan Navy Guards started going up to her room at night-time. I think that's how she met Joe. In the stage-play and the different movies of *Rain,* they had Sadie's lover a white G.I., but it was really Joe. Maugham was fit to be tied about Sadie being next to him in Bella's. He yelled his head off to Bella about the bedlam, but it didn't do him any good. Sadie just kept right on with her love-making with Joe and cranking up the gramophone."

It wasn't difficult to imagine Maugham next door to Sadie, gnashing his teeth and planning his revenge. And he was not to forget the cursed gramophone that was driving him out of his mind: "They heard Davidson's voice, and then the noise of something heavy falling. The music stopped. He had hurled the gramophone on the floor."

Sadie, to escape the condemning, soul-scorching glares of the missionaries, and to spend more time with Joe, took all of her meals in her room, which gave Maugham the occasion to write: "When the trader was gone MacPhail said: 'I shouldn't think she'd find it exactly cheerful having her meals in her room.' "

Ben laughed heartily when I mentioned this to him.

"Oh, I rather think Sadie thoroughly enjoyed eating with Joe in the privacy of her room. Bella broiled wonderful steaks, and there were always desserts of pies and cakes, which Joe particularly went for. And, because it was hot and sticky, Sadie only wore a thin wrapper, and Bella told me that sometimes she didn't wear anything at all, strutting around in front of Joe naked as a jay-bird. She was sure nuts about Samoan fellers. She claimed they were the only men who had ever sexually satisfied her."

Only once in the story did Maugham intimate that Sadie was fornicating with a Samoan: "Don't you think we ought to make Mr. Horn turn her out of here?" asked Mrs. Davidson. "We can't allow her to insult us." "There doesn't seem to be any place for her to go," said MacPhail. "She can live with one of the natives," sneered Mrs. Davidson.

"One night, late, Sadie did a foolish thing," continued Ben. "She was pickled to the gills and talked Joe into going swimming naked with her off the Governor's motor-boat pier. A young Naval lieutenant saw them splashing around in the bay, and reported it to the executive officer the next morning. He issued a memo to the Governor. That was about *it* for Sadie!

"And if that wasn't enough, Sadie hauled Joe over to the Courthouse to try and get a marriage license from Judge Alexander Stronach, a staunch southerner from Florida. Naturally, he turned them down flat, telling her that she'd have to get the application approved by Governor Poyer.

"No, Sadie wasn't deported just because she was drinking

and disturbing the peace. She was kicked off the island because she wanted to associate with the Samoans and marry one of them. Today, I suppose she'd be considered a liberal-minded young lady, with idealistic racial views. But, you must remember that the Navy men here were all mostly from the south, and they looked down upon her as a cheap floosie, a whore, for going to bed with a brown-skinned island man."

Ben settled back in his rattan-chair and smiled reflectively.

"Wouldn't it be interesting to know what happened to Sadie?" he mused. "Where she went, if she's still alive, and how she wound up." He gave me a wry grimace. "She could be a white-haired grandmother, you know." Then he shook his head positively. "No, gals like Sadie never become white-haired grandmothers!"

"Oh, those girls sometimes change for the better," said his wife Lena.

"Possible, not probable," sighed Ben.

I drove in a taxi out to Amanave Village, 18 miles from Pago Pago in the western district of Tutuila. Iosefo Suafo'a, or Joseph, received me in his chief's *fale,* or meeting-house.

When I had settled myself cross-legged on a mat, with my back against a chief's post of the conical-shaped long-house, partaken of a coconut half-shell of the peppery *kava* liquid in the traditional Samoan ritual of greeting, and waited until the Chief evaluated the case of canned tuna I had brought him, I cleared my throat and spoke.

"Chief, would you mind telling me about your remembrances of the American girl known as Sadie Thompson?"

He put his weight against his chief's post, and smiled reflectively.

"Sure t'ing. I damned happy tell you 'bout Sadie Thompson!"

"Don't you remember her real name?"

He scratched his head. "Dat her name. She call herself Sadie . . . Sadie Thompson." He frowned at me. "I vairee sure."

I didn't feel that I should argue this point.

He continued:

"I on'y twenty-four when I meet dat blonde, hot lallapalooza from Honolulu. I jes' orderly boy in Samoan U.S. Navy Guard, runnin' errands for officers between offices an' wireless station. One day lieutenant tell me take young lady from Honolulu, who come down on *Sonoma,* for look-see 'round Station. *Oka-Oka!* Gee Whiz! when I catch gander ob her I know she number-one *fafine* (girl).

"On walk-around she make sweet-talk me. Feel my muscle an' say she bet I vairee strong feller. She tell me dat she t'ink young ensigns an' lieutenants jes' cake-eaters. She tell me come up her room at Bella's, have supper, play gramophone, an' play her uke an' sing Samoan songs to her. After dat I up dere ebry night.

"Sadie tell me, 'Joe, you more bettah getta hell outa *Fita-Fita* Guard an' we take up-boat to Honolulu an' get married.' I say: 'I no got *tupe* (money) Sadie-baby.' She tell me: 'Neber min', Joe honey, no mattuh, I got blentay mazuma. We go over Court-house an' get marriage license.' I say: 'I t'ink more bettah you take it easy, Sadie. I t'ink I catch blentay hell from Navy you do dat.' 'Crap on dem!' Sadie yell. 'We American citizens, dey gotta treat us okay!' But I no t'ink so.

"So I keep goin' up Sadie's room at Bella's ebry night, wind up gramophone, sing, dance, laugh, eat blentay goo' t'ings Bella cook. But all time I no feel good. I figger, any time now I t'ink you catch blentay hell, Iosefo Suafo'a! Officers ride me all a time, Marine sergeant keep tellin' me:

307

'Wha' ta hella-mattuh-you, Joe, you look thin, all-time sleepy?' I sure tired a'right, I neber get 'nough sleep. Dat *fafine* after me all time. *A'ue!* My achin' back! Sometimes I mus' go back barracks get rest-up!"

Joe very shortly was to get his "rest-up"—*permanently!*

The missionaries, the naval officers, the white traders of Pago Pago had all complained to Governor Poyer about Sadie and Joe.

One morning, at six a.m., there was a loud pounding on Sadie's door. Outside Bella Bartley was arguing with two Samoan men.

Sadie reared up in bed. "What the hell is going on out there, Bella?" she demanded.

"It's Chief of Police Jack Hunkin Mailo and Mike Laulu is with him. They're looking for Joe, honey."

"Bushwah! Unless they have a search-warrant tell them to get to hell outa here! I know my constitutional rights!"

Chief of Police Mailo spoke patiently through the closed door. "I'm only doing my duty, Miss. I have an order from the Captain of the Yard to find out if Joe's with you."

"He's here—and so what?"

"Then he must come along with us. That's an order."

"You can all go to hell!"

Joe eased himself out of the rumpled bed, affixed his *lava-lava* more securely. "More bettah I go 'long with Jack and Mike, Sadie-baby," he sighed. "I in Navy, sign articles, mus' obey. If I don't, den I t'ink I catch blentay hell."

Joe descended the stairway with the two native police-men, and above, in a torn dressing-gown, Sadie railed abuse down upon the Chief of Police and his assistant. "You've gotta nerve bothering us! I'll write to President Woodrow Wilson about this!"

Joe was brought before the High Court of American Samoa.

Judge Stronach asked him sternly: "Don't you know it's wrong to go with this *palagi fafine* (white woman), Iosefo Suafo'a, to be with her almost every night in her room, like man and wife?"

Joe hung his head sheepishly.

Sadie leapt to her feet, arms flaying the air. "It's none of your damned business that Joe and me keep company! I'm taking Joe back to Honolulu with me—and we're going to be married!"

Judge Stronach rapped his gavel angrily. "That'll be quite enough, young lady! One more disturbance from you, and you'll be held in contempt of court! I can tell you right now that you'll be going back to Honolulu—*but not with Joe!* He's in the Navy, and you have no right to encourage this Samoan boy in such a thing. So I'm officially notifying you that the Governor has approved an order to deport you to Honolulu on the *Ventura*."

Stunned into silence, Sadie sat down.

Judge Stronach then shook a warning forefinger at Joe. "From now on, Iosefo Suafo'a, you stay away from this *palagi* woman, if you know what's good for you!" And he added crisply: "The Court finds you guilty of fornication and co-habitation, as charged—and fines you $100."

But to this day, Joe has never paid that fine. It would be interesting to know how the High Court of American Samoa balanced their books on that outstanding account!

Joe was confined to his barracks until after the *Ventura* had sailed for Honolulu. Three days before the arrival of this passenger-vessel, Joe received a damp, crumpled note slipped to him by a Samoan guard. It was from Sadie: "Joe, honey, I'm really being sent away on the *Ventura*. When you're ready to come up to Honolulu, I'll pay your fare. Please hurry up and quit the Navy. This is where you can reach me." It was an address in Honolulu.

Sadie wrote Joe four letters from Honolulu, imploring him to get his release from the Navy Guard of Samoa and join her. "I've got plenty of money," she assured him.

The U.S. Navy Captain of the Yard in Pago Pago sat Joe down and had a serious talk with him. He pointed out to Joe that he had eight years' service behind him in striking for the 30-year pensioned retirement. Now, did Joe want to throw that eight years out the window for a blonde whore? Joe wrote Sadie of his decision to remain in the Navy.

"I neber hear from Sadie after dat," sighed Joe.

But on September 30, 1931, Joe was transferred, as a Seaman 1st Class, aboard the deep-sea Navy tug-boat *U.S.S. Ontario,* to be stationed temporarily for overhaul in Pearl Harbor. And on his first shore-leave, Joe rushed to the address that Sadie had given him. He rang the bell at the small hotel, waited a long time, and then an unpleasant, gaunt woman answered the door. "She moved away a long time ago!" she snapped. "No, no, she didn't leave any forwarding address! Her kind never do!"

"So dat was *uma-lava* (finish) for Sadie and me," said Joe, a little mournfully.

I wondered if Joe had read the Maugham short story, *Miss Thompson,* or seen any of the filmed versions.

"*Lei ai!* No! why I mus' read story, or see moon pitch to savvy 'bout dat blonde tomato. Who savvy Sadie better'n me, huh?"

There was a long, brooding silence, and then Joe's shoulders, resting against the High Chief's post, hunched up and then settled down, accompanied by a loud belly-deep groan.

"Damn-hell! I really like know what happen dat Sadie!"
He gave me a quizzical glance. "What you t'ink happen if I
go up Honolulu an' marry Sadie when she tell me?"

It is difficult to conjecture just how Joe would have fared
if he had joined her in Honolulu. One thing is quite certain: he would not now hold his *matai,* or chiefly title, as
High Chief Iosefo Suafo'a of Amanave Village in American
Samoa, with its huge valley, a veritable cornucopia, to feed
him, his family, and his villagers forever. Nor would he be
receiving his Navy pension of $149 each month, or hold in
excellent credit rating his ten thousand dollar life insurance
with the United States Government. Joe today, for a Samoan,
is a man of considerable means.

And, as an added bonus, he does have his titillative memories of one of the most famous blonde prostitutes of literary
history.

20. Ethel
of The Pool—and a Discovery

One morning, in Pago Pago, I met Ben Kneubuhl on his way to the dock to supervise the unloading of a Matson freighter.

"As long as you're here, why don't you drop over to Apia and have a talk with the woman who was the girl in Maugham's *The Pool*," he suggested. "She's still living there, must be over sixty if she's a day, but still a very fine looking *fafine*. She might be able to tell you the year that Maugham was here in Samoa—and a *few other things* besides."

So when the Union Lines *Tofua* called at Pago Pago on its way to Apia, I boarded the passenger-vessel for the overnight voyage.

In response to a note I sent "Ethel," she invited me to tea. And it was with some apprehension that I walked down the seaside road for a first meeting with one of Maugham's perhaps most fictionally maligned, real-life heroines.

She received me in the high-vaulted reception-room that afforded a superb view of the harbor of Apia, very blue under the sun-filled, cloudless sky.

There were a few moments of strained silence, perhaps more on my part, after our greeting, in which all that could be heard was the distant diapason of the southern ocean across the barrier reefs. We both thoughtfully watched a cargo-boat moving in at slow speed from the sea, approaching with caution the narrow coral-bound channel; in the intervening shaded roadway the Samoans passed in graceful, contented indolence.

I knew that she understood that I had not come solely to sip Jasmine tea with a beautiful old lady of Apia.

Then she turned her head and smiled at me, a wonderful radiant warm smile. I was instantly at ease. And in that brief interlude every detail of *The Pool* passed with precise continuity through my mind.

Maugham in no instance had exaggerated her former loveliness, because even now, in her early sixties, she was a stunning part-Samoan woman, a little heavier in figure perhaps, but her classically cut features still retained much of the striking beauty of her girlhood. Her hair, now grey, was carefully arranged. The dress that clung tightly to her youthful figure could only have been designed by a Parisian couturière, and the subtle fragrance of perfume was an expensive blend.

It was obvious that she had groomed herself to meet someone who remembered, and expected to see something of, the ravishing physical qualities that Maugham had so admiringly described. It was her eyes that were remarkable: they were enormous, of an extraordinary deep-brown color, rather mysterious, but with a calm regard of people and circumstance, and, to disconcert, an occasional flirtatious twinkle in their depth, as if still assured of her redundant femininity.

With the inherent friendliness of the Samoan, she informed me that her first name was M——e, which was how I should address her.

We chatted about Pago Pago and Apia gossip for ten minutes or so, and my uneasiness gradually returned. We were both jockeying for the proper equilibrium, so as not to be thrown off balance, regardless of the reason why we had met for tea. Now and again I saw a wary expression in her eyes, and then she would jiggle her slippered foot with impatience, as if with growing irritation that I was so stupid that I imagined she didn't know why I was sitting across from her, rather than sightseeing or on a fishing excursion far out to sea.

It was, therefore, with some relief that I saw a Samoan maid come in the archway to speak with her, and M——e arose and walked across to converse in private. As she moved, quickly, elegantly, I saw that her step was still youthfully paced, and I recalled Maugham's description: "Ethel was lovely as she went about the little house, lithe and graceful like some young animal of the woods, and she was gay."

She came back in a few minutes and sat down.

"Yes, it was nice of you to bring me an *alofa* from old Ben Kneubuhl over in Pago," she said in her low, cultured voice. "In an involved way we are *iaga* (related), on his wife Lena's side. She is a Pritchard, descendant of a long-ago British consul of Tahiti and Fiji, who also spent some time here in Apia."

We were still fencing, and I suddenly decided that complete candour would be the most appropriate strategy for explaining the true reason for my visit.

"I wonder if you remember the year that the British author Somerset Maugham visited Apia?" I asked.

She replaced her cup in its saucer, and it rattled slightly, the only sign of a controlled tremor of emotion. Her eyes clouded for an instant, a flush came to the surface of her

olive complexion, and the sensual Polynesian mouth tightened. Then she settled back in her chair and stared at me
coolly, as if provoked at the advantage I had so brusquely
taken; a cynical smile curled her lips.

She expelled her breath slowly, before she spoke.

"Well, now it's out," she said flatly. "I didn't think you
came to see me just to bring a greeting from Old Ben. He's
really such an old gossip!"

Her fingers toyed with the emerald necklace at her throat.
She averted her head and stared out to sea again, and I saw a
tiny vein in the side of her well-formed neck throbbing faintly.

I felt ashamed now that I had come to disturb her usual
complacency, to draw so abruptly the sutures from a wound
not yet healed.

She still didn't look at me when she said suddenly:

"No, I'm afraid I don't remember the year that Mr.
Maugham was here in Apia. It must have been close to
Christmas, because I had just returned from England. He
stayed at the Central Hotel with a rather handsome travel-
ling-companion—and he was friendly with my first husband.
They met often for drinks at the Central Bar or the British
Club. They talked a lot, about England, I suppose, because
my husband was homesick for London."

Then she lapsed into an icy silence, her eyes narrowed
and unpleasant, the lips petulantly pouted.

I waited.

She inhaled tremulously, turned and faced me.

"There's no point in playing this cat-and-mouse game. And
there's no sense denying that I am the 'Ethel' of this writer's
The Pool, because it's true. I can't stand coyness, least of all
in myself. Everyone of my age here in Apia knows that it
could only be me. And you've made it your mission to know
it, too."

I knew that was all she had to say.

She made no offer to pour more tea, although my cup was empty; an iridescent butterfly from the garden hovered over the plate of tiny sandwiches and cream cookies; the sullen echo of the faraway surf filled the room.

M—e smoothed out the wrinkles of the gown along her trim thighs, then darted a meaningful glance at her diamond-encrusted wrist-watch.

"Gracious, how time flies! I have so many things to do. I must send a girl down to Burns-Philip to shop. I hope you will forgive me . . ."

I knew I was being sent on my way.

On the verandah, she took my hand impulsively, but her smile was too formally gracious to be genuine.

"It was nice of you to come to tea," she murmured. "And when you next see Mr. Maugham, please do thank him for me, for at least some of the complimentary things he wrote about me, my prettiness at that time, for one thing. As for the rest of the story, it's outrageously distorted, that you must believe."

She walked at my side part of the short distance to the steps.

"Well, now that you've met and talked with me, do you really think that I ever could have been the horrible bitch of *The Pool?*"

Then, without waiting for an answer, she was gone.

As I strolled back to Aggie's Hotel along the waterfront roadway, I could picture Maugham proceeding along this same route in his early morning and sunset walks, and how boldly he had usurped and utilized the long-ago, real-life characters of this somnolent South Seas port, most of them dead and buried now and forgotten.

Still, there might be one or two old-timers left, who, if

Maugham dared to make a revisit, would totter up to him, shake a bony fist in his face, and quaver: "You scribbling, meddling bastard! I've kept alive all these years just to punch your God-damned interfering nose!"

And I could imagine Maugham, without a blink of an eye or losing his poise, remarking casually:

"Oh, yes, if it isn't old G——r. I wrote you into *The Pool*, didn't I?"

And so it *would be,* a living, breathing, wrathful prototype out of the story.

Maugham gave punctilious attention in patterning his fictional characters after the genuine human article—that has been too well established already. He made no attempt to camouflage the settings or the authentic activities of his vulnerable victims.

How much was fact and fiction of *The Pool?*

I am inclined to think that this particular story was *all too true.*

I was to spend a considerable number of months more in the Samoan islands, both American and Western, and part of the time I researched in old files to see if I could find out *Sadie's* real name, or to establish the exact date that Maugham and she had arrived in Pago Pago.

I finally wrote an airmail letter to Maugham, who had returned in 1960 from the Orient, requesting that he consult his files to see if he had somewhere written down Sadie's real name, or if he had any confirming data, a bill, an old passport, a letter, a brief notation, on the month and year he had arrived in Samoa.

He replied promptly, from Grand Hotel de l'Europe, in Bad Gastein, Austria, where he had gone again for a rest-cure from the arduous Far East trip, under date of June 8, 1960:

"I was pleased and interested to get a letter from you from Pago Pago. I am afraid I cannot remember what month I was there in 1919—after all, that is a hell of a long time ago. I forget how long I stayed, I only stayed long enough to take the inter-island boat. I spent some months in Tahiti and the neighboring islands.

"I am sure that Sadie Thompson was not the real name of my heroine. I would never have been so foolish as to risk such a thing. She might easily have started an action against me and claimed half a million dollars in damages. I have no idea what happened to my own Sadie Thompson."

I decided that there was only one way to find out Sadie's real name, and the exact time she and Maugham had arrived in Pago Pago. I felt it was important for more than just mere curiosity: it would definitely establish if Governor Poyer was the one who had deported Sadie, and if Judge Stronach was the judge on the High Court of American Samoa. Literary adventuring has always intrigued me. So I continued on to Honolulu, where I was certain I'd find some lead on Sadie.

I consulted the newspaper files, but there was little on Maugham, save a few short items in reference to his literary works or his birthdays. I phoned the British Consul, hoping that he might have something in his files, albeit years back, on Maugham's transit through Honolulu. Maugham was famous at the time he came to the Pacific, and I felt they would surely have had a tea for him at the Consulate or at some home in Honolulu. Nothing.

I contacted the office of the U.S. Immigration and Naturalization Service in Honolulu, requesting a copy of passenger manifests for the year of 1916, which I felt was the year Maugham had gone to Samoa. I was stiffly advised that all records had been sent to San Francisco for micro-filming. When I wrote there, a terse reply came back, notifying me that the records of the Immigration and Naturalization Service are by law and regulation confidential, and that they could not comply with my request.

I wrote to the Matson Navigation Company, the line that absorbed the Oceanic interests, asking if they had any information on Maugham's passage on the *Sonoma*. They couldn't help me. And they had put out many feelers in San Francisco in a sincere effort to assist me.

I communicated with many old residents, hoping they'd remember when Maugham had passed through Honolulu. They knew that he had been here, but couldn't possibly remember the year.

The inconceivable and the monstrous!

Then I had the sense to phone the State Archives of Hawaii, to ascertain what newspapers were published in Honolulu in 1916, that might have run passenger-lists of embarking and disembarking sea voyagers. I was told that the *Commercial Advertiser* had always run the most complete shipping news. And the bound copies were available at the Public Library.

So I went to work, page by page, scanning for any item pertaining to Maugham, a literary tea, a reception at a socialite's Diamond Head home, an interview, anything that might give me a lead.

Hour by hour I turned the yellowed, crumbling pages . . . January . . . February . . . March . . . April . . . on and on, until I began suffering with double-vision from the poor type reproduction, the nerves and muscles in the back of my neck tightening painfully.

May . . . June . . . July . . . August . . . Hell, I thought, what a fruitless search! And was it so important?

I slept a night over it, and then went back with renewed determination September . . . October . . . November . . .

Then I had my first clue! There were accounts of the November raids on the Iwilei red-light district of Honolulu. Maugham had mentioned that he had been in Honolulu when these raids had started. I now turned the pages more slowly.

Then, suddenly, it leapt out at me!

Arrivals from Los Angeles and San Francisco, aboard the *S.S. Great Northern,* among many passengers: *Somerset Maugham and F.G. Haxton!,* November 14, 1916!

Slowly, page by page, poring long over every printed word, I proceeded. And at last I found what I was looking for:

The departure of the Oceanic Steamship Company's *Sonoma,* Monday, December 4, 1916, at 7 p.m. for Australia, via Pago Pago.

And when I saw the list of passengers embarking in Honolulu, I gave a loud exclamation that elicited a reproving stare from the librarian.

It read as follows:

Somerset Maugham, Mr. Haxton, W.H. Collins, *Miss Thompson,* Mr. and Mrs. J.J. Mulqueen.

Maugham had actually used the real name of his heroine-prostitute!

He had even blazoned it for the title of the original short story, *Miss Thompson.* He had written it sometime between 1919 and the end of 1920. Surely, his memory had not been that faulty that he would have innocently used her real name.

One has to be realistic where Maugham's sense of retributive literary justice is involved: Miss Thompson had caused

Maugham many sleepless nights in that wretched boarding-house in American Samoa—and he was making sure she didn't escape unscathed. Arrogance, cynicism, writer's fortitude, whatever you want to label it, Maugham had certainly made himself vulnerable, considering the world wide fame of the story, to a colossal lawsuit for slander and libel. That he had escaped in safety can perhaps be credited once again to his lucky literary star.

21. Emile a Tai Gauguin

Tahiti was still on my itinerary, so, with my work completed in Honolulu, I continued to San Francisco and boarded the Matson luxury-liner *Mariposa* for the ten-day voyage to Tahiti. The island-landfall was equally as exciting as on my first visit. The spires of La Diademe, Tahiti's most ornate crown of sharp peaks, were girdled by fleecy streamers of clouds floating above the valley of Fautaua, where Pierre Loti had frolicked in a pool with his nymphet Polynesian mistress Rarahu; waterfalls performed their careless archings over lush green slopes; there was the exotic fragrance of tropical flowers; dramatic Moorea Island floated like a rough-hewn battlemented castle to starboard.

Many changes had taken place in Papeete: a new *quai* had been constructed some years back: hole-in-the-wall Chinese shops along the waterfront had disappeared, replaced by modern concrete buildings; a new post office had risen on the site of the old one, where my father and I had first glimpsed Emile a Tai; the old two-story wooden-frame building that had once housed the Tahiti Yacht Club and the Cercle Bougainville—where James Norman Hall, Charles Nordhoff, Robert Dean Frisbie, Rupert Brooke, Frederick O'Brien, Maugham, Aldous Huxley, and many nomadic writers, painters and escapists had sipped cocktails while watching the splendour of a sunset behind Moorea Island—had been torn down. And, beyond Papeete, I saw the stark-white coral runway for jets across the Faaa reefs, and the scarred sections along beaches and slopes where hotels were under construction or remodelling to accommodate the new tourist invasion. A half-dozen air-lines were winging in weekly with short-term escapists, lushes and libertines. And the strange ones that the planes missed, more than a dozen vessels, on regular or irregular calls, were transporting to France's *Perle-du-Pacifique*.

I was somewhat disappointed concerning the hustle-and-bustle of the port, and I knew that Maugham would have lamented the encroachments of commercialism that had banished forever the languorous *ambiance;* the old Tiare Hotel, where Maugham had stayed, had long ago been razed, and Johnny Goodings's Aina Parè Hotel on the waterfront had also been demolished. Little remained of the old Tahiti that Maugham and I had known.

And I was wondering what had happened to Emile a Tai, Gauguin's Tahitian son, who had once threatened to reclaim the Gauguin-on-glass from Maugham's Villa Mauresque.

My friend, Ralph Varady, author of *Many Lagoons*, informed me that Emile had long ago degenerated into an inebriated beachcomber.

"The poor fellow became too confused as the years passed. He was made too aware of his birthright; everyone expected too much of him. They expected some incredible artistic talent to manifest itself. He was satisfied at first being a fisherman and a gardener. Then the tourists started photographing him because he was the son of Paul Gauguin, and it wasn't long before the journalists began interviewing him. Stories and photographs about him began to appear in American and European newspapers and magazines. Every travel book on Tahiti mentioned him, usually in derogatory terms as a stupid, gross Tahitian.

"An enterprising tourist bureau here thought that, because he was the son of a world-famous artist, whose paintings were selling for a half-million dollars, it would be a smart promotion idea to use him as a tourist-greeter out at the airport. I think he reported for work the first day, and then disappeared for a week on a beer-bender. He made another attempt, on probation, but instead of delivering a rehearsed greeting in French, Tahitian and pidgin-English, he cadged the tourists for drinks, or scrounged them for a buck or two.

"Next, an enterprising character from Hollywood decided he'd take Emile back to a movie studio and promote him for some sort of a film or TV program. But he changed his mind when saw what a stupendous amount of food and booze Emile could put away. Someone else set him up in a curio shop, to sell carved Tahitian *tikis* (idols) and island handicraft, but Emile traded all the junk for booze, or the merchandise was stolen while he was having a quick one in a nearby bar.

"Then the boss of the stevedore gang down at the dock caught Emile pilfering foodstuffs, and he was arrested and tossed into the *boite*. He had a ravenous appetite, and he made a nuisance of himself begging for handouts at the back-doors of Chinese restaurants. He hung around the local brewery drinking the reject flat Hinano beer. He became quite an eye-sore staggering around town in his flapping shorts, faded, torn Aloha-shirt and frayed pandanus hat. The authorities 'exiled' him to Raiatea Island, hoping the change would do him some good, straighten him out, but he was soon back in Papeete and up to his old tricks."

It was understandable that the French authorities and residents here were embarrassed by the Tahitian son of Gauguin. There was a *rue de Paul Gauguin* and a *Lycée Gauguin* in Papeete, and plans were underway for a museum commemorating the French artist.[1] The consensus of out-raged opinion was that Emile was dragging the revered name of Gauguin through the gutters of Papeete. What many evidently overlooked was that no one had shown the slightest interest, when Emile was in his early formative years, to see that he received some sort of a formal education.

"He's well over sixty," remarked Varady, "and he can't even read or write. All he can do is scrawl the name of 'Gauguin' on the ball-point, crayon, and water-color sketches he sells to the tourists for a dollar apiece."

"He's doing art-work?" I exclaimed.

"Let's just say he doodles on clean sheets of paper, and daubs up pieces of cardboard. Something you'd expect a six-year-old child to do."

"Where can I find Emile?" I inquired.

---

[1] The Musée de Gauguin was formally dedicated in October of 1964, and opened for a preview, in Papeari, on the south coast of Tahiti, about 30 miles down the coast from Papeete, near the Isthmus of Tahiti-iti. It was built with funds donated by the Singer Sewing Machine Company and the Polignac Foundation.

"He usually hangs out at the Oceanic Garage along the waterfront there. On boat-day, and when the planes come in, he makes bamboo fish-traps and sells them to the tourists, along with his 'art-work.' Be prepared to see a big change in Emile from the first time you saw him."

I walked down to the garage. But I saw no one who resembled even remotely the young Emile I had visited in Punaauia in the mid-Thirties. I wandered into the back of the garage. A corpulent Tahitian was snoring on a tattered strip of pandanus matting, like a stranded whale run-aground on a reef, gasping out its last breath. I went back to the front of the garage.

"Can you tell me where I can find Emile a Tai?" I asked the attendant, pointing to the discarded bamboo traps at one side of the entrance.

He jerked his thumb over his shoulder. "That's Gauguin."

The sleeping 325-pound behemoth was Emile a Tai?

"Not a Tai. He calls himself *Gauguin* now." The attendant went back and prodded the gargantuan man's bulging mid-section with his bare foot. "Gauguin, a tourist wants to buy a fish-trap!"

Emile gave a spluttering snort, like a grampus, and rolled over. "Tell him to pick one out and give you two dollars American," he mumbled in French to the attendant.

I approached and squatted down beside him.

He stared at me blankly. "All right then, *Monsieur*, a dollar for a small one."

I extended my hand. "Emile, it's been a long time. My father and I visited you many years ago in your home in Punaauia."

He gave me a limp, sweaty handshake, and pushed himself to a sitting position. "Oh, did you?" He belched resoundingly. "Well, fortune has not favored me since then." He gave me a half-lidded appraisal. "I hope you will buy something, a fish-trap, a sketch signed 'Gauguin.'"

"Yes, of course," I said. "But now why don't you come along with me to Quinn's Bar and have a drink—and talk about old times."

The alacrity with which he got to his gigantic limbs was astonishing. "With pleasure, *Monsieur!*" he cried. "With pleasure! *Merci beaucoup!*"

I noticed the curious stares that followed us down the waterfront street to Quinn's.

And as he sat across from me in a booth and drained a bottle of beer without taking a breath, I had an opportunity to study closely the cruel joke that fate had played upon Emile a Tai. There was not the slightest vestige left of a resemblance to his illustrious father. The nose was huge and beaked, the eyes almost buried in lumpy folds of flesh; the mouth was slack and the gums almost toothless, and three chins filled the open neck of his soiled sport-shirt.

It was almost unbelievable that this human hippo was the slender, introverted, and lonely man I had met almost thirty years ago. I remembered how a writer had described him then: "He is a gentle, sensitive man who bears a marked resemblance to his father. He has the same searching eyes, the same long, determined jawline . . . a steady fellow with none of his father's wild irresponsibility, none of his fanatical devotion to his art . . ."

When the American painter, Robert Lee Eskridge, also author of the travel-book *Manga Reva,* saw the physical change in Emile, he had exclaimed: "What a startling contrast to the slim young man, the Tahitian son of Paul Gauguin, whom I sketched in Tahiti upon my return from Manga Reva in the Gambier Archipelago in 1929!"

And with some irony, I was remembering some of the descriptive passages in Maugham's *The Moon and Sixpence,* in reference to the fictional Emile:

"Then I saw Ata. She was suckling a new born child . . ."

Later:

"She (Ata) called out, and a boy came running along. He swarmed up a tree, and presently threw down a ripe nut . . ."

Then, after a passage of years, Maugham, as the narrator of *The Moon and Sixpence,* asks a French doctor in Papeete:

"What happened to Ata and the child?"

"They went to the Marquesas. She had relations there. I have heard that the boy works on one of Cameron's schooners. They say he is very like his father in appearance."

And, finally, at the conclusion of the novel, Maugham had written:

"I do not know why I suddenly thought of Strickland's son by Ata. They had told me he was a merry, light-hearted youth. I saw him, with my mind's eye, on the schooner on which he worked, wearing nothing but a pair of dungarees; and at night, when the boat sailed along easily before a light breeze, and the sailors were gathered on the upper deck, while the captain and the supercargo lolled in deck-chairs, smoking their pipes, I saw him dance with another lad, dance wildly to the wheezy music of the concertina. Above was the blue sky, and the stars, and all about the desert of the Pacific Ocean."

I had lived too long with the story of Paul Gauguin's tragic life in French Oceania, and the mockery of his native son's existence, not to have felt a strong twinge of sadness as I contemplated the misshapen, bloated, bald-headed Emile, now wriggling his fat fingers coyly at the bar waitress to bring him more bottles of *biere* Hinano.

"Since my first trip here in 1934 or 1935, I've been back

329

here three times," I told him. "I looked for you, and asked for you, but I couldn't locate you."

He reached across the table and patted my hand. "That was *tres gentil* of you to be concerned. But I was most likely in jail, in Raiatea Island, or possibly the hospital. Sometimes I eat too much and drink too much, and my stomach becomes upset."

"Why do you run afoul of the law so much?" I wanted to know.

He grinned. "Oh, for one thing or another. Mostly because they say I make *un fléau public* of myself. A lot of tourists come by where I sit in front of the garage, to buy my fish-traps, to take my photograph, to have me sign 'Gauguin' on slips of paper, menus, plane-tickets, envelopes, match-book covers, bills, even on shirts and ties, or buy one of my pretty pictures. They, of course, pay me a dollar or two, and when I have enough money in my pocket I go off and have some drinks. A few drinks lead to a few more, and so on, and the first thing you know I'm drunk. And as I am a heavy man, the alcohol makes me stagger more, and sometimes I fall down, and sometimes it becomes too much of an effort to get up, and so I sleep where I drop.

"Once I fell off the sea-wall into the bay and the police had to fish me out. It took three of them to haul me up by ropes, and one of them lost his balance and fell in, uniform and all, and he was so provoked about it, and because the crowd was laughing so hard, he insisted that I be taken right away, dripping wet, to jail. Oh, I've had my troubles with the police, that you can believe, and the *boite* has become like a second home to me. I don't think the authorities like to see too much of me, because, once locked up, I have nothing to do but eat, and, as I have an enormous capacity, it upsets the budget for their running-expenses."

"You don't really remember me, do you, Emile?"

He ran a reflective hand over the grey stubble on his chin, searched my face with a guarded expression. "You speak perfect French," he said, now uneasy. "Perhaps you represent a company here where I owe a bill. *Are* you a bill-collector? If so, then I can tell you that you are wasting your time, because business has been bad, and I am broke."

"I visited you in Punaauia many years ago with my father. Your mother was alive then. I've never forgotten that day. We talked about the Gauguin-on-glass that the British writer, *Monsieur* Maugham, found here."

Emile's face darkened. "My memory is now faulty," he admitted. "I don't really remember you. But I have not forgotten that *sacré* Englishman who got away with my father's painting that belonged to me! Ah, if I had only been able to get it back, I would not now be in the sorry condition in which you now see me. I would be able to buy champagne to welcome you back to Tahiti."

He signalled the waitress for more beer. "But this does call for a real celebration. Fancy you coming all the way to Tahiti to see poor penniless Emile Gauguin!" His lips trembled and his eyes flooded with tears. "That you knew me in better days moves me deeply, *Monsieur*."

He drank a bottle of beer in sniffling self-pity. "Now, listen to me, I beg of you. Everyone here has a very low opinion of me, even my eight-or-so children are ashamed of me. I am pointed out as the beachcomber-son of a famous man. Fate just dealt me a low blow, that's all. No one has ever extended to me a helping hand. I am a self-taught man, and I do have a rather decent vocabulary, because I have learned to listen and to retain what I hear. My mind is rather an uncomplicated one, and, like a sponge, it soaks up things remarkably well. The French Government here never showed any interest in my mother or me, to see that we got along, that I went to school and learned how to read and write. As a young man I was a fisherman, but my neighbors laughed at me. 'You,' they sneered, 'the son of a great painter whose pictures sell for so much money, must fish for a living?' And when I started growing vegetables for the Papeete market, they shook their heads and said: 'So the son of the great Gauguin must spread manure to keep body and soul together!' So there you have it, *Monsieur,* that is what I have been up against!

"There are those here in the Government and the French residents, who call me a swindler and a fraud, because I sign the name 'Gauguin' for a souvenir to the tourists, and affix it to my drawings." He banged the table with an empty beer-bottle. "Well, I have the legal right to do so! And the exclusive monopoly here in Tahiti. My father Paul Gauguin had five legitimate children, and four whose birth-papers were signed 'Father Unknown.' Of the three of these four bastards, born here in the islands, I am the only one living today in French Oceania. So if I can turn my father's name of Gauguin to a little profit, I intend to do so! I have a big stomach, and so I like to eat, and I always have a consuming thirst, so I like to drink. On a good boat-day, I can get about $15 from the American tourists, and I spend it all on myself. I think I deserve what little pleasures come my way.

"Now and again some hypocritical Tahitian women will pass by the garage where I am making bamboo fish-traps, and yell at me: 'Have you no shame, you *clochard*! Your children are scattered all around the island!' To them I always say: 'Well, would you prefer I have them here on Quai Bir Hakeim sleeping on the cement floor of this garage, following in their father's bare footsteps?' Oh, they are so quick to moralize! There are really no orphans, illegitimate or neglected children in Tahiti. The Tahitians love children.

"So my children sleep and eat well. Once I tried to interest them in painting, and a French teacher took an interest in them. Adolphe showed promise, and the teacher said that his dark-browns and blues were similar to my father's. Célina had a drawing exhibited in Paris.[2] But they don't paint anymore. They didn't really get much encouragement. And, after all, they have more Tahitian blood than I, so their ambition must be quite watered down, too. And it's foolish to assume that genius is passed on.

"I am the only 'painter' in the family. What I draw, or color with crayon or water-color, I sell for about one dollar American. I know what they say about my art-work. Scrawls from an infantile mind! But no matter which way you look at it, it's a bargain. They take my drawing back home, put it on a wall, and say: 'Look, I have an original Gauguin!'

"And here's something to think about: In 1903 six of my father's paintings sold here in Papeete, at an auction, for one franc each.[3] And an entire lot of paintings and sketches went for ten francs. And if you have the time to look into the Musée de Polynesie here and consult their archives on that auction, you'll find that a package of my father's paintings sold for half a *franc* each.

---

[2] Célina a Tai, in 1953, sent a drawing of her famous grandfather for exhibition in the Paris Pedagogical Museum, along with the art work of colonial children of France. The critics made favorable comments on her work, their kind words perhaps influenced by the knowledge that Paul Gauguin was her grandfather. *France-Soir* of Paris had reported: "The efforts revealed striking gifts that only heredity could explain."

[3] The French *franc* was then worth about twenty cents.

"So what if I am doing my drawing and painting late in life? I am over 60. My father was in his forties when he started painting. Well, he lived and worked in a cool climate, while I am living in a hot island. Things move more slowly here. I should say that I have a decent chance to perhaps finish something someday for which a rich American or European will give me a handsome price. If not, then I won't blow my brains out. I won't go mad with frustration like my father.

"Look at it this way: my father never got along in Tahiti or the Marquesas as well as I do. They tell me that it is written in the books that he was always drunk, but hungry, and the creditors were forever after him to settle accounts. He was unfriendly and unpleasant; he didn't like people around him. It was as if he was always burning with fever to find the different way to paint. He wasn't at peace with the world, or with himself. They say that is the way with a genius. However, I don't know quite what that means. All I know is that my father died wretchedly, and charity buried him in that Calvary Cemetery in Atuana of Hiva Oa Island. So he was put into the ground in the savage cannibal Marquesas Islands far to the north of here.

"You can see for yourself that I am fat and well-fed, and if you had been a bill-collector it would have been useless for you to try and hound me, because I have not a *sou* in the bank nor any tangible property upon which to place a lien, or confiscate, for debts. So I, Emile Gauguin, am not a genius, because I comprehend my limitations. I eat well, I drink well, I sleep well, and I am not tormented by too much of a brain. Usually, I am a man of tranquil temperament.

"The only time I become out of my mind with anger, is when I see a notice on the bulletin-board at the post office that another of my father's paintings has sold for a huge fortune. Then I go around to the bars to drown my misery and chagrin. The last time I went completely out of control. I saw where $364,000 was paid for one of my father's paintings in New York City.[4] When *Maman* was living, I would keep asking her: 'Now, why didn't you just save one of my father's paintings Just one, *just one!*' She would keep telling me that she never saw any beauty or worth in anything Koké painted, so she gave them away, or destroyed them. So when my father's paintings became valuable, you can see what *Maman* and I lived with all the time, mockery, bitterness, regret, frustration. Then there were the paintings that rightfully belonged to us that were stolen, such as the one on the glass panes of the door in the Anani home in Mataiea."

"I have seen that painting in the home of *Monsieur* Maugham in the south of France," I interrupted.

And I described it in detail and where Maugham had installed the priceless neo-impressionistic work.

Emile banged his huge fist down on the table, making the empty beer bottles jiggle.

"Ah, yes, we are back to that thieving *Peretane* again! Well, I have not given up the idea of bringing him into court and getting back that painting!"

I mentioned that Maugham was contemplating, because of the art thefts along the Riviera and his advanced age, including the Gauguin-on-glass among the collection he intended auctioning off later in London, the proceeds ear-marked to establish a fund for deserving artists.

"And how about a part of that money for Emile Gauguin,

---

[4] Rosenberg and Steinberg, art dealers, sold Gauguin's *I Await The Letter* for this amount.

who, under the circumstances, deserves it as much as anyone?" Tears were running down his bloated cheeks. "How
I would love to throw a stone through that Gauguin-on-glass,
just to settle the score!" He smiled wanly through his grief.
"But I will never get within a stone's-throw of it, that I
know. It was destined that I live and die here in Tahiti. But,
then, what better place to die? I have only been away from
Tahiti three times, once in 1918 to New Caledonia, where
I served my military service, once to Raiatea Island, 135
miles from Tahiti, when the *Prefecture-de-Police* ordered it,
and also to the Marquesas Islands.

"I must tell you about that Marquesas trip, *Monsieur*. It
was quite droll, believe me. A fat tourist came to the Oceanic
Garage one day. He said to me: 'Emile Gauguin, I want you
to come with me to the Island of Hiva Oa, to your father's
grave. I have a movie camera and I shall take some film of
you that will be historical.' I had never been to the Marquesas, to see my father's tomb, so I said I would be happy to go.

"So off we sailed on the *Tiare Taporo*. It was a horrible
trip, of course. There was not enough to eat on the *Tiare
Taporo*, and when I complained to the captain of the schooner he said that if he gave me as much as I asked for they'd
be out of provisions before they reached the Marquesas. If I
had known how niggardly the food was going to be, I would
have surely made the American tourist put aboard extra
food for me.

"Well, we finally reached Hiva Oa, and this funny fellow
with his camera took me up to the Calvary Cemetery above
the Bay of Traitors at Atuana. It was a hot, long hike, and
I had to rest a number of times, and it rained a lot. I was not
too happy about it, but he kept telling me to keep moving.

"We found my father's tomb, just a crude, square stone

mound, not too high off the ground, with his name on a marker and the date. The tourist set up his camera, and then told me to start acting. I said: 'What am I supposed to do?' He said: 'Lay your head on the top of the tomb and weep, as if you can't control your grief.' I told him: 'Look, *Monsieur*, I am Emile Gauguin, of no profession, certainly no actor. And, besides, I never knew my father, so how can I be sad about someone I can't even remember.' He said: 'Well, okay, but do something. Just don't stand there! I'm wasting film! Pretend that you're holding a conversation with him.'

"So I stood with my hands on my hips, looking at the tomb, and shouted: *'Bon Jour*, Papa! Listen to me, you, inside there! So I have come at long last to tell you something! I am Emile Gauguin, your big Tahitian son! You know, your unrecognized son! Now, cannot you make some kind of arrangements so I can get some money from some of your paintings? You didn't leave *Maman* and me anything, not even a *sou*. Hello, there now, listen to me! *Mon pere*, why did you beat *Maman* so much with a stick? She told me you were a wild fellow when you had too much to drink. Hello, now, you must remember when *Maman* would hit you on the head with a coconut when you chased the *vahines*.

" 'Now listen well, Papa, I make drawings now, not as good or marketable as yours, to be sure, but not so bad considering. And I sign them *Gauguin* like you. Not *Paul*, but me, *Emile*! Excuse me, Papa, while I laugh! *Aue!* Oh my! My stomach and my backside are shaking like jelly in the sunshine. Here in the islands I am more of a success as a beachcomber than you were as an artist. Anyway, rest well, *Mon pere, dormez-bien!* Hello! Hello! Goodbye! Goodbye!

Tahiti's most famous beachcomber is now saying hail and farewell to Tahiti's most famous painter. If my visits are not frequent here to your tomb, just remember that you never left any money for the trips. So I'll have to do the best I can.'

"*Aue!* It was a hard climb up to the cemetery on the hill, and the walk down was exhausting. I almost died from fatigue! And in the end this crazy American only gave me such a small amount of money for performing like a cinema actor in that Marquesan cemetery!"

Then he seemed to shiver.

"I was happy to leave Hiva Oa on the schooner. I got to thinking how playful and *hohoarearea* (comic) I was there in the cemetery, how disrespectfully I had spoken. We Tahitians fear the dead. My mother told me that my father was a strange one, of bizarre moods, beliefs, and actions. She was sure that his *tupaupau* (ghost) would return to haunt these islands. *Aue!* I would not want to meet his ghost on the lonely beaches of Hiva Oa, especially that I, Emile the beachcomber, was lording it over my father, the great painter."

He sighed asthmatically, drained the last of another bottle of beer.

"Of course, I never knew my father, and what my mother told me of him was of little consequence. I only know, from what people tell me, and what I look at on the bulletin-board they read for me, that my father is one of the world's greatest painters. And that is why the tourists buy my fish-traps and my drawings, or photograph me, or just come to stare at me, as if I am some sort of a rare animal in a zoo. I know what they are thinking: 'Here sits the son of Paul Gauguin, like a fat Buddha, but he is really only a blubbery, drunken beachcomber!' I think hard about my father at times, and I try hard to believe that he is my father, to get into the mood of a son-father relationship, but it is impossible."

The native orchestra on the back platform of Quinn's began playing a wild native dance number. A pretty, shapely *vahine* dragged a drunken tourist into the center of the small floor and began gyrating her hips against his. Emile watched them somberly.

"My father, so I understand, had a fever for the *vahines* of Tahiti and the Marquesas. His models fought to sleep with him. Painting and sexual intercourse were his obsessions. With me, it's eating, drinking and sleeping."

He extended a slip of paper across the table to me. "A rich tourist gave this to me a few months ago. I cannot read. What does it say?"

It was an excerpt from Paul Gauguin's rambling *Intimate Journals:*

> "How much does society owe me?
> A great deal too much.
> Will it ever pay?
> *Never!*"

Digesting this reflective, bitter mood of his father's, Emile nodded his head ponderously, knowingly.

"Ah, *oui*, I suspected that the American, who gave me that piece of paper with the writing, wished to make me angry, to make me unhappy about being the 'forgotten son' of a famous man. Well, to hell with him! As a beachcomber I'll live longer than he will as a man of much money in the bank."

Beer was beginning to bubble out of the corners of his slack mouth and down his chin, dribbling onto the enormous globe of his bare stomach.

"Well, *Monsieur,* I think I have had enough *biere* Hinano for one sitting. Now I must go back and relieve myself. *Excusez-moi si'l vous plait."*

He was gone a long time. When he returned he had two one-dollar bills in his hand.

"I sold a bamboo fish-trap to a steward off the *Mariposa.* I told him to go by and pick one up at the garage. So now I can buy you a drink, which is proper." He sat down heavily, signalled the waitress. "And while I was back there making much peepee, I got a brilliant idea. This is it: why don't I appoint you my personal representative to go and see that English writer who has my painting on glass? You travel much, and you say you know him. I'm sure he would listen to you. You could tell him that I am determined, that I mean business. Perhaps, to avoid unpleasantness, he would settle with me. I would be glad to make it worth your while, if a settlement was arranged, say ten or fifteen percent commission; it could mean a bit of money for you."

"It would be a waste of time," I said, with finality. "The statute of limitations expired years ago. There is not the slightest chance of you doing anything about it. It belongs to *Monsieur* Maugham. He purchased it legally, and no court process could ever reverse that fact. It would be best if you forget about that Gauguin-on-glass."

He sat for a long time, mumbling and sighing over his beer.

At last he said heavily: "Ah, *oui,* deep in my heart I know you are right. I just like to think something could be done about it, that's why I talk all the time about it. You're right, I should forget about it."

He shrugged his shoulders.

"And I suppose I should be satisfied that the *Peretane,* in his book about my father, has made it possible for me to realize a steady income of sorts. The tourists bring his book by now and again, *La Lune et Sixpence,* and ask me to sign 'Gauguin' on the pages where he wrote about me: as a child at my mother's breast, where I climb up a palm for a coconut, how later I worked as a seaman on a schooner between the islands, something about me in a painting my father did, and the last part of the story, where *Monsieur* Maugham gives a long description of me as a young man doing a native dance on the schooner.

"I asked at first if the writer gave me a name, but I found out that he hadn't. Well, in real life, if it comes to a point of law I suppose, I don't have a real name either. But here in Tahiti we always have a name, if not the father's then the mother's last name; everyone born on the island has some sort of a prideful identity with someone."

He arose, with prodigious effort.

"Well, it's a consolation that at least here in Tahiti, it *is* recognized that I *am* the son of Paul Gauguin, and that I am fast becoming a tourist oddity. It's better than being a no-body, even though I do have the social status of a native beachcomber."

He beamed affectionately down upon me.

"And now I must bid you *au revoir.* The tourists will be going back to the *Mariposa,* from their tours, shopping, drinking and sleeping with the *vahines,* and I should be in the front of the Oceanic Garage with my fish-traps, my drawings, in my clean shirt to be photographed, so I can pluck a few dollars from them. *A bientôt.*" He squeezed my fingers in his moist, pulpy hand.

Then he lumbered off, like a good-natured hippo, through the crowd of drinkers and dancers.

In the following days, I stopped occasionally to chat with Emile as he sat in front of the Oceanic Garage fashioning his fish-traps. Sometimes he disappeared for a few days, once for as long as two weeks.

And then one morning I met him coming down the road from the local jail.

"Ah, *oui, oui,* once again I have been on vacation as a guest of *Hotel de Boite.* The same as before: too much to drink, talking too much and ungratefully against the French administration here, saying I was going to reorganize the Pupu Tiama Maohi political party against the *Toe-paus* (French)."

He sighed.

"And the food is getting worse and worse in the jail. I won't be able to take it much longer. This time, I had many hours to think about myself, that I wasn't getting any younger, and that I should be doing something about my predicament.

"I got to thinking about the tourists: they point their cameras at me and I smile; they buy my fish-traps; they get me to sign the books about my father; they buy my drawings and paintings. I sell my art work very cheaply, as you know. Just a dollar or two. It's a very cheap price for them to amuse themselves at my expense, to show a photo of me to their friends back home, and say: 'Have a look at this *caractère,* this fat slob. He is the Tahitian son of Paul Gauguin.' Or they hang one of my drawings or paintings on their wall, so they can say: 'I own a Gauguin.'

"Now if I could only get to America or France, think what I could do with the name of Gauguin, eh, *mon ami,* that is *something* to think about, you must admit. Who knows, perhaps the miracle might take place, the day might come when I will leave Tahiti for a while, and become famous and rich, just to show these doubters, these scoffers here, that the name *Gauguin* means something, even though the strain is now watered down and anaemic in my blood."

As I watched him walk slowly down the road toward the waterfront, I thought: If only someone had taken an interest in him when he was in his early twenties, had provided the means for him to study art seriously, he would have garnered a fortune from the current influx of tourists in Tahiti.

When I returned to Europe, I was to hear from time to time about Emile, through letters from friends. His life in Papeete was of the same routine, brief forays of industry on boat-day, inebriated absences, frequent incarcerations in the local calaboose; a bailing-out by H. Allen Smith, the American humorist, who supplied him with art materials.

A friend wrote me once:

"He has been pulling some hilarious tricks here lately. His art business has been booming. So much so, that he's had to get help to take care of the demand. It is said that he enlisted the aid of second-grade school-children to give him their drawings they do in the classrooms, to which he affixed the name of 'Gauguin.'

"But, the neatest trick of all, was one he got away with at the hospital, where he had to go for a check-up. He had his eye on a plump nurse there, and one day he propositioned her on the verandah. 'I will have to think it over,' she told him. 'And, of course, it would have to be for money. I am poorly paid here as a nurse.'

"A day or so later, the nurse caught him in her room. 'What are you doing here?' she demanded suspiciously. 'I am here to keep my end of the bargain,' Emile told her. 'I am so excited about you, I will give you 500 francs to sleep with me.' She complied immediately.

"It was not until after Emile had left, that, placing the 500 francs in her purse, she found that, coincidentally, there were 500 francs missing. *Emile had paid her with her own money!*

"She complained to the police, and Emile was taken to La Maison d'Arret. But he was held for routine questioning only a short while. The police were in philosophical accord that poetic justice had been served on the Tahitian nurse."

And, finally, a startling announcement: A French woman, one Madame Josette Giraud, a fortyish writer, arrived in Papeete. She had read in a French journal about Emile Gauguin and his bamboo fish-traps, his posings for the cameras of tourists, his crude drawings and paintings. But Emile was missing from his familiar spot in front of the Oceanic Garage. She made inquiries and learned that he had been locked up again in the Papeete Jail for vagrancy. She bailed him out, transported him in a taxi to a small waterfront hotel, and, before she went out to shop for clean clothes, ordered him to take a much-needed shower and shave. Then she took him for a big meal at a Chinese restaurant, and, while he consumed huge platters of lean pork, almond-shrimp, eggs-foo-yung, and fried rice, she talked to him earnestly about his father.

And, as he ate ravenously, Emile listened politely. It was the first time that anyone had ever spoken to him with so much respect, placed any value on his heritage, made him ashamed of his indolent ways. Madame Giraud spoke enthusiastically—and hopefully.

"It is not too late to try to paint honestly," she told him. "You bear the name of Gauguin. At least, make the attempt.

It is better than just being a fat fellow whom the tourists come to gawk at."

The next day she bought him paint brushes, canvases, oils, and told him to transfer any ideas that came to him on the clean white expanses. And the effect of oils on canvas fascinated Emile; he began painting anything that caught his fancy. Some of the results were bizarre, but not unattractive.

And Madame Giraud kept prodding him. "You don't want to die a beachcomber, do you? Then apply yourself! If you want to, there is no limit to which you can't succeed."

And when the time came for Madame Giraud to leave Tahiti, she did not desert Emile.

"Perhaps we will go to Paris," she said enthusiastically, "where your father first started his painting. The *ambiance* will be a big help to you. You will walk in the same streets that your famous father once trod, you will visit the art museums, you will talk to artists and critics, who will tell you many things you never knew about your father. You will see some of his original paintings of Tahiti and the Marquesas. Some of them are of your mother. I will read to you from the many books about your father. You will acquire an awareness of your father and the history of art of his time."

Madame Giraud was certain that she could control the lazy, obese, tippling Emile once she got him away from Tahiti.

I left Tahiti for Europe before she carried him off to civilization.

I was in London in December of 1962 and through the late Spring of 1963. One morning, over coffee, I read an electrifying notice in the *Daily Express*:

An exhibition of more than fifty of Emile Gauguin's canvases was being held at the O'Hana Gallery of Modern Paintings in Carlos Place.

An editorial on the colorful Tahitian paintings said:

"For much of his 62 years, Gauguin's son Emile has led an idyllic, if unfruitful, life on Tahiti. Suddenly he turns to painting and the canvases which arrive from the Pacific produce immense excitement among art lovers.

"It is a remarkable demonstration of the force of heredity; important, perhaps, for the world of art. A considerable talent, untutored, isolated from the stream of thought and technique, could bring a fresh, even unique quality to painting."

I turned to the conservative *London Times*, and the critic called Emile's work "a life document of touching simplicity."

I hurried over to the O'Hana Gallery. But Emile was not there taking bows or signing autographs. But his art-creations were, 61 examples of them, nothing too improved from the twelve that I had bought from him for one dollar each, so long ago in Papeete. There were colorful landscapes, flowers and native *fares*. And all of them were signed with the magical scrawl of *Gauguin!*

Jacques O'Hana, proprietor of the gallery of modern paintings, was very satisfied with the exhibition that had been held from April 25th to May 31st.

"Yes, yes, it's been very interesting. They're selling remarkably well. Twenty-or-so have sold, ranging in price from $700 to $1400. The financial arrangements are in the hands of Madame Giraud. From here the exhibition will be sent to Geneva and Paris.

"Emile's work has no similarity to his father's. His paintings are primitive, childlike almost, but they have something in them of the Australian aboriginal painter, the late Albert

Namatjira." And he added: "His paintings are more of curiosity value rather than future intrinsic investment, but, still, he's on his way. Who can tell what may happen in a few years? It would, indeed, be quite a revelation if the Gauguin talent should suddenly explode out of him."

Where was Emile now?

Jacques O'Hana was not too certain. "I think Madame Giraud took him to America, but where he is just now I cannot say. I don't think she took him to Paris, as originally planned."

I sent an airmail to a friend in Tahiti describing Emile's exhibition at O'Hana's in London.

He wrote back promptly:

"We thought all along down here that he was in Paris, that he had reformed and was drinking very little, and was spending all his time under the supervision of his mentor, Madame Giraud, smearing an assortment of oils on canvases. Now you suspect he is in America.

"However, no one has taken over Emile's place in front of the Oceanic Garage in Papeete, where he once sold his bamboo fish-traps and ball-point and crayon doodlings. There are the skeptics who are sure that he'll be back one of these days to resume his beachcomber's craft for the tourists, grinning hugely and shouting to his friends and acquaintances: 'Ah, yes, I had a magnificent time away from Tahiti, I can tell you! The pretty models fought over posing for me! I ate like a horse, I slept like a baby. People loved me, respected me, spoke well of me. I was a man of some importance, that you can believe. But, finally, it wearied me. So here I am back where I belong—a happy, worry-free beachcomber, recovered completely and permanently, at long last, from the vicious bite of the bug-of-ambition.' "

347

THE SEARCH

It was quite by accident that I was to meet Emile again. And of all places—*Chicago*! I was strolling down North Michigan Avenue late one morning, when I saw a huge man walking away from the entrance of the small Kasha-Heman Art Gallery. I stopped short, with a gasp of astonishment. No mistaking that bulky, misshapen figure!

I hurried and caught up with him. It *was* Emile. And he was smartly attired in a suit of dark material, highly waxed boots, and an expensive necktie. His flabby cheeks and many chins were shiny from a close-shave; he was redolent of spicy cologne. The fingernails of the flabby hand that grasped mine were well manicured, his grin one of professional amiability. I remembered what H. Allen Smith had said, after his first sight of Emile staggering barefooted around Papeete in tattered T-shirt and gaping shorts: "Put him in a suit and he'd look like one of those big board chairmen back east." He was right. Emile had the affluent appearance of a Wall Street broker.

He spoke gently in French, after I had congratulated him on his European art exhibition.

"*Merci, merci beaucoup.* It was nice of you to attend my exhibition in London." He studied me curiously. "Your face looks familiar, which is why I am taking the trouble of stopping and speaking with you, otherwise I am too busy to talk these days. All day I paint, or think about ideas. Did you know that I finished a remarkable painting of Marina City? So large that I had to wear a butcher's apron so that I didn't splash paint on my beautiful sport shirt. And I also am under contract to an art gallery here, the one back there that I just left. Not only that, but I design fabrics, too, exclusive Gauguin textiles." He peered more closely at my face. "I have to admit that I really don't know where I first or last met you.

It seems, however, that we once talked about the Gauguin-on-glass that the British writer took away from Tahiti in 1917."

He shifted a book that he was carrying under one arm. I saw that it was a copy of Maugham's *The Moon and Sixpence*. He noticed my regard, and said quickly:

"Oh, yes, I carry the book about, because people like to see the British writer's references to me when I was a young fellow. It's good for public relations. And, just by coincidence, *Monsieur* Maugham happened to have an auction of thirty-four of the paintings he owned at a place in London, just about the time of my exhibition. Among his collection was the Gauguin-on-glass. But I don't let that bother or worry me anymore. I've been selling my own canvases in Europe, New York City and here, and at a pretty penny, I can tell you. And here in Chicago I am very famous."

"So you intend to remain here?"

"Oh, yes, this is my permanent headquarters now," he replied loftily. "I am under contract to Madame Giraud and her good friend, Madame Kovler, who is a partner in the art gallery. She tells me what she wants for her customers and I paint to order. I, of course, design special things for dress-material, drapery, and such. The company is called *Emile Gauguin Designs*."

Emile was comfortably installed by Madame Giraud in a house out in Maywood, a western suburb of Chicago. His reference to his domicile was extravagant. "Oh, it's quite a mansion, indeed!"

Later, when I saw the early 1920-ish pile of stucco and wood, I surmised that the contents inside were as dated as the exterior. Emile occupied a bedroom on the second floor, furnished cheaply with an ancient bed, austere dresser and straight-back chair. The floor was worn and bare, as were the walls, except for some magazine pin-ups of semi-nude American bathing girls.

A young American couple occupied the home with him, the husband being a young graduate art student, who was teaching Emile some fundamentals in art techniques and sculpturing. And there were two frenetic Siamese cats, a slightly benzedrined Afghan, a small tropical bird, and a temperamental Spanish maid to complete the household. The American couple, Lockhart by name, could not speak French, nor could the maid, and Emile didn't speak a coherent word of English. How they conversed was a miracle, but they seemed to communicate quite well with wild gestures, laughter and pantomimes.

Emile, for amusement, watched TV and listened to the radio, which, being in English, he could not comprehend. "But I like to watch the pictures on TV, particularly the gangster and cowboy movies. And on the radio there is always pretty music; sometimes they play even a Tahitian recording, and I become lonesome for Tahiti and the Oceanic Garage."

His routine was fixed: an early rising at 6 a.m., and, before dressing or eating, a careful rearranging of the furniture of the room. "I must have change every day, so I shift the bed and dresser set all the time. I even repin the pictures on opposite walls, in different patterns. I can't stand monotony. Then I go down to breakfast. I eat the American breakfast, but, believe me, I am starved for raw fish and breadfruit. However, I must diet, because I am slightly affected by diabetes."

Out in the small yard behind the vintage home, enclosed by a high fence and shrubbery, were a concrete goldfish pond, some unfinished sculptures in wood and marble—and a heavy bar-bell.

"I must exercise, because I have to keep my weight down. In Tahiti I was over 300 pounds, but now I weigh only about 235 pounds. So I sleep and paint better now. And Mesdames Giraud and Kovler keep telling me that over-eating is bad for my heart, and that I will have more artistic thoughts and ability on a moderately filled stomach."

The education of Emile Gauguin in America was quite startling, indeed! I remembered what his father Paul Gauguin had written about Emile and the prospects of his education: "The education of Emile! It remains the most difficult undertaking a man has ever attempted. I myself, in my own country, dare not think of it. Here (in Tahiti), enlightened at last, I regard it quite calmly."

Emile's father had intended for him to remain in Tahiti, his school-room being the lagoon and the coral reefs and the deep verdant valleys, his experiences derived from a normal affinity with nature. Emile was supposed to remain a simple Polynesian, without any commercial avarice.

Emile had a number of clippings for me to read of his artistic progress, some good, some bad. One in particular was not too complimentary. A European review had stated bluntly: "He has, we are told, the mind of a child, a fact which takes most of the surprise out of the discovery that he paints like a child."

But there was another review to offset this caustic analysis:

"He is, in an artistic sense, an authentic primitive. Authentic primitives are almost impossible to find any more. They cannot exist in America or Europe. Here everyone has been influenced somewhat—by magazine photos or billboards, if nothing else. A true primitive can only exist in a place like Tahiti, where there are no pictures of any kind (?) Strictly from an academic standpoint, for anyone interested in the process of artistic creation, everything he does is absolutely fascinating."

Jack Paar, on his evening TV variety program, had held up an 8x4-foot painting of Emile's, which elicited only derisive laughter and ridicule from the viewers.

"I was in New York City for a while, and finally Madame Giraud brought me to Chicago. So this is to be my city, because she has big plans for me. And the arrangements she doesn't make for me, Madame Kovler does. They keep me moving, I can tell you! Although I am getting started late, I know I must be patient and try to make something of my life."

One of his letters he treasured. It was from Pierre Gauguin, the grandson of Paul Gauguin, and his nephew, living in Copenhagen. It read, in part:

"My dear Uncle:

"You don't know me, however, I am your nephew, son of your half-brother John. Here in Denmark without even knowing your address I followed your life for 30 years and I have some photos of you in some magazines at the age of 35. What a resemblance to your father and your brothers! I am very happy to have had the chance to write to you thru Mme. Giraud after having seen your exhibit in London. Your paintings impressed me very much.

"I sincerely hope that you will continue to be the great artist you are and to listen only to the practical advices of Mme. Giraud and to discount those who think they understand and know art or those who think they can paint just because they went to art school. If you will continue to express yourself on canvas as you have done in your London exhibit, you will give to the world something very beautiful and completely new in the field of art. In this case the whole world will know that you are truly a descendant of a proud Tahitian family, and of a painter whose talent is appreciated by all the world."

Emile folded the letter reverently and replaced it in his wallet. He nodded and spoke softly. "So I have no other choice but to remain here in Chicago and work hard, to justify the faith and expectations that my friends and family have in me."

Aue! The Emile of Chicago, U.S.A. was a far cry from the Emile of the Oceanic Garage of Papeete!

22. Maugham on Thieves, Age, Death and God

When I next visited Maugham, I found that he had deteriorated sadly, both physically and mentally. He was suffering from sudden blackouts, his memory was impaired, and he couldn't remember names of people, places, or dates. He addressed me as "Gerald" once, another time as "Phillip." With advanced old age deafness was infuriating to him. He who enjoyed listening to friends in stimulating discourse, now had to strain his ears to hear only a small part of what they said.

He was pleased, but amused, about Emile's success.

"I'm happy that he's able to utilize the name 'Gauguin' for a few dollars, even as old as he is. It's the least that destiny can do for him. Maybe he'll be able to earn enough, if too many leeches don't batten onto him and exploit and cheat him, to go back to Tahiti, buy a piece of land, and have all his children and grandchildren around him for a contented old age."

He chuckled. "And it's reassuring to know that he now won't be kicking up a row with me about the Gauguin-on-glass. From now on he'll have to go to its new owner in America about that. An American bought it, so I understand. He even went to Tahiti to see the house where I found it. It broke my heart to sell off my cherished paintings. But there was nothing else to do. Villa Mauresque must surely have been on the imminent time-table of the art gangs operating along the Riviera. It would have been only a matter of a short time when they would have broken into my villa if I had kept them there."

Maugham's introduction to the catalogue of his art collection, which Sotheby's distributed to potential buyers at the auction in London, explained more fully and interestingly his qualms about his private art collection:

"Ladies and Gentlemen:

"You would not have been invited to come here this evening if the owner of a restaurant called La Colombe d'Or on the hills behind Nice had not had a liking for pictures. Painters found it pleasant to work there and it suited them that the proprietor was not unwilling to take a picture as payment for the board and lodging with which he provided them. In course of time he was able to hang pictures on the walls of the large room which served to seat the customers who came from Nice or Monte Carlo to lunch or dine. The food was good and the pictures, so unlike what one was used to, were an attraction. The artists began to be talked about and bold men actually bought their pictures. The owner of the Colombe d'Or was offered good money for those he had, but aware that they brought him customers, he refused to sell.

"One morning when he and his staff awoke to enter upon the day's work he had a shock. During the night burglars had stripped the walls and not a single picture was left. The theft caused a sensation.

"Now, the Mayor of my village of St. Jean knew that I had a collection of pictures and it may be that he thought it would not be to his credit if they were stolen. He called me up and said he would like to come to my house to see what precautions I had taken to keep them in safety. I said I would be glad to see him. He came. I have a large old-fashioned house with French windows and I conducted the Mayor from room to room. When I had shown him all there was to see he smiled and said: 'I have never seen a house that so obviously invites robbers to enter and steal. If you want to keep your pictures you must do something about it.'

" 'What?' I asked. 'There's only one thing you can do,' he answered. 'You must build a strong room and keep your pictures in it.'

"I had not bought pictures for many years to keep them in a strong room, but I saw his point and somewhat unwillingly, and at considerable expense, I turned one of my bedrooms into a strong room.

"I am often away from home, sometimes for a few days, sometimes for several months. Before I leave I have to send for an electrician to take away the top lights, take the pictures out of their frames and put them in the strong room. It is an irksome business and I don't know that it is very good for pictures. When I come home the electrician has again to be sent for, the pictures have to be taken out of the strong room, put back in their frames and hung back in their appointed places. Even if I were only going out to dinner I could not be sure that a thief would not take the opportunity to steal one or two of my pictures. For many years they had

357

given me a great pleasure; now they were an anxiety. I decided to sell them. I hope you will get as much pleasure out of such as you buy tonight as I have got out of them in the past."

"It wasn't easy to part with my Gauguin. It was a rather inspiring sight when I worked in my study. I rarely go in there anymore. When the Gauguin was removed from the window-opening, the room became empty, cheerless and musty, like a vacant chamber in a haunted house."

I sensed the premonition of imminent death in his quavering voice, but not one of fear, just that of wearisome resignation to the inevitable.

"My home and my work no longer exist for me. Old age is the cruelest practical joke that life plays on humanity. There are the artificial defenses, of course, the measures of allaying the final show-down, but the delaying actions merely prolong the farce. There comes the day, as you knew it would, when you'd have to cease the struggle, to reconcile yourself to every damned sort of mental and physical inconvenience inflicted on mankind.

"I once thought I would quietly slip out of life, by my own hand, at about the age of sixty-five. But when I reached sixty-five, I was still interested in peoples and places, and, of course, my writing. I figured I'd wait a few years more, until I was sure I was through with life. But that was a mistake. You never really set the time. You only think about it, procrastinate, and then, before you know what's happening, you're too old to do anything about it. The will is gone and there's no courage left for positive action of any kind. What a damned shame, really! It makes one so damned helpless. I suppose that is why old and senile people whimper and weep so much. They are not suffering as much from a physical pain as they are from a twinge of troubled conscience that they didn't end the degeneration into decrepit old age sooner, when they had the determination. Yes, my friend, my old age is a pretty kettle of fish!

"Dying is the most hellishly boresome experience in the world! Particularly when it entails dying of 'natural causes,' like an exasperating loitering in an empty, desolate street, or on an arid, lonely seashore waiting for an overdue ferry. Now, waiting for death is a maddening hanging onto life.

"My hearing is impaired, and I become irritable and impatient because I think the fault is solely with other people, who I suspect mumble just to annoy and try my patience. I totter and become dizzy when I proceed from one point to another given point. I can't play tennis anymore, or swim in my blue-tiled pool, or dance; I can't concentrate on cards anymore, nor can I write, because the right word always seems to elude me. Sex is finished and over with, which might be the only blessing of old age. Yes, growing old is a very ugly and dirty business!"

Later in the year, I made several attempts to see Maugham, but was informed that he was bed-ridden and seeing no one, not even his closest friends. He would sit up at times in his painted bed, resting against a cushion specially embroidered for him by Marie Laurencin, and look through a volume of drawings which Matisse had given to him, or gaze wistfully out upon the blue Mediterranean, making the comment from time to time that, when he felt better, he must plan another trip.

In pleasant weather he might be assisted out to the terrace to doze for short periods in the sunshine, to smell the varied fragrances of his gardens, or listen to the whispering sounds of bees at work. Sometimes, when the climate was favorable, he would be taken by his secretary-companion, Alan Searle, for motor-trips along the Corniche highways to adjacent Riviera towns to say hello to old friends.

Therefore, it was quite by accident that, in January of 1964, I was able to meet and talk with Maugham. He had on the twenty-fifth of January, in his 90th year, expressed a wish to visit nearby Monte Carlo, even though the energy to dress and withstand the short drive along the coast-road would be gruelling.

"If I don't go this anniversary, I most surely won't be here to go next year," he had told Alan Searle.

I was only accorded a short visit with him. And I knew on this occasion that it was to be our last conversation. On this, his 90th birthday, he was melancholic and depressed, lapsing now and again into mumbling monologues, as if complaining over the expectancy of falling into a comatose state; he had lucid moments, then blank spells. His mind wandered. It was most pitiable. His face seemed wrinkled and dead as a mummy's.

Frequently, however, I was surprised at the strong timbre of his voice. As, for example, when he suddenly inclined his head toward the Monte Carlo Casino, seen through the window.

"I wrote a short story with this setting, called *The Facts of Life*, which was filmed as one of the four stories under the screen-title of *Quartet*. It concerned an eighteen-year-old British tennis player who comes to Monte Carlo to play in the spring tournament. His worried father warned him ahead of time that there were three things he wanted him to abstain from in the gay Riviera resort: gambling, loaning money, and having anything to do with strange, flashy women.

"But circumstances influenced the youth whereby he had to disregard all three cautions. He gambled at the roulette tables of Monte Carlo Casino and won, he loaned money to a beautiful French woman who told him she had lost heavily, and later she invited him to go to bed with her, which he did. When she thought he was sleeping soundly, she stole from his jacket-pocket twenty thousand francs, about $4000 then, the money he had won at roulette.

"But he had witnessed her thievery and saw where she hid the money, in the bottom of a flower pot. When she came back and fell asleep beside him, he arose, recovered his money, and slipped out of her hotel room. Later, when he counted the money, he was surprised to find he had taken six thousand francs of her money too.

"The father was disturbed, when the son, upon his return to England, with some cheek, told him that he considered his advice unsound. And the father had to reluctantly accept the decision of his friends, whom he had gone to for counsel, that his son was 'born lucky, and in the long run that's better than to be born clever or rich.' "

He was silent for a few minutes.

"I've always had the intention of writing a novel about the man, Francois Blanc, the swindling Parisian ex-waiter, who opened the Monte Carlo Casino in 1865, and actually saved the Grimaldis from shuffling off down the long rutted road to the royal poorhouse. Blanc was, indeed, a very interesting man. Lord Brougham, one of England's Lord High Chancellors, once praised him: 'Francois Blanc is the most brilliant financier of our times, and he has astounded me by the profundity of his foresight and calculation.'

"Blanc was a congenital speculator, a lover of gold, a hard and ruthless man, who had the staunch conviction that human beings were obsessed with the mania to be relieved swiftly of their hard-earned, embezzled, inherited, or stolen cash, and that possession of same across his gaming-tables was *all points* of law. He was convinced that only a rogue could win at his gaming-tables. His favorite quotation was: 'For every inch that is not fool is rogue!' Many unlucky gamblers would waylay him to shout hysterically: 'I've lost all my money at your tables, so now I'm going to commit suicide—unless you give me 50,000 francs!' To which Blanc would always coldly reply: 'Good! Come to my office and I'll loan you an excellent pistol.' Oh, he was a *caractère* all right! What a novel I could have written about him, if I could have found the time! He was the one who originally abolished taxes in Monaco. He had a . . ."

He broke off, glanced at me irritably with hooded eyes, his lips compressing sternly.

"Don't expect an invitation to my funeral! There will be no ceremony, no flowers, no caterwauling of hymns, no Holy Henry delivering a mealy-mouthed eulogy. All this I've settled! And I'm to be cremated. I looked into a modern crematorium when I was up in London on my last trip.

"And my clerical critics need not hold the vain hope that there will be a last-minute death-bed conversion to any religious faith. I have not uncovered any evidence in my ecclesiastical researches to cause me to change my agnostic views. I still neither believe in the existence of God, nor in the immortality of the soul. When I do die I know that most people will say: 'Hell, I thought he died long ago.'

"No church, of course, can place any claim to me. I will exit life an atheist, a congenital disbeliever. I've been an atheist ever since I was a young boy, when I learned that God, as acclaimed, could *not* perform miracles, especially where *I* was concerned. It would be sheer hypocrisy to turn to religion, or to believe in God, now. I don't regret ever having rejected any of the religious faiths adopted by the masses."

Maugham's humiliating stammering as a youth deeply disturbed him. Once, on the eve of returning the next morning to school, where he was constantly jeered at by his classmates and bullied by the impatient masters because of his nervous speech affliction, he prayed fervently and tearfully that God would cure him of his vocal impediment. When he assayed speaking the next morning he found that he stammered as badly as ever.

In his autobiographical novel, *Of Human Bondage*, he had his hero, Phillip Carey, pray to be cured of his clubfoot, as he himself had prayed to be cured of his stammering.

In 1894, at the age of twenty, he had written in his note-book:

"The belief in God is not a matter of common sense, or logic, or argument, but of feeling. It is as impossible to prove the existence of God as to disprove it. I do not believe in God. I see no need of such an idea. It is incredible to me that there should be an afterlife. I find the notion of future punishment outrageous and of future reward extravagant. I am convinced that when I die I shall cease entirely to live; I shall return to the earth I came from. Yet I can imagine that at some future date I may believe in God; but it will be as now, when I don't believe in Him, not a matter of reasoning or of observation, but only of feeling."

When he was twenty-seven, he had again written in his notebook:

"I am glad I don't believe in God. When I look at the misery of the world and its bitterness, I think that no belief can be more ignoble."

And later:

"Perhaps all the benefits of religion are counterbalanced by its fundamental idea that life is miserable and vain. To treat life as a pilgrimage to a future and better existence is to disown its present value."

And in 1917:

"Once, at sea, I thought I was in imminent danger of death, and words of appeal arose quite involuntarily to my lips, remains of the forgotten faith of my childhood, and it required a certain effort of will to suppress them and look forward to what might come with an equal mind. I was at that moment within an ace of believing in God, and it required an outraged sense of the ridiculous to save me from surrender to my fear."

During his early medical schooling, he had made a bitter observation:

"I saw men die at the hospital and my startled sensibilities confirmed what my books had taught me. I was satisfied to believe that religion and the idea of God were constructions that the human race has evolved as a convenience for living . . . for the survival of the species . . ."

And he kept returning, in his writings, to the idea of God and immortality over the ensuing years:

"A God who is all-powerful may be justly blamed for the evil of the world, and it seems absurd to consider him with admiration or accord him worship . . . none of the arguments for the existence of God is valid . . . Nor has anyone satisfactorily explained the compatibility of evil with an all-powerful and all-good God . . . When one considers the vastness of the universe, with its innumerable stars and its spaces measured by thousands upon thousands of light years, I am overwhelmed with awe, but my imagination cannot conceive a creator of it.

"The only God that is of use is a being who is personal, supreme and good. I remain an agnostic, and the practical outcome of agnosticism is that you act as though God did not exist . . . There is no reason for life and life has no meaning. We are here, inhabitants for a little while of a small planet, revolving around a minor star which in its turn is a member of one of unnumbered galaxies . . . And if the astronomers tell us truth, this planet will eventually reach a condition when living things can no longer exist upon it and at long last the universe will attain that final stage of equilibrium when nothing more can happen. Aeons and aeons before this man will have disappeared. Is it possible to suppose that it will matter then that he ever existed? He will have been a chapter in the history of the universe as pointless as the chapter in which is written the life stories of the strange monsters that inhabited the primaeval earth . . ."

I recall that Maugham had once remarked cynically to me that man revealed his spirituality more profoundly when he sat down to a hearty and appetizing meal of animal and vegetable matter. And that egotism and vanity motivated most men's endeavors and actions.

In 1944, in his *A Writer's Notebook,* he had written:

"For whether the soul is a conglomeration of qualities, affections, idiosyncrasies, I know not what, or a simple spiritual substance, character is its sensible manifestation. I suppose everyone would agree that suffering, mental or physical, has its effect on character. I have known men who, when poor and unrecognised, were envious, harsh and mean, but on achieving success became kindly and magnanimous. Is it not strange that a bit of money in the bank and a taste of fame should give them greatness of soul? Contrariwise I have known men who were decent and honourable, in illness or penury become lying, deceitful, querulous and malevolent. I find it then impossible to believe that the soul thus contingent on the accidents of the body can exist in separation from it. When you see the dead it can hardly fail to occur to you that they do look awfully dead."

"I had Reverend Davidson rut in bed with Sadie Thompson in *Rain,*" he now told me in this last interview in Monte

Carlo. "Many readers, and of course the clergy, were horrified. I was denounced from many pulpits, there were venomous editorials attacking me. Some said I had set back missionary endeavors around the world a hundred years. It was outrageous, they screamed, that I would have a man of God so compromised with a cheap harlot. Actually, Reverend Davidson was closer to spirituality in bed wildly fornicating with Sadie than at any time of his life. Love, taken on its sensual as well as on its spiritual side, purifies."

Yet, in a reflective mood, he had confessed: "When I look back on my life, with its successes and failures, its endless errors, its deceptions and its fulfillments, its joys and miseries, it seems to me strangely lacking in reality. It is shadowy and unsubstantial. It may be that my heart, having found rest nowhere, had some deep ancestral craving for God and immortality which my reason would have no truck with."

His voice dropped now to such a low pitch that I had to bend closer and strain my ears.

"I know that my days as a living organism are over," he said slowly. "I am as close to death as it's possible for a man to be and still be able to breathe, walk, talk, feel, think. My body, like a too-long used machine, is completely worn out and defective, and there's no repair job possible on it. The organs are beyond salvage or replacement. I'm ready for the human trash-heap. Such a disintegration has to be fatal, either awake or asleep.

"But I don't have the slightest fear of death when it does strike. All of my affairs are in order, and I am resigned. And, as I totter on the brink of the grave, I am of no special anxiety. I agree with La Rochefoucauld that, when you are young, neither the sun nor death can be looked at with a steady eye. But when you are old, you become conditioned to not averting your gaze so readily from the awesome and obvious factors in life. I know that my beliefs in rejecting God and immortality are sound and logical. No great messages from wise men of the world have been forthcoming with proof, to establish the existence of God. Bacon said that men fear death as children fear to go into the dark, and as that natural fear in children is increased with tales, so is the other.

"The only trepidation I've ever had about death is dying aboard a ship and being dumped over the side into the ocean. I could never stomach that terrible prospect. That is why I have remained in my villa these past years, rather than indulging my love of travel and being between ports at sea when death snatches at me. I subscribe to Shakespeare's 'I would fain die a dry death.'

"The day will come," he predicted, in a voice barely above a whisper, "when Christianity will be as archaic as Mayan sun-worship. And I don't think that there are any existing religions to provide a foundation for a new faith for mankind. If the exigencies, the horrors, the worries, the disappointments of life are so unbearable to man that he must have a mollifying belief in a Supreme Being, then a totally new religion must be invented. Clearly, man must have his refuge from despair. Science and philosophy, because they are too specialised branches of knowledge for the masses, would be of little benefit to him. As man must have an opiate to ease himself through life, the prospect of spiritual salvation in the future is not too reassuring.

"Well, anyway, as for myself, I look forward to death as one might contemplate falling off to sleep at night, comfortably and without any anxieties. Lately, every night when I have gone to bed, I have remained awake a short time thinking how nice it would be now if I just couldn't be aroused in the morning.

"When Alan says goodnight to me, I always tell him: 'Just hold the good thought for me, dear loyal friend, that I won't wake up in the morning.' I know it disturbs him a bit my saying that, but that is my wish. 'For there is no God found stronger than death; and death is a sleep.' "

He extended a bony, limp hand for a weak pressure.

"This, of course, will be the last time that we will meet or talk. Think kindly of me now and again. I hope life will continue to treat you pleasantly, and you will enjoy abundant health. That is my wish for you. I have enjoyed our discussions of the South Seas and the Far East, because we have talked and listened with understanding and appreciation for those attractive islands and seacoasts and charming peoples. If *I* was granted one last wish it would be to swim again in the crystalline, cool waters of some South Seas lagoon."

The voice trailed off to a fluttering tiny sigh, his lips trembled, the eyes blinked and closed. I caught faintly breathed, disjointed words: ". . . Death and night . . . wash . . . soiled world . . ."

He was quoting Walt Whitman:

"That the hands of the sisters, Death and Night, incessantly, softly wash again and ever again, this soiled world."

I turned around at the entrance and glanced back at Maugham.

His eyes were open again, and he was smiling rather sardonically in my direction.

I somehow had the impression he was saying to himself:

"I think I've actually succeeded in making him feel sorry for me."

THE WRITINGS OF W.
SOMERSET MAUGHAM

The Writings of
W. Somerset Maugham

The date after each title is the year of its original publication in Great Britain, unless otherwise specified. Dates of
publication of Maugham's plays do not coincide with their
first presentation on the London stages, inasmuch as the
plays were published, in some instances, at later dates.

NOVELS

Liza of Lambeth (1897)
The Making of a Saint (1898)
The Hero (1901)
Mrs. Craddock (1902); new and revised edition (1928)
The Merry-Go-Round (1904)
The Bishop's Apron (1906)
The Explorer (1907)
The Magician (1908)
Of Human Bondage (1915) A new edition was brought out
    in 1946, including a bonus essay "A Digression on the
    Art of Fiction," which Maugham gave as a lecture in
    Coolidge Auditorium, in the U.S. Library of Congress,
    on the occasion of his presenting to the Library of Con-
    gress the original manuscript of *Of Human Bondage,* in
    1946.
The Moon and Sixpence (1919)
The Painted Veil (1925)
Cakes and Ale (1930)
The Narrow Corner (1932)
Theatre (1937)

Christmas Holiday (1939)

Up at the Villa (1941)

The Hour Before the Dawn (1942), published in New York, during World War Two, when he was living in the United States.

The Razor's Edge (1944)

Then and Now (1946)

Catalina (1948)

SHORT STORIES

Orientations (1899)

The Trembling of a Leaf (1921)

The Casuarina Tree (1926)

Ashenden (1928)

Six Stories Written in the First Person Singular (1931)

Ah King (A series of Six Stories) (1933)

Cosmopolitans (1936)

The Mixture as Before (1940)

Creature of Circumstance (1947)

MAJOR COLLECTIONS OF SHORT STORIES

Altogether (1934). This anthology of short stories was published in America under the title *East and West* (1934)

The Complete Short Stories, 3 volumes (1951)

PLAYS

A Man of Honour (1903)

Mrs. Dot (1904)

Lady Frederick (1911)

Jack Straw (1911)

The Explorer (1912)

Penelope (1912)
The Tenth Man (1913)
Landed Gentry (1913)
Smith (1913)
The Land of Promise (1913)
The Unknown (1920)
The Circle (1921)
East of Suez (1922)
Caesar's Wife (1922)
Our Betters (1923)
Home and Beauty (1923)
The Unobtainable (1923); produced also under the title
   Caroline.
Loaves and Fishes (1924)
The Letter (1927)
The Constant Wife (1927)
The Sacred Flame (1928)
The Breadwinner (1930)
For Services Rendered (1932)
Sheppey (1933)
The Noble Spaniard (1953)
The Plays of W. Somerset Maugham, 6 volumes (1931-34)

NON-FICTION, TRAVEL, ESSAYS, AND MISCELLANEOUS COLLECTION
OF ARTICLES.

The Land of the Blessed Virgin (1905)
On a Chinese Screen (1922)
The Gentleman in the Parlour (1930) (The chronicle of a
   trip from Rangoon, Burma to Haiphong, in the then
   French Indo-China.)
Don Fernando (1935); new and revised publication (1950)
The Summing Up (1938)

Books and You (1940)

Strictly Personal (1942) Published in the United States in 1941.

A Writer's Notebook (1949)

The Vagrant Mood (1952)

Ten Novels and Their Authors (1954) (Originally published in America in 1948, under the title *Great Novelists and Their Novels* in 1948)

Points of View (1958)

Looking Back (1962), published as a magazine series, of material largely from his non-fiction books.

Rag-Bag (to be published after his death) This will be a retrospection on his early years, as a young man in London.

Purely for My Pleasure (1962) ; a special volume reminiscing on the interesting experiences concerned with the acquisition of his private art collection.

COLLECTION OF SHORT STORIES AND ESSAYS EDITED BY MAUGHAM

Traveller's Library (New York, 1933)

Teller of Tales (New York, 1939)

Modern English and American Literature (New York, 1943)